LIBRARY OF MONEY AND BANKING HISTORY

The Use of Credit Instruments in Payments in the United States

NATIONAL MONETARY COMMISSION

THE USE OF

CREDIT INSTRUMENTS

IN PAYMENTS IN THE

UNITED STATES

BY

DAVID KINLEY

[1910]

REPRINTS OF ECONOMIC CLASSICS

AUGUSTUS M. KELLEY · PUBLISHERS

NEW YORK 1970

First Edition 1910
(Washington: Government Printing Office, 1910)

Reprinted 1970 by
AUGUSTUS M. KELLEY · PUBLISHERS
New York New York 10001

SBN 678 00546 X

LIBRARY OF CONGRESS CATALOGUE CARD NUMBER
68-27848

PRINTED IN THE UNITED STATES OF AMERICA
by SENTRY PRESS, NEW YORK, N. Y. 10019

61st Congress, 2d Session | SENATE | Document No. 399

NATIONAL MONETARY COMMISSION

THE USE OF CREDIT INSTRUMENTS IN PAYMENTS IN THE UNITED STATES

REPORT COMPILED BY

DAVID KINLEY, Ph. D., LL. D.

University of Illinois

Washington : Government Printing Office : 1910

NATIONAL MONETARY SYSTEM.

NELSON W. ALDRICH, Rhode Island, *Chairman.*

EDWARD B. VREELAND, New York, *Vice-Chairman.*

JULIUS C. BURROWS, Michigan.
EUGENE HALE, Maine.
PHILANDER C. KNOX, Pennsylvania.
THEODORE E. BURTON, Ohio.
JOHN W. DANIEL, Virginia.
HENRY M. TELLER, Colorado.
HERNANDO D. MONEY, Mississippi.
JOSEPH W. BAILEY, Texas.
JESSE OVERSTREET, Indiana.
JOHN W. WEEKS, Massachusetts.
ROBERT W. BONYNGE, Colorado.
SYLVESTER C. SMITH, California.
LEMUEL P. PADGETT, Tennessee.
GEORGE F. BURGESS, Texas.
ARSÈNE P. PUJO, Louisiana.
ARTHUR B. SHELTON, *Secretary.*

A. PIATT ANDREW, *Special Assistant to Commission.*

CONTENTS.

LIST OF TABLES.

THE USE OF CREDIT INSTRUMENTS IN PAYMENTS IN THE UNITED STATES.

Discussions concerning the issue of notes by banking institutions, which largely occupied the attention of students of finance and business men in the eighteenth and the first three quarters of the nineteenth centuries, have been succeeded by equally intense discussions of the amount and influence of credit deposits on the books of the banks, when drawn on by their customers with checks. The fact that the use of checks against deposits renders unnecessary a large amount of money, or currency, attracted attention early in the history of deposit banking, and efforts have been made from time to time to determine the proportion of money, or currency, replaced with checks and credit documents of similar character.[a]

The purpose of these inquiries, of which the investigation here reported is the latest, is a double one. It is desired, in the first place, to find a basis for estimating the proportion of business done by means of credit paper, or the volume of exchanges settled without the direct use of money or currency—in other words, the volume of money which credit instruments enable the country to dispense

[a] In this discussion the phrase "credit documents" or "credit instruments" does not include bank notes.

with, and, therefore, indirectly, the volume of money which the country needs. The second purpose of these inquiries is to shed light on the effect of credit exchanges on the value of money, or the price level.

In all industrial communities exchanges are made in three ways: by direct barter; by direct money payment; and by indirect barter, or exchanges wherein, instead of money, credit documents of some kind are given, which cancel one another partly or wholly, and so render the use of money necessary only for the settlement of balances, if at all.

Not uncommonly it is thought that exchange by direct barter is unimportant in highly advanced communities. The volume of products which is put into market, in any country, is far from being the total volume of its production. A large amount of goods are consumed directly by those who produce them. These goods do not enter at all into the market, and therefore have no direct effect on prices or on the amount of money needed by the country. To be sure, they exercise a potential influence, because in case of a scarcity of supply in any line much that is ordinarily consumed by the producers would be thrown upon the market for sale. In a way, therefore, goods consumed by their immediate producers constitute a barrier against a sudden great advance of prices. This phenomenon is familiar enough to the public in the case, for example, of wheat. The price on the exchanges and in the market is largely influenced by visible and invisible amounts not yet offered for sale. Nevertheless, the volume of goods used directly by those who produce them, exercises, as already remarked, no important direct influence on prices. This is so whether the articles are finished goods ready for the so-called "ultimate consumer" or become the raw material of another intermediate producer, provided, of course, the article is not monopolized by a single producer.

A second portion of the goods produced are sold for money. Many portions of these goods are doubtless sold many times before they reach the consumer. The sale of this volume of goods constitutes a direct demand for money to effect payment, the amount necessary for the purpose depending not only upon the average price, but upon the number of times the goods change hands before reaching the consumer.

Still a third volume of goods produced and entered into market are sold on the basis of a price established by the money exchanges, but are not paid for with money in any form. For a large majority of these purchases checks are given either at the time of purchase or soon after. These checks are deposited with the banks; by means of bookkeeping they are set off against one another, and the balances only call for money payment. Even these balances, however, may not call for the use of money for their settlement; they may, and indeed frequently are, entered to the credit of the owner on the books of his bank, and in time canceled by the payments against him coming in at a later period. Obviously this volume of goods, since it does not call for the direct use of money, enables a community to do away with a large volume of money which would otherwise be necessary. It is not true, however, as some apparently have thought, that no money is necessary for these transactions. In normal times, when business is good and confidence unimpaired, there are always some balances from these transactions the owners of which call for settlement in money, and the banks must keep a reserve against these demands. When confidence is impaired, these balances are likely to be larger, even if the total volume of credit is smaller.

There is no way of determining the relative amounts of business done in the three ways mentioned—by direct barter, direct money payment, and credit paper. No data exist which would enable us to make even an approximate estimate of the first portion or indeed of the second. It is possible, however, to determine with some degree of accuracy the volume of business done by indirect barter or settled with credit paper, for we can get some idea of the amount of business thus done by a study of the statistics of the banks.

The amount of the country's business settled with credit paper has long been a matter of dispute, on which widely different opinions have been expressed. On the one hand, men of affairs, especially in banking and other business circles, impressed as they naturally are with the vast volume of business transacted under their eyes by means of credit paper, have usually overemphasized the importance of credit paper settlements and minimized the importance of the large volume of currency. On the other hand, others, particularly those who from time to time urge upon the public the necessity of a larger volume of currency, have denied that the volume of credit business was as large as claimed and have minimized its influence, urging, on the contrary, the necessity for a larger volume of money. Some of them have gone further and insisted that even if the volume of credit payments were as large as many claim, it is a bad thing to have business done so largely in this way and that it is desirable for the best interests of the country that the volume of credit business should be diminished and that of direct money payment enlarged.

More careful students of the subject, in both of the above groups, have insisted, like Francis A. Walker, upon a middle view. They have admitted freely the claims of the business men, bankers, and others, that over 90 per cent of the "wholesale" business of the country was done by means of checks, drafts, or bills, but have urged that the retail business was mainly done with money; that wages were mainly paid with money, and that the demand for money for these purposes constituted the most important part of the country's need for money.

The second and indirect purpose of the inquiry is to get some light on the amount of money needed and the effect of the volume of credit transactions on its value. The discussion of this topic, however, will be more opportune after we have reached some conclusion concerning the first matter.

METHODS OF INQUIRY.

Three methods have been pursued in the effort to determine the proportion of business done by credit documents. For the sake of brevity these may be referred to as the method of clearing-house statistics, the method of bank deposits, and the method of getting information direct from the merchant.

The clearing-house method.—The first method consists, briefly, in noting the volume of clearings from time to time and their relation to the estimated volume of business done. If the volume of clearings increases more rapidly than the volume of business, obviously the ratio of exchanges settled on the basis of credit paper is increasing. This method was first employed by R. H. Inglis Palgrave, esq., in a paper, "Methods of Banking," published in the Journal of the Statistical Society of London for 1873. Mr. Palgrave took as a measure of the increase in the volume of business, the increase of the aggregate exports and imports of Great Britain, calling the sum of the exports and imports for 1868, 100, or the base. The index number for the aggregate of exports and imports was 102 in 1869, 106 in 1870, 116 in 1871, and 129 in 1872. Meantime the clearings, making the aggregate clearings of 1868 the base, or 100, as in the case of exports and imports, increased to the index number 104 in 1869, 114 in 1870, 138 in 1871, and 171 in 1872. Putting the matter in another way, in 1860 the aggregate exports and imports, or the volume of business, was 137 to every thousand of clearings. In 1869 it was 134 to the thousand, in 1870 it was 128, in 1871 it was 115, in 1872 it was 103.

This method is not satisfactory. It merely shows the general tendency of credit paper payments and they can not to any degree show the character of the business done.

It is doubtful, too, whether this method is applicable in the United States, for, in the first place, we have been for years constantly establishing new clearing houses in places where banks formerly exchanged checks by sending them to one another with their own messengers. In other words, our credit system is growing all the time. Moreover, it is becoming more refined and perfect.

Again, this method would hardly be applicable to the United States, because the volume of our exports and imports is affected by changes in our tariff legislation, whereas in England that element of disturbance is not present.

Another method of using the clearing-house returns for the purpose of determining the proportion of credit paper and business payments was employed by Prof. Willard Fisher.[a]

The method is to determine the amount of credit paper in the total clearings. This may be done by computing from the amount of credit paper that passes through the clearing house the amount that is probably received by all the banks of the country, both those which are members of clearing houses and those which are not. This sum, whatever it is, is then to be compared with the estimated purchasing power of money in active circulation; that is to say, the amount of the money outside the banks, multiplied by its velocity of circulation or the probable number of times it changes hands to effect a given volume of business in a given time.

Prof. Willard Fisher, using this method, came to the conclusion that probably money and credit transactions stood, at the time he wrote, in the ratio of about 1 to 1.

[a] See Journ. Pol. Econ., 3:391ff.

Although the theory of this method is excellent, some of the necessary data is very difficult to get. We can determine the total clearings with approximate exactness, but the velocity of circulation is something about which, at present, we know very little, if anything. Our estimates of the amount of money in circulation are also very approximate. Our Treasury Department gives the estimate from month to month, and the figures are doubtless as good as can be obtained. Nevertheless they are very unreliable.

The bank-deposit method.—The second method of determining the proportion of business done by credit paper is that of finding the proportion of checks and other credit instruments in the bank deposits. The general theory underlying this method is that the deposits in the banks represent in character and volume the receipts of the merchants or tradesmen; that these receipts are, of course, from their customers and, therefore, represent fairly the means of payment used by the customers. This method is the one which has been most extensively employed, especially in the inquiries made in this country, in 1881, 1890, 1892, 1894, and 1896.

Of course, the questions obviously arise whether the bank deposits do fairly represent the receipts of the merchants for sales, and whether the business done by the merchants, the statistics of whose bank deposits are collected, are really representative of the whole business of the country. These and other points will be discussed in connection with the details of the present report. It is important to bear in mind, however, that, while the deposits of the merchants may fairly enough represent the habits of their customers as to paying by check and, therefore, the volume of their business paid for in this way, the habits of their customers will depend on a variety of circumstances. In England, for example, banks do not usually accept small accounts. Consequently, the average size of the checks drawn in England is larger than is the case where many banks are glad to take almost any account that may be offered. Our multitude of small banks facilitates the carrying of small accounts and the payment by check. Of course, the largest checks in the English banks, as in our own, are those used in stock-exchange transactions. In 1885 Mr. Lubbock [a] selected 1,500 checks which passed through his bank, representing a total sum of £871,000 and giving an average for each check of £579. This was on a settling day and included stock-exchange checks. On an ordinary day 1,000 checks examined gave an average of £299. Again, 8,500 clearing checks gave an average of over £300. Mr. Lubbock remarked that checks on bankers who do not clear are much smaller in amount, but do not generally represent commercial transactions. By this he undoubtedly means what we might call wholesale trade and stock exchange dealings. He reported that 1,000 checks of this kind averaged £80 each. Again, 5,848 checks on country banks gave an average of £28 each, and this is the lowest that Mr. Lubbock mentions. A little later, Mr. Palgrave said that "the number of checks under £5 is so small as not materially to supplant the use of coin, which is chiefly used for retail trade and wages." [b]

[a] Journ. Statis. Soc., 28:364.

[b] Idem, 36:86.

In 1881 R. W. Barnett, esq., wrote that "out of 10,000 checks passing through the country clearing it was ascertained recently that 25 per cent were for less than £5, whilst the average of the whole was less than £30."[a] In this country checks are not infrequently drawn for as small amounts as 50 or even 25 cents, and occasionally for less, although the average is much higher. Hence, it is obvious that the field of the check is a far larger one with us than it is in England. Merchants' deposits will therefore represent more accurately the methods of payment in this country than would be the case in England. Consequently, greater reliance can be placed on the returns from our banks for the purpose of such an inquiry. Less allowance has to be made with us in the study of bank deposits for business of merchants who do not bank than would be the case in England.

The fact that we use checks for smaller sums than the people of other countries is shown, too, by the large number of cases in which wages are paid by check, as seen by Tables XX to XXV. The total amount of wages paid by check in the week ending March 16, so far as returns were made, aggregated $40,595,874. Many of these checks, doubtless most of them, were for amounts much smaller than people in England would think of drawing checks for.

Still again, our small banks do not as a rule require customers to carry a fixed balance. While that practice is doubtless necessary and has grown considerably in large places, our country banks seldom require it. As has already been remarked, this facilitates the keeping of

[a] Journ. Inst. Bankers, 2:78.

small accounts and promotes what may be called the "check habit."

From all these considerations it would seem that the method of securing bank deposits for determining the proportion of business done on credit is more likely to yield accurate results in this country than elsewhere. When we come to discuss the deposits of retail merchants, reasons will be given for thinking that their bank deposits really do represent the character of their business receipts. Hence it is not necessary to go into that subject here.

Method of getting information direct from merchants.—A third method of studying this subject is that of securing direct replies from merchants. This is impracticable on a large scale. Multitudes of merchants, especially those whose business is small, do not keep accounts which would give a clear idea of the character of their receipts. No means exist for the collection of such data by any central authority or authorities, or to afford any guaranty of their accuracy when collected. This method of studying the subject can be used only in a small measure in checking up the other methods. It has been used for this purpose in the present inquiry. A number of cases will be mentioned where the merchants themselves have reported their receipts so that it is possible to determine exactly the proportion of credit paper in a month's business.

HISTORY OF INQUIRIES PREVIOUSLY MADE.

As has been remarked, attention was early directed to inquiries concerning the volume of credit transactions, more especially the volume of business transactions settled by means of credit paper.

ENGLISH INVESTIGATIONS.

The Slater inquiry.—So far as the present writer knows, the first important information on the subject of the proportion of credit documents used in business payments was furnished in a report of the committee of the House of Commons appointed to investigate the crisis of 1857. The report includes an analysis of the operations of the banking house of Morrison, Dillon & Co., as furnished by Mr. William Slater, for the year 1856. Mr. Slater had furnished the committee a statement of the receipts and payments of his bank, classified so as to show the proportion in which £1,000,000 of receipts and expenditures were made in money and in credit documents, respectively. The information furnished was as follows:[a]

Receipts:		
Bankers' drafts and mercantile bills, payable after date	£533,596	
Checks payable on demand	357,715	
		£891,311
Bank of England notes	68,554	
Country bankers' notes	9,627	
Gold	28,089	
Silver and copper	1,486	
Post-office orders	933	
		108,689
Grand total		1,000,000
Payments:		
Bills of exchange	302,674	
Checks on London	663,672	
		966,346
Bank of England notes	22,743	
Gold	9,427	
Silver and copper	1,484	
		33,654
Grand total		1,000,000

[a] MacLeod's Theory and Practice of Banking, 1:299.

The Babbage inquiry.—The next attempt to secure statistics showing the proportion in which checks and other credit instruments enter into business payments was made by Charles Babbage, esq., who read a paper before the Statistical Society of London in 1855 on "An Analysis of the Statistics of the Clearing House."[a] This inquiry was made by what has been called above the "clearing-house method." Mr. Babbage attempted, among other things, to determine "the proportion of payments made in bank notes by the public, both in town and in the country." It appeared from the data secured by Mr. Babbage at that time that the percentage of credit paper varied with the volume of the clearings; or, as he puts it, "the larger the clearing the smaller the percentage of bank notes used in the operation." He found that 5.49 per cent of the bank notes occurred in the average of the thirty largest total clearings, this average being £4,553,600; while 8.45 per cent occurred in the average of the thirty smallest clearings, which average was £2,006,800. He found that of the clearings discussed by him, the average for the days of settlement on the English Stock Exchange was £4,504,400, of which 6.42 per cent were bank notes; the average for the days of settlement at the foreign stock exchange was £4,148,900, of which 5.66 per cent were bank notes; that for settlement days of inland bills of exchange amounted to £4,092,100, of which 6.61 per cent were notes.

The Palgrave inquiry.—The next inquiry probably was that of W. Langton, esq., general manager of the Manchester and Salford Bank, Manchester, England. Mr. Langton

[a] Journ. Statis. Soc. of London, 19:28ff.

reported figures in 1873 to R. H. Inglis Palgrave, esq., for the years 1859, 1864, and 1872, and other figures furnished at a later date by Mr. T. R. Wilkinson for Professor Jevons. Mr. Palgrave reported on the matter in an address entitled "Notes on Banking in the United Kingdom, Sweden, Denmark, and Hamburg," etc., read before the Statistical Society of London in February, 1873.[a]

Mr. Palgrave reported from Mr. Langton's figures that in 1859 cash payments, or payments in coin and notes, were about 53 per cent of the total turnover of his bank; in 1864, 42 per cent, and in 1872, 32 per cent. By turnover Mr. Langton meant the total receipts and total out-payments of his bank. These figures show a gradual increase in the proportion of credit paper. Mr. Langton pointed out what most investigators since have ignored, the influence of the amount and manner of payment of wages on the proportionate use of credit paper.

In the article in which he quotes the figures of Mr. Langton, Mr. Palgrave also attempts to show in a general way the growth of credit exchanges by the use of clearing-house statistics, the method which has been described above. He remarks, "If we compare the general circumstances, we shall see how completely the circulation of the country has in recent times passed from being a circulation in notes to being a circulation in cheques."[b]

He points out in this article that the increase in bank clearings has been greater than the increase in the country's trade, and thus infers that an increased proportion

[a] Journ. Statis. Soc., 36:27ff. [b] Idem, 36:80.

of the country's business was settled through the banks by credit paper.

The Lubbock inquiry.—The next important inquiry into the subject was that made by Sir John Lubbock and reported to the Statistical Society in June, 1865.[a] The article is entitled "Country Clearing."

Sir John took the amount of £23,000,000, the sum which passed through his bank during the last few days of the year 1864, analyzed it, and found it was made up as follows:

	Amount.	Per cent.
Clearing	£16,346,000	70.8
Checks and bills not passing through clearing	5,394,000	23.4
Bank of England notes	1,137,000	4.9
Coin	139,000	.6
Country notes	79,000	.3
Total	23,095,000	100.0

This showing was at Sir John Lubbock's own bank in Birmingham. In order to ascertain the practice as to method of payments in London, Sir John took the amount of £17,000,000 paid in by his London customers and found that it was made up as follows:

	Amount.	Per cent.
Checks and bills on clearing bankers	£13,000,000	77.4
Checks and bills on ourselves	1,600,000	9.5
Checks and bills on other banks	1,400,000	8.3
Bank of England notes	674,470	4.0
Country bank notes	9,470	.1
Coin	117,927	.7
Total	16,802,000	100.0

[a] Journ. Statis. Soc., 28: 361.

In discussing the last table, Sir John is of the opinion that the amount of bank notes is too large, because the note account includes notes drawn by the bank itself to replenish its daily supply and in so far did not represent bills paid in by customers. He deducted this amount, £266,000, but added as the amount of notes paid in for collection, discounts, and loans on security the sum of £2,460,686. With these alterations made he came to the conclusion that "out of £19,000,000 credited to our town customers, £408,000 consisted of bank notes, £79,000 of country bank notes, and £118,000 of coin," making the percentages 96.8 for checks and bills, 0.6 for coin, and 2.6 for bank notes.

The Martin inquiry.—In 1880 John Biddulph Martin, esq., banker, read a paper before the Institute of Bankers [a] entitled "An Inquiry into the History, Functions, and Fluctuations of Bank-Note Circulation in the United Kingdom, Continental Europe, and the United States." In this, after quoting the figures of Mr. Slater, Mr. Babbage, and Mr. Lubbock, he gave the percentages of receipts in his own bank for six working days in each month. The dates selected were from the 20th to the 26th, as nearly as might be, so "as to avoid the disturbing influences of the fourth and of the stock exchange settling day." Mr. Martin's figures are for 1878–79 and are as follows:

	Receipts.	Payments.
	Per cent.	*Per cent.*
Bills and checks	96.5	96.9
Notes	2.6	2.1
Coin	.9	1.0

[a] Jour. Inst. Bankers. 1: 273ff.

The Pownall inquiry.—Some figures for London in 1864 are reported by G. H. Pownall, esq., in an article read before the Institute of Bankers, in 1881, entitled "Proportional Use of Credit Documents and Metallic Money in English Banks." [a]

Mr. Pownall reports the following returns as made up from the "Town Counter" in 1864: Coin, 0.6 per cent; notes, 2.6 per cent; checks and bills, 96.8 per cent. He gives the following tables as a result of his inquiry:

Proportional amounts of different kinds of money and credit.

Documents received by country banks in 261 places:	Per cent.
Gold (sovereigns and half sovereigns)	12.41
Silver (with or without copper)	2.79
Bank of England notes	10.16
Country bank notes	1.78
Cheques on the same town or district	26.75
All other cheques and bills	46.11
	100.00

	Documents received by banks in—		
	61 agricultural places.	Towns excluding agricultural places.	The metropolitan area.
	Per cent.	*Per cent.*	*Per cent.*
Gold (sovereigns and half sovereigns)	8.86	14.07	25.218 (gold and silver)
Silver (with or without copper)	1.82	3.24	
Bank of England notes	3.58	13.22	10.982
Country bank notes	2.92	1.25	00.040
Cheques on the same town or district	30.71	24.90	22.494
All other cheques and bills	52.11	43.32	41.266

The first table shows that in the country banks in 261 places in Great Britain nearly 73 per cent of the deposits on a certain day were in checks and bills, 27 per cent being checks on the same town or district. Mr. Pownall

[a] Jour. Inst. Bankers, 2:629.

further makes a careful classification to show the relative use of credit paper in agricultural towns and the metropolitan area. From the second of his tables it appears that nearly 83 per cent of the deposits in 61 agricultural places were in checks and bills, 68 per cent were of a similar character in the towns, and 64 per cent in the metropolitan area.

Mr. Pownall's article shows that at the time at which he wrote the deposits of checks and bills in banks in the suburbs of Manchester were a little over 45 per cent. He further classified the proportional receipts of money and credit paper received by the banks of Manchester and its suburbs according to the trades, including cotton, wool, iron, pottery, and silk. He finds that in the bank receipts from these trades the proportion of checks and bills was as follows: Cotton, 61.5; wool, 68.9; iron, 67.9; pottery, 71.8; silk, 65.7. Other valuable details are given in this excellent article, but it is not necessary to repeat them here because the English practice differs somewhat from our own in the minimum amount for which checks are commonly drawn.

CRITICISM OF ENGLISH INQUIRIES.

The English investigations, although interesting, are hardly comparable in extent with those of this country or valuable as a basis for conclusions applicable to this country. For, in the first place, the number of banks from which statistics were obtained was small in each inquiry. In the second place, the classes of people who use the banks in England are only the larger merchants the great business firms, and wealthy individuals. The

English banks would not show as large a proportion of small checks as the deposits of our own banks. This was certainly true at the time the English investigations referred to were made, for it was not until 1854 that it was legal to issue drafts for a less sum than 20s., and "long after that time great uncertainty appears to have existed on the subject."[a] Moreover, we know from these inquiries that when they were made wages were paid and retail trade carried on more largely with coin, which forms so large a proportion of the English circulation.

Another defect of the English statistics is their comparatively non-representative character. With the exception possibly of those gathered by Mr. Pownall, the statistics presented by the various writers are, so to speak, "sample cases," and it may be doubted whether they were representative. They certainly represent fairly the practice of merchants and the wealthy classes in England with reference to the use of bank accounts and the issue of checks. Can we be sure that they represent the method of making payments used by the larger proportion of the English people, or that used in settling the larger proportion of British trade? Finally, there is no doubt that the returns given by most of the writers include such items as "bills paid in for collection and discount, loans on security," and other items which should not be included if what we are trying to determine is the volume of business payments made from day to day by credit paper.

[a] R. W. Barnett, "Effect of the Development of Banking Facilities Upon the Circulation of the Country," Jour. Inst. Bankers, 2:78.

AMERICAN INVESTIGATIONS.

The Garfield inquiry.—Our next information on this subject comes from a former President, then a Representative, James A. Garfield. In his speech on Resumption, November 16, 1877, he stated that when serving as chairman of the Committee on Banking and Currency, in 1871, he had become interested in the matter and had asked the Comptroller of the Currency to secure for him data on the proportionate use of credit paper and money from 52 selected banks. His remarks as to the results are as follows: "I selected three groups. The first was the city banks. The second consisted of banks in cities of the size of Toledo and Dayton, in the State of Ohio. In the third group, if I may coin a word, I selected the 'countriest' banks—the smallest that could be found at points away from railroads and telegraphs. The order was that those banks should analyze all their receipts for six consecutive days, putting into one list all that can be called cash—either coin, greenbacks, bank notes, or coupons—and into the other list all drafts, checks, or commercial bills. What was the result? During these six days $157,000,000 were received over the counters of the 52 banks and of that amount $19,370,000—12 per cent only—in cash, and 88 per cent—that vast amount representing every grade of business—was in checks, drafts, and commercial bills."[a]

The inquiry of 1881.—In 1881 John J. Knox, while he was still Comptroller of the Currency, made an inquiry into the proportion of bank receipts made by credit paper on two dates, June 30 and September 17, 1881.[b] His

[a] Congressional Record, Nov. 16, 1877, p. 462.
[b] See Report of Comptroller of Currency, 1881.

request for statistics was made of the national banks only, and called for classified returns of all their receipts and payments. In June, 2,106 national banks were in operation and 1,966 sent in replies. In September, 2,132 banks were in operation and all sent in returns. The following table gives a summary of the results:

Analysis of national-bank receipts, June 30 and September 17, 1881.

Items.	June 30 (1,966 banks).		Sept. 17 (2,132 banks).	
	Amount.	Per cent.	Amount.	Per cent.
Checks, drafts, and bills	$261,271,666	91.77	$271,036,525	91.85
Clearing-house certificates	9,582,500	3.36	6,592,337	2.24
Paper money	11,554,747	4.06	13,026,570	4.36
Gold coin	1,864,105	.65	4,078,044	1.38
Silver coin	440,998	.16	500,301	.17
Total	284,714,016	100.00	295,233,779	100.00

It appears that on the date of the first inquiry the gold coin in the receipts of the banks concerned was sixty-five one hundredths of 1 per cent, and the total receipts of silver coin were sixteen one hundredths of 1 per cent, while the paper currency amounted to 4.06 and credit documents to 91.77 per cent.

The Comptroller's conclusion from the June inquiry was that 95.13 per cent of the total receipts of the banks were in credit documents. Curiously enough, however, he includes clearing-house certificates among the credit documents. It is not clear why this should be done.

On September 17 of the same year, the date of the second inquiry, Mr. Knox found that of the receipts of 2,132 banks there were 1.38 per cent in gold coin, 0.17 per cent in silver, 4.36 in paper, and 91.85 per cent in checks, drafts, and bills. His conclusion from the later figures was that 94.09 per cent of the receipts of the banks was in credit documents, including as before clearing-house certificates.

In this inquiry the Comptroller was careful to classify separately the returns from banks in New York City and other reserve cities and the banks elsewhere. In the June inquiry the proportion of credit documents in the banks not in reserve cities was 81.72 per cent, as against 98.7 per cent in New York City and 94.38 per cent in the other reserve cities. The September inquiry gave for the respective classes 81.74 per cent, 98.8 per cent, and 92.35 per cent. These figures thus show the inaccuracy of the statement not infrequently made in the past that over 90 per cent of the whole business of the country was done with credit documents. The 81 per cent of the "banks elsewhere" should have made students suspicious.

The Comptroller further presented a table showing the proportion of checks, drafts, and bills in the receipts of the two dates selected, by States. This table shows that according to the inquiry of June, 1881, 92 per cent was the largest proportion of credit documents in the banks of any State or Territory and was accredited to New Jersey, and the smallest percentage appeared in the returns of Wyoming, as 33.6 per cent. In the inquiry of September of the same year, New Jersey again appears with the largest percentage of credit documents, 91 per cent; while Nevada shows the smallest, only 8.2 per cent. Both in the case of Wyoming and Nevada the amounts from which the percentages were drawn were so insignificant that the two places may be left out of the consideration. In general, the tables showed that checks in the bank returns of the States which reported in the year 1881 largely ran between 65 and 85 per cent.

The inquiry of 1890.—The inquiry of 1881 was not repeated until 1890, when the Comptroller, Mr. E. S. Lacey, thought it wise to secure further information. Accordingly he asked 3,438 national banks to classify their receipts for July 1 and September 17. The blank sent out called for total receipts, distinguishing clearing-house certificates and exchanges for clearing house from checks, drafts, and other credit paper. The results obtained were presented in the usual tables, from which it appears that the total receipts of the 3,364 banks from which replies were received for July 1, were $421,824,726. Of this sum 44.90 per cent was in checks, drafts, etc., excluding exchanges for clearing house. Including clearing-house paper, the percentage was 92. The following table [a] gives the details for both dates:

Character of receipts.	July 1, 1890 (3,364 banks).		September 17, 1890 (3,474 banks).	
	Amount.	Per cent.	Amount.	Per cent.
Gold coin	$3,726,605	0.89	$3,702,772	1.13
Silver coin	1,352,647	.32	1,399,991	.43
Gold treasury certificates	6,427,973	1.52	6,159,305	1.88
Silver treasury certificates	6,442,638	1.53	5,908,714	1.81
Legal-tender notes	7,881,786	1.87	7,665,666	2.34
National-bank notes	5,244,967	1.25	4,371,778	1.34
United States certificates of deposit for legal tenders	520,000	.12	105,000	.03
Checks, drafts, etc	189,408,708	44.90	168,803,756	51.58
Clearing-house certificates	4,391,177	1.04	2,428,834	.74
Exchanges for clearing house	194,290,203	46.06	126,596,873	38.68
Miscellaneous	2,138,022	.50	135,562	.04
Total	421,824,726	100.00	327,278,251	100.00

[a] Finance Report for 1890, p. 383.

Returns were presented as usual for the reserve cities and the banks outside of reserve cities. The total receipts of the banks were $94,000,000 less in September than in July, and practically all of this was in items "which represent substitutes for money." The larger proportion of it was in clearing-house certificates and exchanges. The percentage of checks, drafts, etc., actually received by the banks was larger in September, as the table shows, although the total receipts were less. Other tables classified the facts in different ways to bring out the comparison between them and the data obtained in 1881. It is to be noted, however, that one-half of the total receipts came from 47 banks in New York City.

The inquiry of 1892.—This inquiry, like the two preceding ones, was based on reports obtained from national banks. The purpose of the Comptroller, Mr. A. B. Hepburn, in making the inquiry was "to furnish reliable data from which the public could see and realize how small a percentage of business transactions are represented by actual money, and how impossible it is for the Government to furnish a volume of currency sufficient to meet the wants of the people at all times—that is, in times of general distress or quasi-panic." The Comptroller goes on to say: "Over 90 per cent of all business transactions are done by means of credit. When the public lose confidence and credit is impaired and refused, over 90 per cent of all business transactions are directly affected. It is easy to realize how impossible it is for the remaining 10 per cent of money to carry on the business of the country without monetary stringency and financial distress."[a]

[a] Comptroller's Report, 1892, p. 32.

Of the 3,759 banks from which reports were requested, data were secured from 3,473 in time for use in the Comptroller's report. These data gave the total receipts of the banks on September 15 and the following table gives a brief summary of the results:

Class of receipts.	Amount.	Per cent.
Gold coin	$2,907,017	.88
Silver coin	1,372,054	.41
Certificates, gold, and silver	9,944,355	3.00
United States notes and bank notes	14,661,266	4.43
Currency certificates	2,210,000	.67
Checks, etc	154,959,059	46.79
Clearing-house certificates and exchanges [a]	145,151,462	43.82
Total	331,205,213	100.00

[a] Includes "miscellaneous" items of $586,000.

The Comptroller draws the conclusion that 9.39 per cent of transactions are represented by "cash," and 91.61 by checks, bills, etc. He presents a table showing the receipts of the national banks in the central reserve cities, and the proportion of credit instruments, together with figures for 3,144 country banks. From this table it appears that the country banks received 73.93 per cent of their receipts in checks, on September 15, 1892. The tables show the somewhat astonishing fact that while the percentage of total receipts formed by checks was 46.79, the percentage of checks in the receipts of the country banks was 73.93. The percentage of checks in 48 New York banks was 28.43, in 21 Chicago banks 52.12, and in 8 St. Louis banks 42.26. The large aggregate proportion of "credit payments" reported for the reserve cities is made by the machinery of the clearing-house exchanges.

From another table given in this report it appears that the smallest percentage of checks in the receipts of banks on the date in question was in Oklahoma Territory, where it was 42.37; the largest was 95.64 in the returns from Arizona, while Connecticut showed 92.3, Colorado 92.11, and Rhode Island 92.04.

The Comptroller calls attention to the fact that as contrasted with the inquiry of 1881 the returns of 1892 for New York City indicate "a marked increase in the amount of paper currency received." The amount in the returns of September, 1881, was sixty-five one-hundredths of 1 per cent, while in the returns of 1892 it was 7.53 per cent. He noted also a marked diminution in the proportion of receipts of checks and drafts as between the two dates, "the average per cent for the two days in 1881 being 2.91 per cent greater than the average for the two days in 1890; September 15, 1892, is 3.28 per cent less than September, 1890."

The inquiry of 1894.—The conclusion from the inquiries thus far discussed, as it was given in the public press and elsewhere, was to the effect that over 90 per cent of the business of the country was done on a credit basis, so that the need for money was small. During the next few years the monetary agitation was intense and this statement in its broad form was severely challenged, less as a matter of fact, however, than because of the inference drawn from it. It was urged, not only by those who were insisting on a larger volume of currency, but by careful students of the question, that the large proportion of credit transactions shown by bank receipts did not by any means disprove the need for a larger volume of currency. It was urged, as Francis A. Walker[a] pointed out, that "in spite of barter and in spite of credit a very large part, in most countries by far the largest part, in many countries almost the whole, of retail trade is still conducted by the use of money; and this is after all the vital thing."

The statement that the world over retail trade is conducted by the use of money is in the main correct. In order to test it the present writer suggested to the Comptroller of the Currency, Hon. James H. Eckels, the expediency of making an inquiry into the character of deposits made in the national banks of the country by selected classes of retail traders. The classes selected were those on whose goods between 70 and 80 per cent of the income of the laboring people of the country is spent, as shown by the reports of the Commissioner of Labor in 1890–1892. Accordingly a blank was prepared by the writer and sent out by the Comptroller, asking the national banks of the country to give their deposits in gold, silver, gold certificates, silver certificates, treasury notes, checks and other instruments of credit, made on May 15, 1894, by retail grocers, butchers, clothiers, furniture dealers, and fuel dealers. Replies were received from 2,465 national banks out of a total of 3,774. The aggregate deposits returned were $5,999,065, of which 58.9 per cent was in checks and store orders, and 41.1 per cent in various kinds of money. These figures indicated that the belief that checks did not enter largely

[a] Francis A. Walker, Discussions in Economics and Statistics, 1: 204.

into retail trade was a mistaken one. The returns, however, were on the whole meager, and two years later the writer again urged the Comptroller of the Currency to institute a similar inquiry on a much larger scale. The Comptroller kindly consented, and the result was the inquiry of 1896.

The inquiry of 1896.—The inquiry of 1896 was planned along the lines of that of 1894 for the purpose of determining if possible the proportion of credit paper received in what is commonly called "legitimate trade" as distinguished from speculative transactions. It was desired, moreover, to test the statement so commonly made that the large proportion of credit documents shown in the bank returns was practically due to wholesale trade and speculation. Accordingly a blank was prepared by the writer and submitted to the Comptroller of the Currency and afterwards sent out by him to all banking institutions in the country, calling for the deposits made by retail dealers, wholesale dealers, and all other depositors, in gold, silver, currency, and checks. Certain supplementary questions were added in order to get, as it were, a side light on the returns. These questions were as follows:

1. Does the above statement show the usual proportion of checks, drafts, etc., to total deposits? If not, please indicate how much it differs therefrom.

2. Is it customary in your community to pay wages by check?

3. Are wages as a rule paid weekly or monthly in your community?

The circular also called for the total number of depositors and amount of individual deposits, and the cash on hand classified in the usual way. The request, like that of 1894, was for deposits, not receipts. The date selected was the settlement day nearest the 1st of July. Of nearly 13,000 banking institutions of all classes then in existence, 5,700 sent replies, of which 5,530 were in such shape as to be useful for the purposes of the inquiry. Of these, 3,474 were from national banks and the remainder from state, private and savings banks, and loan and trust companies. The number of replies from private and savings banks and loan and trust companies was comparatively small, so that in writing up the report they were included with the state banks. The returns were analyzed by the writer of this report and presented in numerous tables in the report of the Comptroller for 1896. It is unnecessary here to go into great detail in reviewing the report. Suffice it to say that the grand total deposits of the 5,530 banks was $302,936,232. Of this amount 0.6 per cent was in gold, 0.5 per cent in silver, 6.3 per cent in currency, and 92.5 per cent in credit paper.

Of the retail deposits the aggregate was $26,536,930, and of this amount 2.4 per cent was in gold, 3.2 per cent in silver, 26.7 per cent in currency, and 67.4 per cent in checks. Of the aggregate retail deposits about $15,000,000 were in the six States of Illinois, Massachusetts, Missouri, New York, Ohio, and Pennsylvania, leaving between $11,000,000 and $12,000,000 for the rest of the country. The smallest percentage of checks in retail deposits was shown by Indian Territory, with 52.7 per cent; New Hampshire was next, with 53.2 per cent, while the largest percentage of checks was in Kentucky, which had 77.4 per cent.

The bank returns were supplemented with data secured directly from merchants in several places and also with certain calculations as to the probable practice and expenditures of various classes of people. After all allowances, including the omission of $100,000,000 from the deposits of "all others" to allow for speculative transactions, the conclusion was reached that 80 per cent was a fair estimate of the total proportion of the deposits of the day made in credit paper.

CRITICISM OF THESE AMERICAN INQUIRIES.

The first obvious criticism to be made upon the earlier inquiries in this country is that they called for the total receipts of the banks on a given day. Receipts, of course, are different from deposits,[a] for they include checks presented for collection and not credited until the collection is made. The percentage of credit transactions is calculated too commonly, moreover, on the basis of the inclusion of clearing-house certificates.

Still, again, the returns in the earlier inquiries in this country were criticised because they were received from a limited number of banks. National banks only were used, but at the times when the investigations were made these banks formed a larger proportion of the total number of banks in the country than they do now.

The report of the inquiry of 1894 is to be criticised for not giving aggregate of deposits as well as percentages, and for the omission of the percentages of deposit by the various classes of dealers. The present writer, who made that report, did not realize at the time how helpful the percentages would have been if classified by trades.

[a] The word "deposits" was used in the inquiries of 1894, 1896, and 1909.

A criticism which has been made on the inquiry of 1896 is that the returns were obtained for a settlement day. Deposits on such a day would, it is urged, show a larger proportion of credit paper than on other days. This criticism will be discussed later on in connection with the present investigation, as will also the further question whether bank deposits of merchants may be taken fairly to represent the method of payment of their customers.

THE PRESENT INQUIRY.

The questions.—The present inquiry is undertaken by the National Monetary Commission in connection with its attempt to secure all possible information as a basis for its report to Congress. After careful consideration and consultation with a number of bankers and students of finance, and representatives of the Commission, as well as the Comptroller of the Currency, it was decided to adhere to the general form of the inquiry of 1896. It was desired to secure for purposes of comparison the deposits classified as at the earlier date, and certain additional information was asked for in order to throw some side light on the inquiry. Following is the circular letter and blank form which was sent out by the Comptroller:

TREASURY DEPARTMENT,
Washington, March 1, 1909.

To the Cashier:

SIR: The National Monetary Commission, created by an act of Congress on May 30, 1908, is seeking information concerning the bank deposits and the proportion of payments made on an average throughout the country from day to day by means of checks and similar instruments of credit. On several occasions in the past the Comptroller has made requests of this kind, but the last such inquiry was made thirteen years ago. It is desired on this occasion to obtain returns as complete and representative as possible and to get a response not only from the national banks but from state and private banking institutions of all kinds. Similar inquiries are being made for the Monetary Commission during the current year in England, France, Germany, and other European countries for purposes of comparison with the practice in our own country. For this reason, and on account of the importance of the present investigation and of the purpose for which it is to be used, it is earnestly requested that the recipients of the accompanying blank will give it their best attention and return it promptly to the Comptroller in the inclosed envelope which does not require postage.

Information is desired as to the number and classification of depositors, methods of paying wages, etc., as indicated in the questions relating thereto. The statistics asked for will be published only in a general summary, the figures for the individual banks being treated as confidential.

Trusting that your institution will give me all the information asked for and that you will find it possible to transmit your report promptly after March 16, I am,

Yours, very respectfully,

LAWRENCE O. MURRAY,

Comptroller of the Currency.

[Please fill out this blank after the close of business March 16, 1909.]

MARCH 16, 1909.

LAWRENCE O. MURRAY,

Comptroller of the Currency, Washington, D. C.

SIR: I submit herewith the information requested in your letter of March 1:

1. Deposits made in this bank on March 16, 1909:

[Cents omitted.]

Deposits to credit of—	Gold coin.	Silver coin.	Paper currency.	Checks, drafts, etc.	Total.
	$	$	$	$	$
Retail dealers					
Wholesale dealers					
All other depositors					
Total					

2. Estimated amount of pay rolls paid by the customers of this bank in cash for the week ending March 13, 1909 .... $........
3. Estimated amount of pay rolls paid by the customers of this bank by check for the week ending March 13, 1909 ....
4. Aggregate amount of individual deposits at close of business on March 16, 1909 ....
5. Aggregate amount of other deposits, including the balances of other banks and the deposits of city, State, or national governments on March 16, 1909 ....
6. Total number of accounts, exclusive of bank and government accounts, on March 16, viz: Number.
   - Accounts with balances under $500 ....
   - Accounts with balances between $500 and $2,500 ....
   - Accounts with balances over $2,500 ....

To indicate the character of your bank, please put check-mark (✓) opposite the proper name in list below:

National bank.
State bank.
Mutual savings bank.
Stock savings bank.
Private bank.
Loan and trust company.

Respectfully,

______ ______ Cashier.
______ ______ City.
______ ______ State.

The deposits made on March 16 were called for. This date came on Tuesday, so that the returns of the present inquiry are not those of a settlement day, and consequently are free from the objection made in connection with the previous inquiry, that bank deposits on settlement days usually show a larger proportion of checks than on other days. This objection had been anticipated in the report made to the Comptroller in 1896, and an effort was made at that time to determine whether there was any important variation in the deposits of the bank from day to day throughout a month or two. As shown in that report, the writer got information from several banks showing the proportion of credit paper in their deposits daily for from thirty to sixty or ninety days. As a result of this inquiry he formed the opinion that there was no important difference in the proportion of credit paper on settlement days and other days. The reason may be that there is no such thing as a general settlement day the country over. At any rate, the present returns for a nonsettlement day show a higher proportion of credit paper in the retail class of deposits than was shown by the deposits for a settlement day in 1896. The time of year chosen was simply a matter of convenience for those making the inquiry. As shown by the circular, certain supplementary questions were added, as had been done in 1896. The first of these was a request for the estimated amount of pay rolls paid by the customers of the bank in cash for the week ending March 13, and also the amount paid by check. The blank also called for the aggregate amount of individual deposits at the close of business, and the aggregate amount of other deposits, including the balances of other banks and the deposits of city, State, or National Government, if any.

Finally, a request was made for a statement of the number of accounts with balances under $500, the number with balances between $500 and $2,500, and the number with balances over $2,500. The blank was sent out by the Comptroller to all the banking institutions of the country known to him. The replies were sent, of course, to the Comptroller and forwarded by him to the writer for classification, analysis, and report.

It may not be out of place to say a word about the amount of labor involved in putting the material into shape for use. The blanks were received by the writer early in May. They were arranged by States and classes of banks, and the replies from each State numbered serially. The returns were then tabulated on large ruled sheets, each bank being given a separate entry for the replies for each question. The figures were arranged in columns to correspond to the columns of the circular of inquiry; but three columns were used for the specie—one for gold, one for silver, and one for the total specie. The last column on the sheet was the sum of the specie, currency, and checks from each bank. The columns were then added independently, and in every case of course the column of totals had to equal the sum of the footings of the specie, currency, and checks. Where a discrepancy was found, the error was run down, until it is believed that the figures, as finally presented, are very free from mistakes.

From these primary tables supplementary tables were made, as shown by the report, presenting the data in various ways from various points of view. The other data called for in the circular were also tabulated, but it is not necessary to go into the details of the method of manipulation.

The percentages are made out to one decimal place. They were found mostly by the slide rule and Crelle's Rechentafeln, but a few were found by actual division. Where the figure is less than 0.1 per cent, it is omitted. For this reason a figure sometimes occurs for the per cent of total specie when none is given for gold and silver separately.

Before taking up a discussion of the present returns, it is interesting and worth while to make some preliminary remarks concerning the general character of the statistics, the attitude of the banks toward the inquiry, and the character and form of the replies.

In the first place, all questionnaires and inquiries by means of circulars are under suspicion among some people. It is the opinion of some that it is impossible to frame a questionnaire which will elicit the points that are of importance to the inquiry. Of course it is true, as those familiar with statistical investigations need not be told, that it is quite impossible to prepare a form so phrased as to preclude the likelihood of misinterpretation or to secure information so accurate as to cover all possible variations in the conditions that it seeks to investigate. It almost seems as if common words were turned into stumbling blocks by the mere fact of being used in a formal way. It is exceedingly difficult to get a uniform interpretation of even simple questions and terms. The present investigation is no exception to these experiences.

For example, in the inquiry of 1896 the question was asked: "Is it customary in your community to pay wages by checks?" Objection has been made to the phraseology of this question by one keen critic, Prof. E. W. Kemmerer.[a] He thinks that the information obtained at that time as to the proportion of wages paid by check was inadequate because the word "customary" might be interpreted to mean either "a custom" or "the custom" and that small States were given as much importance as large ones in the table.

It is always possible, of course, for students to take a sentence and find various meanings for a word. It is very doubtful, however, whether one man in a thousand in the community would misunderstand the use of the word customary in this question. The business man, when asked such a question, does not stop to analyze the possibility of various interpretations. If asked what is the custom in your community with reference to a certain matter, he will give an answer which conveys his impression of what is the general practice. He will not stop to say that Jones always does this, but Smith never does. The idea that he will convey in his answer is that if the majority or a considerable proportion of the people do this way, then this is the custom of the community. A question to be sent out for purposes of this kind must be framed in ordinary language and from the point of view of the

[a] Money and Prices, Cornell Studies, 1907, p. 106.

people who read it and not from the point of view of possible critical analysis by professors and other students.

Still it seemed better to change the phrasing of the questions with reference to wage payment. It can hardly be said, however, that the present information on this topic points to a more definite conclusion.

General discussion of the statistics.—In reading over statistics so voluminous and drawn from so many different sources one naturally wonders whether, after all, the figures are very reliable or of great utility. It is true, of course, of statistical matter generally that it presents a case or a subject only partially and with a great many imperfections and defects. Nevertheless, if the figures are carefully collected and properly grouped and interpreted, there is no doubt that such collections of figures as we are about to discuss present a picture of the general conditions of activity which they are designed to represent and from which they are drawn. It is important that we be certain of their general accuracy, the honesty with which they are given, and the honesty with which they are grouped and manipulated. Assuming these conditions, we may rely on the conclusions as presenting the general features at least of the situation.

It is often assumed by critics of such investigations that the statistics can not be relied on because the banks are not interested in such inquiries and are careless about making returns. The writer, having examined all the returns in the present inquiry, as well as in that of thirteen years ago, and having read the numerous letters which correspondents have sent, without being requested to do so, in connection with their returns, is convinced that there is not only a widespread interest in the inquiry, but that the correspondents have been careful as a rule to give the figures as accurately as they could, according to their understanding of the question. In the present inquiry, the interest of the correspondents has been evinced in many ways. In one of the larger cities of the country, for example, representatives of the banks associated in the clearing house, on receiving these blanks, were sufficiently interested to get together and discuss the purpose and meaning of the questions and decide upon a plan whereby the replies from that city would be based upon a uniform interpretation. Several letters written by individual bank officers express their interest, indicating that although the compilation of the returns required a good deal of time and therefore subjected the bank to considerable expense, they were glad to comply with the request. Indeed, the general interest of all classes of banks is shown by the large number of replies. The interest extended not only to national bank officers but to the officers of other classes of banks. The officers of some banks who by mischance failed to receive blanks, nevertheless having seen notices of the inquiry and the form of the blank in the newspapers, sent in the information wanted. The examining officers of the state banks in the various States, such as the state auditors, also evinced great interest and were very helpful in the inquiry by urging upon the banks under their jurisdiction a full and prompt compliance with the Comptroller's request. For all of this willing response the commission, the writer, and the public in general certainly owe a debt of gratitude to those who went to so much trouble.

The day selected.—In the inquiry of 1896 the day selected for securing information was the settlement day nearest the first Monday of July. It has been objected by critics of the report of 1896 that a settlement day is not representative of the ordinary day-to-day deposits of the business men of the country, particularly of the retail tradesmen. Supplementary inquiries made in 1896 seemed to show that there really was little or no difference in the proportion of checks and other credit documents deposited from day to day throughout a month or two and the percentage determined by the returns of the banks on the day chosen. The writer is convinced that this is true, not only from having gone through the books of several banks at the time of the inquiry of 1896, but as a result of considerable inquiry here and there among bankers. The returns of the present inquiry confirm this opinion. The day selected is not a settlement day, yet the proportion of credit documents in retail trade runs even higher than it did in 1896 or in 1894.

Of course the habits of the people in the matter of paying by check may have changed somewhat in that time; but even if so, it is doubtful whether it can have changed so greatly.

Moreover we must remember that a good many monthly accounts are probably settled with money instead of checks. If a person is in the habit of paying by check, he would very likely pay a month's account or a day's purchase of any importance with a check.

If he is in the habit of paying money, he will pay both accounts with money.

As indicated in what has just been said, other critics have urged that one day, whether a settlement day or a nonsettlement day, is not enough to give a fair idea of the character of the receipts of business men, to say nothing of the habits of the people of the country in settling accounts. No reason has ever been given for this opinion, excepting that one day is one day out of three hundred and sixty-five in the year. It should be noted, however, that the various inquiries have been made on different dates, and the results have been substantially the same. It should be noted further, as remarked in the preceding paragraph, that so far as a direct inquiry has been made upon this point the testimony of bankers and the evidence from their books is that one day is typical. There are many banks in the country of which this is not true.

If the settlement day selected in 1896 were not typical, because it would show an undue proportion of checks in the deposits, a nonsettlement day ought to show an undue proportion of cash. The opposite is the fact. If one day which was a settlement day was not typical, one day which is a nonsettlement day ought to be as nontypical in the opposite direction. The contrary is the fact brought out by the figures in the present inquiry.

In discussing the returns of settlement days, moreover, we must not forget that a settlement day is not the same for all classes of business, nor for all classes of purchasers, nor for all parts of the country. Many retail business men consider a customer sufficiently prompt if he settles a month's account within ten days after receiving his bill, while others expect payment the next day. Not a few accounts are settled semi-monthly, instead of monthly, and still others are settled quarterly. There is ground for thinking that the distribution of settlement days is such as to reduce materially what would otherwise be a disproportion of the amount of credit paper in bank deposits on those days.

We may fairly conclude therefore that for purposes of such inquiries almost any day will do, because of the vast extent of our country, the large number of banking institutions that send replies, and the multifariousness of the business involved. The habits of our people and the customs of widely separated communities are likely to be very different from what they would be if our population were condensed into a small area, like England or Belgium.

General criticism of the replies.—As has been remarked, the inquiry was sent to all the banking institutions in the country known to the Comptroller. This number was about 25,000. Notwithstanding the interest and care exhibited, there were, of course, a great many who filled out the blanks carelessly and with an apparent lack of appreciation of the public importance of such an inquiry and the moral obligation on individual citizens to do what they can to help on the progress of enlightenment in all matters of such public interest. Perhaps the most surprising thing in the study of the returns was the necessity of checking up additions, because of the numerous errors in addition made in the original blanks. This defect has been noticed in earlier inquiries. There was not a very large number of such blanks, but the fact that there were some and that there was no certainty as to when an error would be found made it necessary to check up all. Of the total number of blanks sent out, 12,190 were returned. Of this number 698 were rejected, leaving 11,492 which were used in making the report.

The reasons for the rejection of nearly 700 blanks were numerous. Some gave all deposits as retail deposits, some gave them as wholesale only, some gave them as the deposits of "all others," and some entered only aggregate deposits on the day in question. When a blank was found which had entries only under retail deposits it was scrutinized to determine whether the entry was correct or whether the total deposits of the day had been entered under the head of "retail." In many cases accompanying letters gave a clew to the determination of this question. Where there was any doubt the returns were calculated in the "all others" rather than in the "retail." The number rejected on this account was not very large.

The same remarks apply to those which returned all deposits as wholesale, all others, or aggregate. There were some cases in which this was a correct return, as accompanying letters showed.

Blanks which gave the aggregate deposits of gold coin, silver coin, currency, and checks, without classifying them according to depositors, were not used. It may be said, however, that in no case did any one of these present any striking differences from the general run of the replies in regard to the proportion of credit documents in the aggregate deposits. A good many of the blanks were rejected because the aggregate deposits of the day were all entered under one head instead of being classified. For example, one blank from West Virginia reported a receipt of nearly $250,000 in gold coin from the three classes of depositors on the 16th day of March. Farther on in the blank the aggregate deposits at the close of business on the day in question are given as a trifle over $200,000. The inaccuracy of such a statement is too obvious to need comment.

In the case of a good many rejected blanks the persons who made them out evidently read them carelessly, for they gave the same figure for the deposits of the day as is given lower down in the blank for the aggregate deposits of the bank at the close of business.

One or two made the strange and inexplicable mistake of giving not the deposits of the day, but the aggregate deposits of the bank, and yet returned them classified as gold, silver, currency, etc., for different classes of dealers.

Probably, however, the largest proportion of those rejected were thrown out because they gave no information at all in answer to the first question, but filled out carefully the answers to the other questions. These are helpful, however, in discussing the later questions. Probably half or more of the rejections were due to this cause.

As already stated, some banks returned all deposits under "retail," and others all under "wholesale." Where possible, these were properly entered. But in so far as deposits returned as retail were not really so and were not detected as not being so, the total retail deposits, of course, will be too large. The same is true of the total wholesale deposits in so far as the same cause of error was at work, but the error in either case is trifling. It can not amount to more than a few thousand dollars in the total retail deposits or in the total wholesale. The probability is that if there is any error due to bad classification by the correspondents, it tends to make the deposits accredited to "all other" depositors large at the expense of the others, for the reason that it is easier to enter the returns under "all others" than to classify them. The figures given for retail trade, however, are without doubt representative of retail trade as that phrase is commonly understood.

Twenty were received too late for use, and the seven blanks received from Alaska and Hawaii were not used because they were so few that their use would reveal the business of individual banks. Moreover, they were hardly germane to the purpose of the discussion, and they show no marked differences from those received from banks on the continent.

It is worth while noting that of the blanks rejected the proportion of the national banks is smaller than that of any of the others. Of the national bank replies 1.7 per cent were rejected, of those of the state banks 7.4, of those of the private banks 12.3, of those of the stock savings banks 13, of those of mutual savings banks 14.5, of those of the loan and trust companies 7.2, and of the total 5.5.

The national banks are more accustomed to making out forms, and probably they are in a position to answer such questions more easily than any of the other classes of banks. On the whole, there seemed to be a large amount of careless answering from the state and private banks. Obviously, the questions in some cases were not carefully read. It will be noticed that of the 385 stock savings banks from which replies were received 183 were in Iowa, and it was the stock and the mutual savings banks whose replies were most commonly defective.

Many of the cashiers of the savings banks evidently thought that it was not the intention to have them answer the first question on account of the classification of depositors and so omitted it altogether. Nevertheless, they gave some valuable information in connection with the other questions. The following table shows the total number of replies received and the number rejected in considering question 1. The number of banks giving replies is afterwards entered only in the tables of aggregates because not all banks gave returns for all classes of depositors. The States with the largest percentages of rejections of replies of "all banks" are Arkansas and Rhode Island, each having 14.2.

TABLE I.—*Number of replies received and number rejected.*

State or Territory.	National banks.		State banks.		Private banks.		Savings banks.				Loan and trust companies.		Total.	
							Stock.		Mutual					
	Received	Rejected.	Received.	Rejected.	Received.	Rejected.	Received.	Rejected.	Received	Rejected.	Received.	Rejected.	Received.	Rejected.
Alabama	60	1	48	3	4	3	0	0	0	0	0	0	112	7
Arizona	11	0	13	3	0	0	1	0	0	0	0	0	25	3
Arkansas	28	1	70	12	3	0	1	0	0	0	3	2	105	15
California	118	4	177	20	7	1	78	6	1	0	2	0	382	31
Colorado	86	2	30	5	23	2	1	0	0	0	5	0	145	9
Connecticut	78	2	14	0	1	0	0	0	54	11	10	0	157	13
Delaware	26	0	4	0	0	0	0	0	2	0	4	1	36	1
District of Columbia	10	0	5	0	0	0	5	0	0	0	4	0	24	0
Florida	26	0	31	3	4	0	2	0	0	0	0	0	63	3
Georgia	68	2	113	13	9	3	3	0	0	0	0	0	193	18
Idaho	29	0	32	1	1	0	1	0	0	0	4	0	67	1
Illinois	342	5	287	7	222	19	6	0	0	0	4	0	861	31
Indiana	207	2	166	13	106	9	1	1	6	0	50	10	536	35
Iowa	228	5	174	6	95	14	183	25	0	0	2	1	682	51
Kansas	169	2	348	25	6	0	1	0	0	0	1	0	525	27
Kentucky	113	2	172	20	0	0	2	0	0	0	1	0	287	22
Louisiana	28	2	49	1	0	0	2	0	0	0	0	0	79	3
Maine	69	1	12	0	0	0	0	0	37	5	19	1	137	7
Maryland	95	0	24	4	2	1	6	0	7	1	8	1	142	7

TABLE I.—*Number of replies received and number rejected*—Continued.

State or Territory.	National banks.		State banks.		Private banks.		Savings banks.				Loan and trust companies.		Total.	
							Stock.		Mutual.					
	Received.	Rejected.	Received.	Rejected.	Received.	Rejected.	Received.	Rejected.	Received.	Rejected.	Received.	Rejected.	Received.	Rejected.
Massachusetts	189	1	0	0	3	1	0	0	135	22	28	1	355	25
Michigan	85	0	176	15	57	13	18	1	0	0	1	1	337	30
Minnesota	228	4	360	29	3	0	2	1	4	1	2	0	599	35
Mississippi	25	0	69	7	1	0	6	2	0	0	0	0	101	9
Missouri	102	3	415	25	30	4	2	0	0	0	17	1	566	33
Montana	33	0	18	0	5	0	0	0	0	0	0	0	56	0
Nebraska	168	3	281	20	5	0	7	1	0	0	0	0	461	24
Nevada	9	1	6	1	1	0	0	0	0	0	0	0	16	2
New Hampshire	54	0	6	1	0	0	6	0	21	5	1	0	88	6
New Jersey	153	2	14	0	0	0	0	0	15	0	43	4	225	6
New Mexico	26	3	4	0	0	0	1	0	0	0	0	0	31	3
New York	387	5	118	5	23	6	0	0	95	6	59	1	682	23
North Carolina	47	0	65	6	1	0	6	3	0	0	6	0	125	9
North Dakota	94	2	129	5	0	0	0	0	0	0	0	0	223	7
Ohio	319	3	182	13	78	7	17	4	0	0	6	2	602	29
Oklahoma	168	8	151	11	0	0	0	0	0	0	0	0	319	19
Oregon	47	1	32	1	8	1	1	1	0	0	0	0	88	4
Pennsylvania	687	5	109	5	21	1	8	0	10	0	128	2	963	13
Rhode Island	21	0	6	2	0	0	0	0	13	5	9	0	49	7

South Carolina	23	1	52	7	0	0	0	0	0	0	3	2	78	10
South Dakota	74	3	130	11	8	0	1	0	0	0	0	0	213	14
Tennessee	70	5	55	8	0	0	5	1	0	0	1	0	131	14
Texas	365	12	30	4	20	7	1	1	0	0	0	0	416	24
Utah	17	1	17	3	2	0	2	0	0	0	0	0	38	4
Vermont	50	1	6	0	1	0	3	0	9	2	7	0	76	3
Virginia	90	2	68	4	1	0	3	1	0	0	1	0	163	7
Washington	39	0	66	3	5	1	1	1	0	0	1	0	112	5
West Virginia	68	2	60	5	0	0	1	0	1	1	2	0	132	8
Wisconsin	104	0	225	15	2	1	0	0	0	0	1	1	332	17
Wyoming	18	0	12	0	1	0	1	1	0	0	0	0	32	1
Total	5,551	99	4,630	342	759	94	385	50	409	59	432	31	12,167	675
Alaska	1	1	3	3	1	1	0	0	0	0	0	0	5	5
Hawaii	2	2					0	0	0	0	0	0	2	2
Unclassified as to kind of bank and therefore not used													5	5
Returned entirely blank													11	11
Grand total													12,190	698

CLASSES OF BANKS REPORTING.

In all previous inquiries on this subject, excepting that of 1896, no effort was made to get returns from banks other than national. The courteous treatment accorded the inquiry of the Comptroller in 1896 showed clearly that bankers of all classes would be glad to give information. Accordingly, as has been stated, the inquiry was sent to all classes of banks and the interest of state banking officers was enlisted to promote the cooperation of the state and private banks of the different States.

A few words of explanation concerning the classification of banks is therefore desirable. There was no difficulty, of course, with the national banks. Every bank with a national charter knew how to classify itself.

In a few cases banks thought they could not be classified under any of headings in the circular, and therefore entered themselves under the head of "foreign bank." There were not more than half a dozen of these, and as they are probably operating under state charters they were classified as state banks. The mutual savings banks, as that term is understood in Massachusetts, and the trustee savings banks, as the phrase is used in New York, were classed together. Some bank officers in New York, however, seemed to think that the savings banks of New York could not be properly classified under any of the headings of the circular. Whatever reasons there may be for holding this view, for the purposes of this inquiry they should be classed with those of Massachusetts. In some cases a bank properly entered itself under more than one head. Two or three could say that they were state banks, stock-savings banks, and loan and trust companies. Obviously, what was meant was that they were loan and trust companies operating under a state charter and doing a savings-bank business in addition to their commercial business. They were classified as loan and trust companies.

It developed that a great many national banks are carrying savings accounts. These were obviously separated in the reports from the commercial accounts in practically all cases. In answering question 4 of the circular, however, many banks included the savings and commercial accounts without distinction.

Of course, the classification of deposits by retail dealers, wholesale dealers, and all others was hardly applicable to the mutual savings banks. Returns from the savings banks under the head of "all others" alone would have been entirely satisfactory, since, of course, people who deposit in savings banks do so as individuals and not as classes of business men. Nevertheless, savings banks evidently endeavored to classify their deposits exactly as the circular called for. While, for purposes of discussion by and by, we shall find their total deposits the thing of most importance without reference to the classification, it is interesting to note that a good many tradesmen are using the savings banks.

It is interesting to notice, too, the distribution of the kinds of banks from which replies were received. The state banks figure less prominently in the Eastern States than in the Middle West, Northwest, and Southwest. In the New England States and in New York, New Jersey,

Pennsylvania, Delaware, Maryland, Ohio, and Texas the national banks are much in excess of the state banks, in number. The difference is much less in Illinois, Indiana, Iowa, Louisiana, and Oklahoma, while the state banks which replied largely outnumbered the national banks in California, Georgia, Kansas, Louisiana, Michigan, Minnesota, Mississippi, Missouri, Nebraska, North Carolina, North Dakota, South Carolina, South Dakota, and Wisconsin.

Of the 759 private banks from which replies were received 675 were in ten States. Illinois had the largest number, 222; Indiana came next with 106; and the other 8 in order were Iowa 95, Ohio 78, Michigan 57, Missouri 30, New York 23, Colorado 23, Pennsylvania 21, and Texas 20.

Of the 385 replies from the stock-savings banks, 183 came from Iowa and 113 from California, Michigan, and Ohio together. The remaining 89 are pretty evenly distributed throughout the country.

Of the 409 replies from mutual savings banks, under which head cooperative savings banks of all kinds not organized for profit of stockholders were included, 135 came from Massachusetts, 95 from New York, 54 from Connecticut, 37 from Maine, and the rest were scattering. It is to be noted, however, that so far as the returns of this inquiry show, this class of banks is confined to the New England States and New York, California, Delaware Indiana, Maryland, Minnesota, New Jersey, Pennsylvania and West Virginia.

The distribution of these through the country at large is much more uneven than that of the stock-savings banks.

Loan and trust companies reported from all the states excepting Alabama, Arizona, Florida, Louisiana, Mississippi, Montana, Nebraska, Nevada, New Mexico, North Dakota, Oklahoma, Oregon, South Dakota, Texas, Utah, Washington, and Wyoming. The states from which the loan and trust companies are absent are in the main those which may be said to be without great commercial development.

CLASSES OF BUSINESS AND CUSTOMS AS TO METHODS OF PAYMENT.

It seems pretty obvious that it would be difficult to mention any class of business, in any kind of community, even in "retail trade," of which it could be said with assurance that no part of its receipts were in the form of credit documents. Given a community in which the habit of paying by checks is well developed, the question whether a given purchase will be paid for in that way depends principally on two things, its amount and time of payment. If the sale is a "cash sale" it is likely to be paid for with a check according as its value is $1, $5, or more. By some people the dollar purchase would be paid for by check The instances are not few in which checks are drawn for sums smaller than $1. If, on the other hand, the sale is a "charged sale" to be settled at the beginning of the following month or at the end of some designated credit period, it will very likely be paid for with a check, if the purchaser is in the habit of paying with checks; otherwise it will be paid with money; for it seems to have been forgotten in all statements about the disproportion of credit paper in the deposits of so-called settlement days that even a month's account will be paid with money by people who are not in the habit of using checks. It is probably true, however, that the larger proportion of charged sales are made by people who are in the habit of paying with checks.

If, now, we consider the character of various kinds of retail business it will be evident that we might guess beforehand that in certain kinds of business the proportion of credit paper received in payment would be pretty large, while in others it would be pretty small or entirely disappear. No evidence exists to show that it disappears altogether in any kind of business, although it undoubtedly does vanish in the case of a great many individual stores in every business. A short discussion of some of these points will help us.

The grocer's sales to the people who enter his store from day to day are both cash sales and charged. A cash sale of such a character that the purchaser will likely take the goods with him will almost always be paid for with money, even in communities where most of the customers are personally known. If it is a sale, for example, to a family whose income is $15 or $20 a week and it is charged, it will very likely be paid for with money, provided the family is of the wage-earning class. It is just as likely to be paid with a check as with money if the purchaser belongs to the professional or semiprofessional class. A bookkeeper or clerk whose total yearly income is \$1,000 is not unlikely to be a check user, whereas a carpenter or bricklayer with the same annual wages will not be.

Now, single purchases made in the average-sized grocery in a country town are moderate in value, and yet of sufficient value to justify payment by checks in a large number of cases by people who are in the habit of paying in that way. The individual purchases at any one time in a confectionery store or the ordinary drug store, on the other hand, assuming again that the customer is known, are usually so small that if they are cash sales they will very likely be paid for in money. One does not draw a check to pay for a dish of ice cream or a dime's worth of candy, or a bottle of medicine filled on a physician's prescription. The small sales when charged, however, make an aggregate which makes the use of the check evident. If, however, the purchase is one that aggregates \$1, \$5, or more, even though a cash sale, it may be paid by check.

If we consider the business of the furniture dealer, we see that the average purchase here is considerable, so that we would expect a larger proportion of checks in his payments than in the case of the druggist, for example. It is evident that if the total receipts of the business in a community such as we have in mind are made up mostly from a large number of sales, each small in volume, we are likely to find a larger proportion of money. But "small in volume" is a relative term. What would be a small single sale here would be a large one, for example, in many a small shop in Berlin. What is in the writer's mind in using the phrase "small sale" may be described, perhaps, as a sale less than $5. Consequently we would expect a large proportion of checks also in the receipts, for example, of custom tailors, jewelers, coal dealers, and lumber dealers. The average purchase in the field of each class of these is considerable. The confectioner, the barber, the notion store, on the other hand, each has a small average single sale. Here we would expect the volume of checks received in payment to run down.

Circumstances alter considerably if we take the case of a large city like New York or Chicago, where customers are nearly all personally unknown to the sellers of the goods. A stranger would not think of going into Wanamaker's in Philadelphia, or R. H. White's in Boston, or Marshall Field's or "The Fair" in Chicago, and offering to pay a $5 purchase with a check. Of course, this is done. It is not, however, done without trouble. The percentage of checks in the receipts of certain stores in the Loop district of Chicago, to be given later on, may therefore be taken as a fair average of the proportion of payments made with checks by the middle class of people, in so far as they purchase at places where they are not personally known. Many of them will pay bills at other places, however, with checks. Consequently the average given for these stores can not be taken as the true average of the proportion of payments made with checks even by this class of people. It is too low. We must remember, too, that although the purchasers in these stores represent the great group of the middle-class purchasers, the total volume of their purchases may be less than that of a smaller class above them and that the average percentage of check payments for the whole country is raised by the latter.

If one would find the store in which the proportion of cash reaches its maximum, he should seek a store each of whose single purchases is of small value, like cigars or candy or "knick knacks;" whose clientele is exclusively of the class of day laborers and people unknown personally to the dealer. One would find such a store on lower State street in Chicago, or on Milwaukee avenue, or on the east side in New York. Even here, however, the chance customer of means, whom the dealer is glad to welcome once in a while, will come in and give his check for a box of cigars, or enough Christmas toys to make a group of children in a neighborhood house happy at some season of the year, or for some purchase arising from unusual circumstances of that kind. In fact, the retail trade of the country shows that the habit of paying by check has probably reached down in some measure to all economic classes of the community whose income is $1,000 or more, provided they are other than what are classified as manual laborers.

THE RETAIL RETURNS.

The following table shows the retail returns of the present inquiry:

TABLE II.—*Retail deposits in national banks, state banks, private banks, loan and trust companies, stock savings banks, and mutual savings banks.*

NATIONAL BANKS.

States.	Gold.	Silver.	Total specie.	Currency.	Checks.	Total.	Gold.	Silver.	Specie.	Currency.	Checks.
							P. ct.	*P. ct.*	*P. ct.*	*P. ct.*	*P. ct.*
Alabama	$3,517	$20,178	$23,695	$87,056	$261,261	$372,012	0.9	5.4	6.3	23.4	70.2
Arizona	5,985	2,132	8,117	6,950	30,313	45,380	13.2	4.7	17.9	15.3	66.8
Arkansas	1,305	4,628	5,933	18,364	82,000	106,297	1.2	4.3	5.5	17.2	77.3
California	199,789	38,872	238,661	80,611	919,359	1,238,631	16.1	3.1	19.2	6.5	74.3
Colorado	44,121	14,461	58,582	92,993	420,970	572,545	7.7	2.5	10.2	16.2	73.6
Connecticut	1,638	9,567	11,205	232,078	376,864	620,147	.3	1.5	1.8	37.5	60.6
Delaware	136	1,402	1,538	25,327	42,772	69,637	.2	2.0	2.2	36.4	61.4
District of Columbia	242	3,082	3,324	96,323	103,546	203,193	.1	1.5	1.5	47.5	51.0
Florida	1,057	35,556	36,613	77,954	199,672	314,239	.3	11.4	11.7	24.8	63.5
Georgia	4,105	23,917	28,022	109,958	272,053	410,033	1.0	5.8	6.8	26.8	66.3
Idaho	7,875	3,247	11,122	9,389	60,263	80,774	9.7	4.0	13.7	11.6	74.7
Illinois	35,863	57,065	92,928	602,747	2,174,040	2,869,715	1.3	2.0	3.2	21.1	75.7
Indiana	30,712	51,161	81,873	281,447	551,950	915,270	3.4	5.6	9.0	30.7	60.3
Iowa	18,697	29,296	47,993	137,287	579,089	764,369	2.5	3.8	6.3	17.9	75.8
Kansas	8,684	22,927	31,611	104,250	407,058	542,919	1.6	4.2	5.8	19.2	74.9
Kentucky	8,229	22,448	30,677	91,740	310,189	432,606	1.9	5.2	7.1	21.2	71.6
Louisiana	272	9,313	9,585	60,284	172,990	242,859	.1	3.8	3.9	24.8	71.2
Maine	245	3,251	3,496	70,607	133,244	207,347	.1	1.6	1.7	34.0	64.3
Maryland	973	11,941	12,914	209,019	332,645	554,578	.2	2.2	2.4	37.6	59.9
Massachusetts	2,967	31,234	34,201	608,545	2,356,772	2,999,518	.1	1.0	1.1	20.3	78.6
Michigan	7,754	14,617	22,371	134,145	472,468	628,984	1.2	2.3	3.5	21.4	75.1
Minnesota	30,698	26,277	56,975	160,326	725,490	942,791	3.3	2.8	6.1	17.0	76.9

Mississippi	1,050	8,213	9,263	26,935	69,986	106,184	1.0	7.8	8.7	25.4	65.9
Missouri	17,424	30,050	47,474	274,687	1,027,432	1,349,593	1.3	2.2	3.5	20.1	76.4
Montana	7,084	6,585	13,669	27,071	144,696	185,436	3.8	3.5	7.3	14.6	78.1
Nebraska	15,488	24,225	39,713	121,448	498,106	659,267	2.4	3.7	6.0	18.4	75.6
Nevada	4,415	1,685	6,100	1,428	14,670	22,198	19.9	7.6	27.5	6.4	66.1
New Hampshire	665	3,792	4,457	67,035	148,230	219,722	.3	1.7	2.0	30.5	67.4
New Jersey	7,324	12,207	19,531	386,752	820,192	1,226,475	.5	1.0	1.5	31.5	67.0
New Mexico	5,150	3,539	8,689	19,881	98,969	127,539	4.0	2.8	6.8	15.6	77.6
New York	14,629	40,408	55,037	1,010,342	6,921,758	7,987,137	.2	.5	.7	12.7	86.6
North Carolina	1,135	10,623	11,758	43,844	126,105	181,707	.6	5.8	6.4	24.1	69.5
North Dakota	365	4,829	5,194	36,295	115,329	156,818	.2	3.1	3.3	23.1	73.6
Ohio	49,283	60,744	110,027	539,494	1,353,109	2,002,630	2.4	3.0	5.4	27.0	67.6
Oklahoma	2,088	17,834	19,922	75,414	293,836	389,172	.6	4.6	5.2	19.4	75.4
Oregon	53,404	8,453	61,857	12,199	324,476	398,532	13.4	2.1	15.5	3.1	81.4
Pennsylvania	89,373	80,745	170,118	1,240,070	2,984,995	4,395,183	2.0	1.8	3.9	28.2	67.9
Rhode Island	265	1,883	2,148	43,934	66,009	112,091	.2	1.7	1.9	39.2	58.9
South Carolina	317	7,178	7,495	24,617	79,289	111,401	.3	6.4	6.7	22.2	71.1
South Dakota	5,955	4,513	10,468	29,732	114,781	154,981	3.7	2.7	6.4	19.1	74.5
Tennessee	1,982	19,175	21,157	113,217	273,813	408,187	.5	4.7	5.2	27.7	67.1
Texas	12,442	67,267	79,709	272,237	838,381	1,190,327	1.0	5.7	6.7	22.8	70.5
Utah	14,290	5,914	20,204	19,684	92,428	132,316	10.8	4.5	15.3	14.9	67.8
Vermont	125	4,694	4,819	51,536	130,248	186,603	------	2.4	2.4	27.6	70.0
Virginia	5,039	12,038	17,077	109,838	317,611	444,526	1.1	2.7	3.8	24.8	71.4
Washington	58,379	10,313	68,692	24,780	367,118	460,590	12.7	2.2	14.9	5.4	79.7
West Virginia	2,574	4,520	7,094	43,005	121,247	171,346	1.5	2.6	4.1	25.2	70.7
Wisconsin	14,386	17,714	32,100	143,759	449,044	624,903	2.3	2.8	5.1	23.0	71.9
Wyoming	3,265	1,925	5,190	10,035	69,236	84,461	3.8	2.3	6.1	11.8	82.1
Total	802,760	907,638	1,710,398	8,066,669	28,846,102	38,623,169	2.1	2.3	4.4	20.9	74.7

TABLE II.—*Retail deposits in national banks, state banks, private banks, loan and trust companies, stock savings banks, and mutual savings banks*—Continued.

STATE BANKS.

State.	Gold.	Silver.	Total specie.	Currency.	Checks.	Total.	Gold.	Silver	Specie.	Currency.	Checks.
							P. ct.	*P. ct.*	*P. ct.*	*P. ct.*	*P. ct.*
Alabama	$1,352	$5,779	$7,131	$26,601	$54,683	$88,415	1.5	6.6	8.1	30.1	61.8
Arizona	4,370	988	5,358	7,510	22,545	35,413	12.3	2.8	15.1	21.2	63.7
Arkansas	1,760	6,305	8,065	18,649	91,989	118,703	1.5	5.3	6.8	15.6	77.6
California	175,387	26,779	202,166	30,031	712,124	944,321	18.6	2.8	21.4	3.2	75.4
Colorado	12,157	1,926	14,083	6,789	44,341	65,213	18.6	3.0	21.6	10.4	67.9
Connecticut	127	1,919	2,046	45,960	155,499	203,505	------	.9	1.0	22.6	76.4
Delaware	--------	120	120	1,768	3,502	5,390	------	2.2	2.2	32.8	65.0
District of Columbia	20	336	356	10,874	8,095	19,325	.1	1.8	1.9	56.3	41.8
Florida	160	4,197	4,357	13,858	37,717	55,932	------	7.5	7.8	24.6	67.5
Georgia	3,620	22,439	26,059	48,385	82,706	157,150	2.3	14.3	16.6	30.7	52.7
Idaho	3,965	1,908	5,873	6,348	29,149	41,370	9.6	4.6	14.2	15.4	70.4
Illinois	29,242	24,483	53,725	432,700	1,584,304	2,070,729	1.4	1.2	2.6	20.9	76.5
Indiana	21,012	17,024	38,036	80,466	177,383	295,885	7.1	5.8	12.8	27.2	60.0
Iowa	2,839	9,019	11,858	56,188	171,018	239,064	1.2	3.8	5.0	23.5	71.5
Kansas	4,185	12,873	17,058	65,576	265,812	348,446	1.2	3.7	4.9	18.7	76.4
Kentucky	9,610	24,425	34,035	77,954	234,583	346,572	2.8	7.0	9.8	22.5	67.7
Louisiana	62	10,041	10,103	40,655	102,103	152,861	------	6.6	6.6	26.6	66.7
Maine	135	410	545	15,339	31,628	47,512	.3	.9	1.2	32.2	66.6
Maryland	402	1,387	1,789	19,453	28,433	49,675	.8	2.8	3.6	39.1	57.3
Michigan	6,545	18,517	25,062	158,170	340,252	523,484	1.2	3.5	4.7	30.2	65.1
Minnesota	26,115	19,736	45,851	129,517	323,986	499,354	5.2	4.0	9.2	25.9	64.9
Mississippi	801	11,084	11,885	24,449	88,343	124,677	.6	8.9	9.5	19.7	70.7

Missouri	11,610	44,159	55,769	213,760	971,410	1,240,939	.9	3.6	4.5	17.2	78.3
Montana	7,140	2,201	9,341	13,894	86,688	109,923	6.6	2.0	8.5	12.6	78.9
Nebraska	3,226	12,155	15,381	75,332	298,973	389,686	.8	3.1	3.9	19.3	76.8
Nevada	3,725	1,130	4,855	1,492	24,472	30,819	12.2	3.7	15.8	4.8	79.4
New Hampshire	------	360	360	2,462	3,514	6,336	------	5.7	5.7	38.8	55.5
New Jersey	242	948	1,190	35,151	47,755	84,096	.3	1.1	1.4	41.8	56.8
New Mexico	160	174	334	1,109	2,786	4,229	3.8	4.1	7.9	26.2	65.9
New York	29,603	59,115	88,718	1,116,060	2,565,583	3,770,361	.8	1.6	2.4	29.6	68.0
North Carolina	60	1,085	1,145	10,103	27,722	38,970	.1	2.8	2.9	26.0	71.1
North Dakota	202	5,010	5,212	32,911	89,065	127,188	.2	3.9	4.1	25.9	70.0
Ohio	27,099	27,009	54,108	230,169	465,981	750,258	3.6	3.6	7.2	30.8	62.0
Oklahoma	90	4,632	4,722	37,883	35,173	77,778	.1	6.0	6.1	48.7	45.2
Oregon	21,961	4,078	26,039	4,916	94,847	125,802	18.3	3.2	20.7	3.9	75.4
Pennsylvania	14,410	13,500	27,910	189,570	278,807	496,287	2.9	2.7	5.6	38.2	56.2
Rhode Island	20	423	443	9,786	26,009	36,238	.1	1.2	1.3	27.0	71.7
South Carolina	705	14,326	15,031	41,732	83,602	140,365	.5	10.2	10.7	29.7	59.6
South Dakota	840	5,006	5,846	30,999	83,935	120,780	.7	4.2	4.9	25.7	69.4
Tennessee	1,905	6,288	8,193	21,161	121,470	150,824	1.3	4.2	5.5	14.0	80.5
Texas	275	2,660	2,935	12,737	37,915	53,587	.5	5.0	5.5	23.8	70.7
Utah	10,405	2,533	12,938	7,908	77,815	98,661	10.5	2.6	13.1	8.0	78.9
Vermont	40	301	341	11,188	30,283	41,812	.1	.7	.8	26.7	72.5
Virginia	1,069	5,461	6,530	42,870	96,793	146,193	.7	3.8	4.5	29.3	66.2
Washington	38,445	8,283	46,728	18,407	186,045	251,180	15.3	3.3	18.6	7.3	74.1
West Virginia	1,192	5,756	6,948	35,809	77,004	119,761	1.0	4.8	5.8	29.9	64.3
Wisconsin	19,138	13,185	32,323	160,880	455,780	648,983	3.0	2.0	5.0	24.8	70.2
Wyoming	210	695	905	3,049	29,041	32,995	.6	2.1	2.7	9.3	88.0
Total	497,638	462,168	959,806	3,678,578	10,888,663	15,527,047	3.2	3.0	6.2	23.8	70.0

TABLE II.—*Retail deposits in national banks, state banks, private banks, loan and trust companies, stock savings banks, and mutual savings banks*—Continued.

PRIVATE BANKS.

States.	Gold.	Silver.	Total specie.	Currency.	Checks.	Total.	Gold.	Silver.	Specie.	Currency.	Checks.
							P. ct.	*P. ct.*	*P. ct.*	*P. ct.*	*P. ct.*
Alabama		$126	$126	$12	$49	$187		67.4	67.4	6.4	26.2
Arkansas	$200	74	274	1,011	1,070	2,355	8.5	3.1	11.6	42.9	45.4
California	1,260	296	1,556	147	4,570	6,273	20.1	4.7	24.8	2.3	72.9
Colorado	575	364	939	2,786	8,733	12,458	4.6	2.9	7.6	22.3	70.1
Connecticut	5	28	33	1,629	12,623	14,285		.2	.2	11.4	88.4
Florida		157	157	821	3,397	4,375		3.6	3.6	17.9	77.7
Georgia		223	223	589	1,208	2,020		11.0	11.0	29.1	59.8
Idaho		4	4	290	3,845	4,139		.1	.1	7.0	92.9
Illinois	5,202	8,273	13,475	77,706	209,593	300,774	1.7	2.7	4.4	25.8	69.8
Indiana	3,090	6,190	9,280	28,416	64,506	102,202	3.0	6.1	9.1	27.8	63.1
Iowa	235	2,913	3,148	11,548	59,817	74,513	.3	3.9	4.2	15.5	80.3
Kansas	100	624	724	2,544	5,837	9,105	1.1	6.9	8.0	27.9	64.1
Maryland				100	426	526				19.0	81.0
Massachusetts		244	244	2,652	2,346	5,242		4.7	4.7	50.6	44.7
Michigan	1,730	3,895	5,625	27,508	34,628	67,761	2.5	5.8	8.3	40.6	51.1
Minnesota	30	95	125	304	2,695	3,124	.9	3.1	4.0	9.7	86.3
Mississippi		179	179	22	2	203		88.1	88.1	10.8	1.0
Missouri	125	809	934	3,481	12,246	16,661	.8	4.8	5.6	20.9	73.5
Montana	110	105	215	1,101	2,247	3,563	3.1	3.0	6.0	30.9	63.1
Nebraska	10	103	113	585	2,125	2,823	.4	3.6	4.0	20.6	75.4
New York	190	854	1,044	10,779	16,980	28,803	.6	3.0	3.6	37.5	58.9
North Carolina	30	120	150	291	1,058	1,499	2.0	8.0	10.0	19.4	70.6

Ohio	1,225	1,644	2,869	9,046	50,266	62,181	1.9	2.6	4.5	14.5	81.0
Oklahoma	------	15	15	40	95	150	------	10.0	10.0	26.7	63.3
Oregon	495	164	659	107	1,996	2,762	17.9	5.9	23.8	3.9	72.3
Pennsylvania	280	907	1,187	9,442	34,848	45,477	.6	2.0	2.6	20.7	76.6
South Dakota	20	171	191	1,479	10,496	12,166	.1	1.3	1.4	12.1	87.5
Texas	30	6,416	6,446	15,402	19,086	40,934	.1	15.7	15.8	37.6	46.6
Utah	15	78	93	98	2,179	2,370	.6	3.3	3.9	4.1	92.0
Vermont	------	5	5	150	315	470	------	1.0	1.0	32.0	67.0
Virginia	------	1,057	1,057	10,782	14,973	26,812	------	4.0	4.0	40.2	55.8
Washington	665	91	756	506	4,736	5,998	11.1	1.5	12.6	8.4	79.0
Wisconsin	------	35	35	472	2,188	2,695	------	1.3	1.3	17.5	81.2
Wyoming	25	------	25	180	1,898	2,103	1.2	------	1.2	8.6	90.2
Total	15,647	36,259	51,906	222,026	593,077	867,009	1.8	4.2	6.0	25.6	68.4

LOAN AND TRUST COMPANIES.

							P. ct.	P. ct.	P. ct.	P. ct.	P. ct.
Arkansas	$115	$528	$643	$2,067	$1,952	$4,662	2.5	11.3	13.8	44.3	41.8
Colorado	135	233	368	1,093	21,302	22,763	.6	1.1	1.7	4.8	93.4
Connecticut	5	1,755	1,760	36,440	73,055	111,255	------	1.7	1.7	32.7	65.6
Delaware	15	28	43	2,260	1,977	4,280	.3	.6	1.0	52.8	46.2
District of Columbia	------	------	------	10,100	19,044	29,144	------	------	------	34.6	65.4
Idaho	435	229	664	791	2,469	3,924	11.1	5.8	16.9	20.1	63.0
Illinois	880	773	1,653	13,970	27,386	43,009	2.1	1.8	3.9	32.5	63.6
Indiana	2,427	2,527	4,954	10,608	40,148	55,710	4.4	4.5	8.9	19.0	72.0
Maine	75	675	750	59,708	50,713	111,171	.1	.6	.7	53.7	45.6
Maryland	------	146	146	717	2,692	3,555	------	4.0	4.0	20.2	75.8
Massachusetts	986	10,053	11,039	249,123	706,868	967,030	.1	1.0	1.1	25.7	73.1
Minnesota	200	135	335	2,557	14,108	17,000	1.2	.8	2.0	15.0	83.0

TABLE II.—*Retail deposits in national banks, state banks, private banks, loan and trust companies, stock savings banks, and mutual savings banks*—Continued.

LOAN AND TRUST COMPANIES—Continued.

States.	Gold.	Silver.	Total specie.	Currency.	Checks.	Total.	Gold.	Silver.	Specie.	Currency.	Checks.
							P. ct.	*P. ct.*	*P. ct.*	*P. ct.*	*P. ct.*
Missouri	$790	$2,557	$3,347	$27,678	$153,259	$184,284	0.4	1.3	1.7	15.1	83.2
New Hampshire		32	32	1,180	3,116	4,328		.7	.7	27.3	72.0
New Jersey	1,452	4,922	6,374	140,253	288,446	435,073	.3	1.1	1.4	32.2	66.4
New York	4,762	12,133	16,895	326,705	1,474,229	1,817,829	.3	.6	.9	18.0	81.0
North Carolina	55	2,286	2,341	7,568	21,551	31,460	.2	7.3	7.4	24.1	68.5
Ohio	2,332	651	2,983	10,182	15,007	28,172	8.3	2.3	10.5	36.1	53.4
Pennsylvania	20,411	16,825	37,236	247,305	662,742	947,283	2.2	1.8	3.9	26.1	69.9
Rhode Island	182	2,204	2,386	67,983	72,660	143,029	.1	1.6	1.7	47.5	50.8
South Carolina		135	135	1,089	355	1,579		8.6	8.6	68.9	22.5
Vermont	140	354	494	9,160	34,662	44,316	.3	.8	1.1	20.6	78.3
Washington	800	500	1,300	2,000	15,000	18,300	4.4	2.7	7.1	10.9	82.0
West Virginia	40	273	313	4,534	5,508	10,355	.4	2.6	3.0	43.8	53.2
Total	36,237	59,954	96,191	1,235,071	3,708,249	5,039,511	.7	1.2	1.9	24.5	73.6

STOCK SAVINGS BANKS.

States.	Gold.	Silver.	Total specie.	Currency.	Checks.	Total.	Gold.	Silver.	Specie.	Currency.	Checks.
							P. ct.	*P. ct.*	*P. ct.*	*P. ct.*	*P. ct.*
California	$10,510	$1,289	$11,799	$2,502	$24,012	$38,313	27.4	3.4	30.8	6.5	62.7
Colorado		23	23		93	116		20.0	20.0		80.0
District of Columbia		55	55	781	819	1,655		3.3	3.3	47.2	49.5
Georgia	10	224	234	336	621	1,191	.7	18.9	19.6	28.2	52.2
Illinois	435	1,144	1,579	8,218	8,311	18,108	2.4	6.3	8.7	45.4	45.9

Iowa	4,590	8,173	12,763	36,172	104,059	152,994	3.0	5.3	8.3	23.7	68.0
Kansas	640	115	755	376	321	1,452	44.2	7.9	52.1	25.8	22.1
Kentucky	15	17	32	120	71	223	6.7	7.6	14.3	53.8	31.8
Louisiana	----	58	58	826	68	952	----	6.0	6.0	86.8	7.2
Maryland	----	98	98	2,749	5,836	8,683	----	1.1	1.1	31.7	67.2
Michigan	916	1,829	2,745	30,227	65,272	98,244	.9	1.9	2.8	30.8	66.4
Mississippi	----	31	31	100	43	174	----	17.9	17.9	57.4	24.7
Missouri	----	10	10	177	5,002	5,189	----	.2	.2	3.4	96.4
New Hampshire	2	36	38	848	216	1,102	.2	3.3	3.5	77.0	19.5
Ohio	230	613	843	4,577	3,365	8,785	2.6	7.0	9.6	52.1	38.3
Pennsylvania	225	48	273	2,748	1,136	4,157	5.4	1.2	6.6	66.1	27.3
South Dakota	110	25	135	100	800	1,035	10.6	2.4	13.0	9.7	77.3
Tennessee	110	983	1,093	7,589	10,035	18,717	.5	5.2	5.7	40.6	53.7
Vermont	----	72	72	1,281	10,676	12,029	----	.6	.6	10.5	88.9
Virginia	----	10	10	155	21	186	----	5.4	5.4	83.3	11.3
West Virginia	160	450	610	2,480	1,100	4,190	3.8	10.7	14.5	59.2	26.3
Total	17,953	15,303	33,256	102,362	241,877	377,495	4.8	4.0	8.8	27.1	64.1

MUTUAL SAVINGS BANKS.

							P. ct.	P. ct.	P. ct.	P. ct.	P. ct.
Maine	$20	----	$20	$55	$215	$290	7.0	----	7.0	19.0	74.0
Massachusetts	----	----	----	50	----	50	----	----	----	----	----
Maryland	----	$9	9	264	48	321	----	3.0	3.0	82.5	14.5
Minnesota	----	43	43	80	229	352	----	12.0	12.0	23.0	65.0
New Jersey	25	1	26	504	----	530	5.0	----	5.0	95.0	----
New York	1,025	98	1,123	8,669	368	10,160	10.1	.9	11.1	85.2	3.7
Pennsylvania	----	2	2	322	464	788	----	----	----	40.9	58.9
Total	1,070	153	1,223	9,944	1,324	12,491	8.5	1.2	9.7	79.7	10.6

TABLE III.—*Aggregate deposits of retail dealers, all classes of banks, by States.*

Locality.	Gold.	Silver	Total specie.	Currency.	Checks.	Total.	Gold	Silver.	Specie.	Currency.	Checks.
							P. ct.	*P. ct.*	*P. ct.*	*P. ct.*	*P. ct.*
Alabama	$4,869	$26,083	$30,952	$113,669	$315,993	$460,614	1.1	5.6	6.7	24.6	68.5
Arizona	10,355	3,120	13,475	14,460	52,858	80,793	12.8	3.8	16.6	17.9	65.5
Arkansas	3,380	11,535	14,915	40,091	177,011	232,017	1.5	5.0	6.5	17.3	76.2
California	386,946	67,236	454,182	113,291	1,660,065	2,227,538	17.4	3.0	20.4	5.1	74.5
Colorado	56,988	17,007	73,995	103,661	495,439	673,095	8.5	2.5	11.0	15.5	73.5
Connecticut	1,775	13,269	15,044	316,107	618,041	949,192	.2	1.4	1.6	33.4	65.0
Delaware	151	1,550	1,701	29,355	48,251	79,307	.2	1.9	2.1	37.2	60.7
District of Columbia	262	3,473	3,735	118,078	131,504	253,317	.1	1.3	1.4	46.7	51.9
Florida	1,217	39,910	41,127	92,633	240,786	374,546	.4	10.7	11.0	24.7	64.3
Georgia	7,735	46,803	54,538	159,268	356,588	570,394	1.4	8.2	9.6	27.8	62.6
Idaho	12,275	5,388	17,663	16,818	95,726	130,207	9.4	4.2	13.6	12.9	73.5
Illinois	71,622	91,738	163,360	1,135,341	4,003,634	5,302,335	1.4	1.7	3.1	21.4	75.5
Indiana	57,241	76,902	134,143	400,937	833,987	1,369,067	4.2	5.6	9.8	29.2	61.0
Iowa	26,361	49,401	75,762	241,195	913,983	1,230,940	2.2	4.1	6.3	19.5	74.2
Kansas	13,609	36,539	50,148	172,746	679,028	901,922	1.5	4.1	5.6	19.1	75.3
Kentucky	17,854	46,890	64,744	169,814	544,843	779,401	2.3	6.0	8.3	21.5	70.2
Louisiana	334	19,412	19,746	101,765	275,161	396,672	.1	4.9	5.0	25.5	69.5
Maine	475	4,336	4,811	145,709	215,800	366,320	.3	1.2	1.5	39.7	58.8
Maryland	1,375	13,581	14,956	232,302	370,080	617,338	.2	2.2	2.4	37.6	60.0
Massachusetts	3,953	41,531	45,484	860,370	3,065,986	3,971,840	.1	1.0	1.1	21.6	77.3
Michigan	16,945	38,858	55,803	350,050	912,620	1,318,473	1.3	2.9	4.2	26.6	69.2
Minnesota	57,043	46,286	103,329	292,784	1,066,508	1,462,621	4.0	3.1	7.1	20.1	72.8
Mississippi	1,851	19,507	21,358	51,506	158,374	231,238	.8	8.4	9.2	22.3	68.5
Missouri	29,949	77,585	107,534	519,783	2,169,349	2,796,666	1.1	2.7	3.8	18.6	77.6

Montana	14,334	8,891	23,225	42,066	233,631	298,922	4.8	2.9	7.7	14.1	78.2
Nebraska	18,724	36,483	55,207	197,365	799,204	1,051,776	1.8	3.5	5.3	18.8	75.9
Nevada	8,140	2,815	10,955	2,920	39,142	53,017	15.3	5.3	20.6	5.5	73.9
New Hampshire	667	4,220	4,887	71,525	155,076	231,488	.3	1.8	2.1	30.9	67.0
New Jersey	9,043	18,078	27,121	562,660	1,156,393	1,746,174	.5	1.1	1.6	32.2	66.2
New Mexico	5,310	3,713	9,023	20,990	101,755	131,768	4.1	2.8	6.9	15.9	77.2
New York	50,209	112,608	162,817	2,472,555	10,978,918	13,614,290	.4	.8	1.2	18.2	80.6
North Carolina	1,280	14,114	15,394	61,806	176,436	253,636	.5	5.6	6.1	24.4	69.5
North Dakota	567	9,839	10,406	69,206	204,394	284,006	.1	3.5	3.6	24.4	72.0
Ohio	80,169	90,661	170,830	793,468	1,887,728	2,852,026	2.9	3.1	6.0	27.8	66.2
Oklahoma	2,178	22,481	24,659	113,337	329,104	467,100	.5	4.8	5.3	24.3	70.4
Oregon	75,860	12,695	88,555	17,222	421,319	527,096	14.4	2.4	16.8	3.1	80.1
Pennsylvania	124,699	112,027	236,726	1,689,457	3,962,992	5,889,175	2.2	1.9	4.1	28.8	67.1
Rhode Island	467	4,510	4,977	121,703	164,678	291,358	.2	1.5	1.7	41.8	56.5
South Carolina	1,022	21,639	22,661	67,438	163,246	253,345	.4	8.5	8.9	26.6	64.5
South Dakota	6,925	9,715	16,640	62,310	210,012	288,962	2.3	3.3	5.7	21.6	72.7
Tennessee	3,997	26,446	30,443	141,967	405,318	577,728	.7	4.5	5.2	24.5	70.3
Texas	12,747	76,343	89,090	300,376	895,382	1,284,848	1.0	6.0	7.0	23.0	70.0
Utah	24,710	8,525	33,235	27,690	172,422	233,347	10.6	3.6	14.2	11.9	73.9
Vermont	305	5,426	5,731	73,315	206,184	285,230	.1	1.9	2.0	25.5	72.5
Virginia	6,108	18,566	24,674	163,645	429,398	617,717	1.0	3.0	4.0	26.5	69.5
Washington	98,289	19,187	117,476	45,693	572,899	736,068	13.4	2.7	16.1	6.3	77.6
West Virginia	3,966	10,999	14,965	85,828	204,859	305,652	1.3	3.5	4.8	28.0	67.2
Wisconsin	33,524	30,934	64,458	305,111	907,012	1,276,581	2.6	2.5	5.1	23.9	71.0
Wyoming	3,500	2,620	6,120	13,264	100,175	119,559	2.9	2.2	5.1	11.2	83.7
Total	1,371,305	1,481,475	2,852,780	13,314,650	44,279,292	60,446,722	2.3	2.4	4.7	22.1	73.2

TABLE IV.—*Aggregate retail deposits, all classes of banks, by banks.*

	Gold.	Silver.	Total specie.	Currency.	Checks.	Total.	Gold.	Sil-ver.	Specie.	Cur-rency.	Checks.
							P. ct.	*P. ct.*	*P. ct.*	*P. ct.*	*P. ct.*
National banks	$802,760	$907,638	$1,710,398	$8,066,669	$28,846,102	$38,623,169	2.1	2.3	4.4	20.9	74.7
State banks	497,638	462,168	959,806	3,678,578	10,888,663	15,527,047	3.2	3.0	6.2	23.8	70.0
Private banks	15,647	36,259	51,906	222,026	593,077	867,009	1.8	4.2	6.0	25.6	68.4
Loan and trust companies	36,237	59,954	96,191	1,235,071	3,708,249	5,039,511	.7	1.2	1.9	24.5	73.6
Stock savings banks	17,953	15,303	33,256	102,362	241,877	377,495	4.8	4.0	8.8	27.1	64.1
Mutual savings banks	1,070	153	1,223	9,944	1,324	12,491	8.0	1.3	9.3	78.4	12.3
Total	1,371,305	1,481,475	2 852,780	13,314,650	44,279,292	60,446,722	2.3	2.4	4.7	22.1	73.2

DISCUSSION OF TABLES.

Retail deposits of national banks.—These returns are classified, as has been indicated, by banks and classes of deposits. Of the national banks 5,452 sent in replies which were used. The aggregate amount deposited by retail dealers in these banks on the day in question was $38,623,169. Of this total, $28,846,102, or 74.7 per cent, was in checks; $8,066,669, or 20.9 per cent, in currency; and $1,710,398, or 4.4 per cent, in coin. The State in whose deposits the largest per cent of checks appears is New York, with 86.6 per cent. The State showing the smallest per cent was Rhode Island, with 58.9 per cent. Thirty States show a percentage of credit instruments in retail deposits of 70 or more. Sixteen show a percentage higher than 60 and less than 70.

Retail deposits of state banks.—The retail deposits of the state banks aggregated $15,527,047 from 4,288 banks. The checks amounted to $10,888,663, or 70 per cent, as compared with 74.7 of the national banks. The currency amounted to $3,678,578, or 23.8 per cent; the specie to $959,806, or 6.2 per cent, almost equally divided between gold and silver. The highest per cent shown by the returns of any State was 88 in the case of Wyoming. It should be noted, however, that the aggregate deposits of the 12 banks reported for Wyoming were only $32,995. The State whose returns show the lowest per cent among the state banks is Oklahoma, with 45.2 per cent. Twenty-two States returned percentages of 70 or more, but less than 88, while seventeen show percentages of 60 and less than 70. The lowest percentage of checks in deposits was that of the state banks in the District of Columbia. The figure is 41.8. It will be noted that the percentages of the District of Columbia were lowest for the national banks also. It will be noted also that Wyoming, which stands highest in the per cent of checks returned in the state banks, stands second with 82.1 per cent according to the returns from the national banks.

Retail deposits of the private banks.—The number of private banks whose returns were used was 665. The aggregate deposits returned to the credit of retail dealers was $867,009. Of this amount $593,077, or 68.4 per cent, was in checks. The highest percentage returned was that of Idaho, 92.9. This, however, was from only one bank. Utah returned 92 per cent from two banks; Wyoming 90.2 per cent from one bank. More than one-third of the total returns were from 203 private banks in Illinois; and these show 69.8 per cent of checks and other credit paper deposited. Mississippi makes the very remarkable showing of 1 per cent of credit documents, but the returns are from only one bank and aggregate only $203. The figure therefore has no significance for the average.

Fourteen States and the District of Columbia gave no returns from private banks. Nineteen of those replying returned percentages of checks higher than 70. Six showed percentages between 60 and 70 and nine between 50 and 60. Aside from that of Mississippi, already noted, the lowest per cent of checks in the deposits was in Alabama, 26.2. Here, again, only one bank was represented.

If we consider only those banks of this group which returned deposits of $10,000 or more from not less than eight banks—those of Colorado, Illinois, Indiana, Iowa, Michigan, Missouri, New York, Ohio, Pennsylvania, South Dakota, and Texas—we find that the percentages range from 51.1 in Michigan to 87.5 in South Dakota.

Retail deposits of loan and trust companies.—Of these institutions 401 reported aggregate retail deposits of $5,039,511 made on the day in question. Of this amount $3,708,249, or 73.6 per cent, were in checks; $1,235,071, or 24.5, in currency; and $96,191, or 1.9, in specie, the silver being $23,717 more than the gold. No usable returns of this class were received from Alabama, Arizona, California, Florida, Georgia, Iowa, Kansas, Kentucky, Louisiana, Michigan, Mississippi, Montana, Nebraska, Nevada, New Mexico, North Dakota, Oklahoma, Oregon, South Dakota, Tennessee, Texas, Utah, Virginia, Wisconsin, or Wyoming.

The largest per cent snown, 93.4, was in the State of Colorado, from 5 banks. Missouri comes next with 83.2 per cent from 16 banks. Minnesota stands next with 83 per cent from 2 banks. New York has 81 per cent from 58 banks.

Pennsylvania, with returns from 126 banks, shows 69.9 per cent. It is noticeable that in this group there are five States which show more than 80 per cent of retail deposits of these companies.

The lowest per cent returned is 22.5 from one bank in South Carolina, whose deposits of this class on the day in question were $1,579. The array of percentages in the loan and trust companies shows a greater variation than in the case of the three preceding classes of banking institutions.

Retail deposits of stock savings banks.—The aggregate deposits of this class returned by 335 of the stock savings banks were $377,495. Of this amount $241,877, or 64.1 per cent, was in checks; $102,362, or 27.1 per cent, was in currency; $33,256, or 8.8 per cent, was in specie, pretty evenly divided between gold and silver, but with a preponderance in favor of the gold on account of the California deposits. The highest percentage of credit instruments returned in the retail deposits of this class of banks was 96.4 from two banks in Missouri with aggregate deposits of $5,189.

The lowest percentage, 7.2 per cent, is shown by the deposits of two banks in Louisiana aggregating $952. Two banks in Virginia with $186 deposits show 11.3 per cent of checks. Six banks in New Hampshire with deposits of $1,102 show 19.5 per cent; two in Colorado and Vermont show percentages of 80 and 88.9 per cent, respectively. Four States give percentages higher than 70 and four between 60 and 70.

Of the States which sent replies from three or more banks New Hampshire had 19.5 per cent of credit paper in $1,102 deposits in six banks.

It should be noted, of course, in considering the returns of the stock saving banks, that while these are commercial banks with active checking accounts in the West, in States like Mississippi, Louisiana, and New Hampshire, they are probably more for savings accounts proper.

Retail deposits of the mutual savings banks.—That the mutual savings banks returned any deposits for retail dealers as such is due doubtless to the literalness with which the officers of a few of these banks interpreted the circular of inquiry. Strictly speaking, the deposits in the mutual savings banks should all be included in one class. Nevertheless, as a matter of interest, they are presented with the same classification as in the case of the other banks.

We find that $12,491 are returned as deposited by retail traders. Of this amount $1,324, or 10.6 per cent, was in checks; $9,944, or 79.7 per cent, in currency; $1,223, or 9.7 per cent, in specie, $1,070 of this being in gold, practically all deposited in the New York banks. The amounts involved are so small that the returns have no significance whatever, of course, as referring to the class of dealers to whom they are accredited.

We shall find the same thing true of the depositors classified as wholesale dealers in the mutual savings banks. Therefore the important table for this class of banks is the "all others."

Aggregate retail deposits.—Tables III and IV show the aggregate retail deposits according to the usual classification, by states and classes of banks.

The aggregate retail deposits were $60,446,722. Of this amount $44,279,292, or 73.2 per cent, were in credit documents, as against 67.4 per cent in 1896; $13,314,650, or 22 per cent, were in currency, and $2,852,780, or 4.8 per cent, were in specie, pretty evenly divided between gold and silver. The largest volume of deposits is in the returns of the national banks and the percentage of checks in these deposits is 74.7, the highest shown by any class of banks. The loan and trust companies come next with 73.7 per cent, but their total deposits were only about one-eighth of those of the national banks. The third in order of percentage is the state banks and the percentage of credit paper in their deposits is 70 in aggregate deposits of fifteen and one-half millions, or about 40 per cent of the deposits of the national banks. The private banks, with aggregate retail deposits of $867,009, show 68.4 per cent of checks, while the stock savings banks, with deposits of $377,495, show $64.1 per cent of checks. The mutual savings banks show 12.3 per cent in checks in deposits of $12,491. The returns of the mutual savings banks are of no importance in the discussion of retail deposits as such.

What now do these figures mean? What is the significance of this 73.2 per cent, which, on the basis of the returns, is the proportion of checks deposited by retail merchants? The real interest of such an investigation as this centers on these retail deposits. There has never been any dispute of the statement that 90 per cent of the wholesale transactions of the country are settled ordinarily by means of credit paper. The contention has been that the method of settlement of wholesale payments gave no indication of the habits of the people with reference to the use of money and checks. To meet this point the inquiries of 1894, 1896, and 1909 have sought to secure a classification of the deposits of the retail merchants.

It is very clear that we can not take the figures on the basis of the returns as representing exactly the proportion of payments made by the people of this country with checks in their retail purchases. Various allowances and corrections must first be made before we can reach anything like a satisfactory conclusion.

ALLOWANCES AND CORRECTIONS.

Banks not heard from.—The number of banks whose reports were used, as already indicated, was 11,491; the total number of different kinds of banking institutions in the country at the time of this inquiry is not exactly known. The report of the Comptroller of the Currency, from year to year, purports to give the number of national, state, private, and other banks, and for the year 1908 the number given is 25,000. There are some so-called banks, however, which are not banks in the ordinary sense of the word. For example, a good many stock brokers have deposits of their customers waiting for opportune investments. They may or may not allow interest on these accounts. They advertise themselves, however, as doing a banking business. The accounts are not checking accounts, nor are they intended to be accounts as ordinarily understood.

On April 28, 1909, about six weeks after the date on which the deposits were called for in this inquiry, there were 6,926 national banks reported as in active operation. Of the whole number, 5,551 replied in some form to this inquiry, and the returns of 5,452 have been used—that is, 80 per cent were heard from. If the aggregate retail deposits of the banks not heard from is in the ratio of their number to the whole number, the amount to be added to the deposits received, in order to get the aggregate retail deposits of all the national banks on the date in question, would be about $9,655,000, making the aggregate deposits by retail dealers in all the national banks of the country on the date in question about $48,285,000.

The Comptroller's report in 1908 gave the aggregate number of state banks reporting as 11,220. Of this number 4,630, or 41 per cent, sent in returns, of which 4,302 were used. The aggregate retail deposits of this number was $15,527,047. If we increase the deposits of the retail dealers of the state banks for the nonreporting banks in the proportion of those reporting, the retail deposits for all the state banks of the country would be about $38,000,000. This is probably too large.

By similar processes of calculation the deposits of private banks by retail dealers on the day in question, after allowance is made for nonreporting banks, would be $1,150,000. For stock savings banks, which are really commercial banks, the figures would be $750,000 for the aggregate of retail deposits on the day in question. For loan and trust companies the retail deposits thus figured would be $7,600,000. We need not include the mutual savings banks. The total is $95,000,000.

It is doubtful, however, whether it is fair to increase the deposits of state banks and private banks in the ratio of the number reporting to the number not reporting, for the state and private banks which sent in replies were probably in the main located in the larger places. The 11,220 state banks reported by the Comptroller had $2,937,129,598 of deposits. This is an average of $261,000 for each state bank. The average individual deposits of the national banks on April 28 last per bank was $656,000. The relative commercial importance of the national bank and the state bank, measured by the individual deposits, is therefore in the ratio of to 2.5 to 1. It is probably greater than this. In allowing, then, for deposits for nonreporting state banks it would be fair to add a smaller sum per bank than the average shows. Moreover, since these nonreporting state banks were probably the smaller banks, the amount to be added to the check deposits should be proportionately larger, because, as we shall see later, the proportion of checks in the deposits of banks in agricultural communities runs very high, and it is in the agricultural communities of the West that we find the stronghold of the small state commercial banks.

When we have allowed for the aggregate deposits of the nonreporting banks, we are confronted with the question what proportion we shall put in the column of checks and other credit documents. It has been urged in the past in the discussion of this topic that the nonreporting or smaller banks will likely show the largest proportion of cash in their deposits, and that on that account, in making allowances for their returns, the proportion of cash entered as against the amount of checks should be larger. The present inquiry does not bear out that contention, but .rather the opposite, as the returns from agricultural districts show.

After we have made allowances for the nonreporting banks in the column of checks for each class of banks and added the proportion shown by the percentage derived from the returns of those which sent in replies, we have a grand aggregate of deposits of retail dealers on the day of our inquiry amounting to $95,000,000, of which about 70 per cent were in checks.

Allowances for possible excess of checks.—Do these bank deposits give a true view of the payments in retail trade? Do the payments by merchants into their banks fairly represent the payments received for sales of goods? The merchants can deposit only what they receive. If they deposit checks from their customers, this fact can only mean that the customers give them checks in payment of some transactions or other. Were the checks given wholly in payment for goods bought? If not, for what other reasons were they given and to what extent? There are several sources from which the retail dealers might get checks which show in their bank deposits. In the first place, merchants cash checks for their customers and friends as a matter of accommodation. So far as this was done on the day in question, the proportion of checks in the merchants' deposits would be too large. How much too large we do not know. In the few cases in which the writer has made inquiry he has been told that from 5 to 10 per cent would cover any error due to this cause. Ten per cent, the larger of the two figures, was given by one of the largest retail dealers in Chicago. It is hardly to be believed that so large a percentage is common. One can hardly believe that the retail stores of the country cashed nearly $10,000,000 of checks as a matter of accommodation for their friends on the day of our inquiry; yet this is what they must have done if they cashed 10 per cent. In the smaller stores where the inquiry was made the percentage ran down to nothing. If we allow 5 per cent for this source of error, we shall, in the opinion of the writer, be doing enough and more.

In the next place, the merchants often cash "pay checks" or take them in payment of bills or purchases which are less than the face value of the checks and give the balance to the customer in money. Very likely some checks of this class are included in the deposits of the retail dealers. They could not have amounted to much, however, for the day of the inquiry was Tuesday, and it is likely that pay checks received on Saturday would have been turned into the banks by Monday. The correction for this source of error for the day in question must be insignificant.

In the third place, we must remember that merchants do not all deposit daily. The deposits made by some merchants represent the receipts of from two to six days, and even longer. In so far as the accumulated receipts of several days appear in the returns, our ratio might be affected. It is doubtful, however, whether any allowance need to be made for this possible source of error. For, in the first place, the dealers who do this are those whose business is small and who are not within convenient reach of a bank; in the second place, they are just as likely to deposit checks as cash; and, in the third place, Tuesday is an unlikely day for such deposits. There is no reason to think that the proportion of cash and checks in their receipts from day to day would show large variation. In the opinion of the writer, no correction needs to be made on this account.

It has been urged also as a possible source of error that many dealers pay their wages to employees and other expenses with the money receipts of the day and deposit the balance. In so far as merchants follow this practice the proportion of checks in their deposits would be too large. We have no way of checking such an error. In some instances a firm draws a check against itself for its pay roll and other expenses. The cash is taken out of the day's receipts and the check deposited in the bank. This and similar methods of wage payment would swell the proportion of the merchants' checks. It is difficult to believe, however, that the amount involved can be very great as compared with the total deposits of the retail merchants. But however great or small the amount, it would be reduced to a minimum in the returns of the present inquiry, because the day of the week selected would not be a pay day, to a large extent, anywhere in the country. For this source of error, again, therefore, we need make no correction. It is more probable that a small error occurs from paying out money for certain other expenses than wages on the day in question. We must remember, however, that the merchant has a bank account and that he is just as likely, perhaps more likely, to pay his bills with checks as with cash. No extensive inquiry on this point has been made. In the few cases in which the writer was able to ask the question, he found that dealers other than those whose business was exceedingly small preferred to pay with checks because they can keep better track of their payments.

Finally, it is urged that checks may pass through several hands before they reach the merchants and are deposited by them in the banks, and that they may be deposited in several banks on the same day before reaching the place where they are finally paid. Such duplications, however, could not occur in the "deposits" of retail merchants, because these deposits contain the checks which they themselves have received from customers and other individuals. These duplications will appear in the "all others" class if these should include the deposits of banks and bankers. No correction needs to be made for such a cause of error, therefore, in the retail figures.

Ignorance of business of depositors.—Perhaps the first point that needs to be settled in the discussion of these returns is who are "retail dealers." The term, of course, is somewhat indefinite. Ordinarily, we think of the retail dealer as one who sells directly to the consumer. He is generally the purveyor of what are called finished goods to those who are themselves to make use of them in final consumption. Even this is not quite accurate, but the phrase certainly conveys to most people pretty definitely the idea expressed above. Even when we have agreed upon a meaning of the term there still is difficulty from the fact that some merchants do both a wholesale and retail business, and do not, perhaps can not, always keep their accounts separate. There is no reason to think, however, that any error occurs in the returns from confusion as to the meaning of the term "retail dealer." As was pointed out in the discussion of 1896, the question where, for example, we shall class the jobber or the lumber merchant, depends upon the community, the extent of the business, and the point of view.

Another possible source of confusion in the returns may arise from the impossibility that banks in large places with a large number of customers can know the business of each individual. In all but the larger cities it is very likely true that this would not be the case, and that the banks would be able to classify with fair accuracy. From the care with which replies were evidently made as a rule it is fair to infer that the banks in the larger cities entered as retail dealers only those of whom they felt sure. Therefore, whatever error there may be in the returns on account of ignorance of the business of particular depositors is likely to arise from the inclusion among "all other" depositors of retail dealers whose business was not known. For it is in that third group that the unknown would be classified.

RETAIL RETURNS BY GEOGRAPHICAL DIVISIONS.

It is interesting to classify the returns by the geographical divisions of the census with a view to detecting any evidence of differences in the practice of paying by checks in different sections of the country. Of the whole sixty-odd millions of deposits returned, $27,000,000 were in the North Atlantic Division and 75 per cent were in checks. The North Central Division had a total of something over $20,000,000, of which 72.5 per cent were in checks. The South Atlantic Division, with aggregate deposits of $3,325,000, had 63.8 per cent in checks. The South Central Division shows retail returns of $4,400,000, of which 69.9 per cent were in checks. The deposits of the Western Division were over $5,000,000, with a percentage of 75.7 in checks. The average is 73.2. Following are the tables:

TABLE V.—*Retail deposits, by geographical divisions, of national banks, state banks, private banks, loan and trust banks, stock savings banks, and mutual savings banks.*

NATIONAL BANKS.

Geographical division.	Gold.	Silver.	Total specie.	Currency.	Checks.	Total.	Gold.	Silver.	Specie.	Currency.	Checks.
							P. ct.	*P. ct.*	*P. ct.*	*P. ct.*	*P. ct.*
N. Atlantic Div	$117,231	$187,781	$305,012	$3,710,899	$13,938,312	$17,954,223	0.7	1.0	1.7	20.7	77.6
S. Atlantic Div	15,578	110,257	125,835	739,885	1,594,940	2,460,660	.6	4.5	5.1	30.1	64.8
N. Central Div	235,309	343,418	578,727	2,565,617	8,467,896	11,612,240	2.0	3.0	5.0	22.2	72.8
S. Central Div	30,885	169,056	199,941	745,247	2,302,456	3,247,644	.1	6.2	6.3	22.9	70.8
Western Div	403,757	97,126	500,883	305,021	2,542,498	3,348,402	12.1	2.9	15.0	9.1	75.9
Total	802,760	907,638	1,710,398	8,066,669	28,846,102	38,623,169	2.1	2.4	4.5	20.9	74.6

STATE BANKS.

Geographical division.	Gold.	Silver.	Total specie.	Currency.	Checks.	Total.	Gold.	Silver.	Specie.	Currency.	Checks.
							P. ct.	*P. ct.*	*P. ct.*	*P. ct.*	*P. ct.*
N. Atlantic Div	$44,577	$76,976	$121,553	$1,425,516	$3,139,078	$4,686,147	0.9	1.7	2.6	30.5	66.9
S. Atlantic Div	7,228	55,107	62,335	224,852	445,574	732,761	1.0	7.5	8.5	30.7	60.8
N. Central Div	152,053	208,176	360,229	1,666,668	5,227,899	7,254,796	2.1	2.9	5.0	23.0	72.0
S. Central Div	15,855	71,214	87,069	260,089	766,259	1,113,417	1.4	6.4	7.8	23.5	68.7
Western Div	277,925	50,695	328,620	101,453	1,309,853	1,739,926	16.0	2.9	18.9	5.8	75.3
Total	497,638	462,168	959,806	3,678,578	10,888,663	15,527,047	3.2	3.0	6.2	23.7	70.0

TABLE V.—*Retail deposits, by geographical divisions, of national banks, state banks, private banks, loan and trust banks, stock savings banks, and mutual savings banks*—Continued.

PRIVATE BANKS.

Geographical division.	Gold.	Silver.	Total specie.	Currency.	Checks.	Total.	Gold.	Silver.	Specie.	Currency.	Checks.
							P. ct.	*P. ct.*	*P. ct.*	*P. ct.*	*P. ct.*
N. Atlantic Div	$475	$2,038	$2,513	$24,652	$67,112	$94,277	0.5	2.2	2.7	26.1	71.2
S. Atlantic Div	30	1,557	1,587	12,583	21,062	35,232	.1	4.4	4.5	35.7	59.8
N. Central Div	11,767	24,752	36,519	163,089	454,397	654,005	1.8	3.8	5.6	24.9	69.5
S. Central Div	230	6,810	7,040	16,487	20,302	43,829	.5	15.5	16.0	37.6	46.4
Western Div	3,145	1,102	4,247	5,215	30,204	39,666	7.9	2.8	10.7	13.1	76.2
Total	15,647	36,262	51,906	222,026	593,077	867,009	1.8	4.2	6.0	25.6	68.4

LOAN AND TRUST COMPANIES.

Geographical division.	Gold.	Silver.	Total specie.	Currency.	Checks.	Total.	Gold.	Silver.	Specie.	Currency.	Checks.
							P. ct.	*P. ct.*	*P. ct.*	*P. ct.*	*P. ct.*
N. Atlantic Div	$28,013	$48,953	$76,966	$1,137,857	$3,366,491	$4,581,314	0.6	1.1	1.7	24.7	73.6
S. Atlantic Div	110	2,868	2,978	26,268	51,127	80,373	.1	3.5	3.6	32.7	63.7
N. Central Div	6,629	6,643	13,272	64,995	249,908	328,175	2.0	2.0	4.0	19.8	76.2
S. Central Div	115	528	643	2,067	1,952	4,662	2.5	11.3	13.8	44.3	41.8
Western Div	1,370	962	2,332	3,884	38,771	44,987	3.1	2.1	5.2	8.6	86.2
Total	36,237	59,954	96,191	1,235,071	3,708,249	5,039,511	.7	1.2	1.9	24.4	73.7

STOCK SAVINGS BANKS.

							P. ct.	P. ct.	P. ct.	P. ct.	P. ct.
N. Atlantic Div	$227	$156	$383	$4,877	$12,028	$17,288	1.3	0.9	2.2	28.2	69.6
S. Atlantic Div	170	837	1,007	6,501	8,397	15,905	1.1	5.3	6.4	40.9	52.7
N. Central Div	6,921	11,909	18,830	79,847	187,130	285,807	2.4	4.2	6.6	27.9	65.5
S. Central Div	125	1,089	1,214	8,635	10,217	20,066	.6	5.4	6.0	43.0	51.0
Western Div	10,510	1,312	11,822	2,502	24,105	38,429	27.4	3.4	30.8	6.5	62.7
Total	17,953	15,303	33,256	102,362	241,877	377,495	4.7	4.1	8.8	27.1	64.1

MUTUAL SAVINGS BANKS.

							P. ct.	P. ct.	P. ct.	P. ct.	P. ct.
N. Atlantic Div	$1,070	$101	$1,171	$9,600	$1,047	$11,818	9.1	0.9	10.0	81.1	8.9
S. Atlantic Div	---------	9	9	264	48	321	------	3.0	3.0	82.5	14.5
N. Central Div	---------	43	43	80	229	352	------	12.0	12.0	23.0	65.0
Total	1,070	153	1,223	9,944	1,324	12,491	8.6	1.2	9.8	79.6	10.6

TOTAL OF RETAIL DEPOSITS OF ALL CLASSES OF BANKS.

							P. ct.	P. ct.	P. ct.	P. ct.	P. ct.
N. Atlantic Div	$191,593	$316,005	$507,598	$6,313,401	$20,524,068	$27,345,067	0.7	1.1	1.8	23.1	75.1
S. Atlantic Div	23,116	170,635	193,751	1,010,353	2,121,148	3,325,252	.7	5.1	5.8	30.4	63.8
N. Central Div	412,679	594,941	1,007,620	4,540,296	14,587,459	20,135,375	2.1	2.9	5.0	32.5	72.5
S. Central Div	47,210	248,697	295,907	1,032,525	3,101,186	4,429,618	1.1	5.6	6.7	23.3	69.9
Western Div	696,707	151,197	847,904	418,075	3,945,431	5,211,410	13.3	2.9	16.3	8.0	75.7
Total	1,371,305	1,481,475	2,852,780	13,314,650	44,279,292	60,446,722	2.3	2.4	4.7	22.1	73.2

These percentages are striking. Can it be possible that with so large a negro population, in which the use of checks practically does not exist, the method of payment of a community for its purchases can be fairly represented by the percentages of the South Central and the South Atlantic divisions? The answer is, as before, that the real consideration is the proportion of purchases, not the proportion of the number of people who use checks. It is true that there are millions of negroes in these two divisions. It is equally true that in the distribution of wealth their share is very small and that their purchases must be correspondingly so. We must remember, too, that a large number of plantation negroes and workers in the lumber districts of the South are still paid to a considerable extent by orders for goods on the stores of the companies for which they work. Indeed, one might almost use these averages as a basis for a study of the distribution of wealth as well as of method of payments.

CHECKS IN CITIES AND AGRICULTURAL DISTRICTS.

Reserve cities.—It is sometimes said that the use of checks is greatest in the cities. Those who claim that most of the proportion of business done by means of checks is composed of stock-exchange transactions, transactions between banks and wholesale business houses, have inferred that a small proportion of check payments would be found in the country districts.

In order to test this view, the percentages have been calculated for the principal reserve cities [a] by themselves, and for the rest of the country.

[a] There seems nothing to be gained by calculating the returns for all the reserve cities separately.

The returns are shown for the various classes of banks in these reserve cities in order that no undue weight may be attached to the class of banks that do most of the business. An inspection of Table VI shows that these reserve cities had $24,191,414 of retail deposits and that of these, 80 per cent were in checks. The national banks in these reserve cities had $15,198,436, of which 84.2 per cent were in checks. The state banks in the same cities had $6,035,175, of which 70.8 per cent were in checks. The private banks had $44,206, of which 47.8 per cent were in checks. The loan and trust companies in these cities had $2,824,387 of the retail deposits, of which 78.6 per cent were in checks. The stock savings banks had $79,050 of retail deposits, of which 59.3 per cent were in checks and the mutual savings banks had $10,160, with 3.6 per cent in checks.

TABLE VI.—*Retail deposits at representative reserve cities in national banks, state banks, private banks, loan and trust companies, stock savings banks, and mutual savings banks.*

NATIONAL BANKS.

City.	Gold.	Silver.	Total specie.	Currency.	Checks.	Total.	Gold.	Silver.	Specie	Currency.	Checks.
							P. ct.	*P. ct.*	*P. ct.*	*P. ct.*	*P. ct.*
Chicago	$12,502	$11,980	$24,482	$307,607	$1,286,252	$1,618,341	0.8	0.7	1.5	19.0	70.4
New York	4,539	6,548	11,087	309,765	5,504,098	5,824,950	.1	.1	.2	5.3	94.5
St. Louis	9,740	6,401	16,141	170,831	524,073	711,045	1.4	.9	2.3	24.0	73.7
Albany	200	949	1,149	22,990	124,774	148,913	.1	.6	.7	15.5	83.8
Baltimore	846	7,888	8,734	158,689	226,265	393,688	.2	2.0	2.2	40.3	57.5
Boston	343	4,051	4,394	154,100	1,707,096	1,865,590	------	.2	.2	8.3	91.5
Brooklyn	740	955	1,695	82,666	53,680	138,041	.5	.7	1.2	59.9	38.9
Cincinnati	4,981	6,025	11,006	85,107	301,921	398,034	1.3	1.5	2.8	21.4	75.8
Cleveland	5,027	3,211	8,238	63,507	354,236	425,981	1.2	.7	1.9	14.9	83.2
Columbus	5,725	6,126	11,851	46,853	64,820	123,524	4.6	5.0	9.6	37.9	52.5
Dallas	1,430	4,707	6,137	17,820	75,777	99,734	1.4	4.7	6.1	17.9	76.0
Detroit	1,155	2,077	3,232	25,144	137,827	166,203	.7	1.2	1.9	15.2	82.9
Fort Worth	275	3,325	3,600	19,182	63,496	86,278	.3	3.9	4.2	22.2	73.6
Galveston	50	1,001	1,051	3,890	12,837	17,778	.3	5.6	5.9	21.9	72.2
Houston	410	2,822	3,232	13,162	41,665	58,059	.7	4.9	5.6	22.7	71.7
Indianapolis	10,327	10,769	21,096	61,946	131,142	214,184	4.8	5.1	9.9	28.9	61.2
Louisville	4,702	5,340	10,042	28,663	112,422	151,127	3.1	3.5	6.6	18.9	74.5
New Orleans	197	4,189	4,386	39,676	117,245	161,307	.1	2.6	2.7	24.6	72.7
Philadelphia	21,169	14,235	35,404	359,694	1,014,097	1,409,195	1.5	1.0	2.5	25.5	72.0
Pittsburg	7,915	10,403	18,318	101,408	772,274	892,000	.9	1.2	2.1	11.4	86.5
San Antonio	235	1,893	2,128	9,610	33,635	45,373	.5	4.2	4.7	21.2	74.1
Savannah	35	693	728	2,831	2,167	5,726	.6	12.1	12.7	49.5	37.8

Waco	35	2,584	2,619	8,086	29,467	40,172	------	6.4	6.4	20.2	73.4
Washington	242	3,082	3,324	96,323	103,546	203,193	.1	1.5	1.5	47.5	51.0
Total	92,820	121,254	214,074	2,189,550	12,794,812	15,198,436	.6	.8	1.4	14.4	84.2

STATE BANKS.[a]

							P. ct.	*P. ct.*	*P. ct.*	*P. ct.*	*P. ct.*
Chicago	$21,923	$11,091	$33,014	$313,370	$1,283,699	$1,630,083	1.3	0.7	2.0	19.2	78.8
New York	23,221	46,685	69,906	759,000	1,952,756	2,781,662	.8	1.7	2.5	27.3	70.2
St. Louis	3,943	4,814	8,757	88,801	163,313	260,871	1.5	1.8	3.3	34.1	62.6
Total	49,087	62,590	111,677	1,161,171	3,399,768	4,672,616	------	------	------	------	------
Albany	30	64	94	3,682	7,787	11,563	.2	.6	.8	31.8	67.4
Baltimore	250	562	812	11,000	11,650	23,462	1.0	2.4	3.4	47.0	49.6
Brooklyn	1,762	4,124	5,886	201,235	358,045	565,166	.3	.7	1.0	35.6	63.4
Cincinnati	1,527	7,412	8,939	29,749	75,741	114,429	1.3	6.5	7.8	26.0	66.2
Cleveland	10,781	5,026	15,807	69,759	164,089	249,655	4.3	2.0	6.3	27.9	65.8
Columbus	405	666	1,071	6,536	21,382	28,989	1.4	2.3	3.7	22.6	73.7
Detroit	10	106	116	1,666	2,140	3,922	.3	2.7	3.0	42.5	54.5
Houston	55	942	997	5,646	17,578	24,221	.2	3.9	4.1	23.4	72.5
Indianapolis	75	100	175	749	2,755	3,679	2.1	2.7	4.8	20.4	74.8
Louisville	7,465	3,774	11,239	29,427	95,988	136,654	5.5	2.8	8.3	21.5	70.2
New Orleans	12	1,263	1,275	18,246	35,333	54,854	------	2.3	2.3	33.3	64.4
Philadelphia	365	491	856	13,761	19,178	33,795	1.0	1.5	2.5	40.7	56.8
Pittsburg	1,682	2,532	4,214	27,181	41,204	72,599	2.3	3.5	5.8	37.4	56.8
Savannah	60	2,919	2,979	7,663	9,604	20,246	.3	14.4	14.7	37.8	47.5
Washington	20	336	356	10,874	8,095	19,325	.1	1.8	1.9	56.3	41.8
Total	73,586	92,907	166,493	1,598,345	4,270,337	6,035,175	1.2	1.5	2.7	26.5	70.8

[a] The cities omitted from this and the following lists made no reports for these classes of banks.

TABLE VI.—*Retail deposits at representative reserve cities in national banks, state banks, private banks, loan and trust companies, stock savings banks, and mutual savings banks*—Continued.

PRIVATE BANKS.

City.	Gold.	Silver.	Total specie.	Currency.	Checks.	Total.	Gold.	Silver.	Specie.	Currency.	Checks.
							P. ct.	*P. ct.*	*P. ct.*	*P. ct.*	*P. ct.*
Chicago	$862	$762	$1,624	$14,481	$16,697	$32,802	2.6	2.3	4.9	44.2	50.9
Galveston	30	359	389	2,079	1,936	4,404	.8	8.2	9.0	47.1	43.9
San Antonio	------	2,500	2,500	2,000	2,500	7,000	------	35.7	35.7	28.6	35.7
Total	892	3,621	4,513	18,560	21,133	44,206	2.0	8.2	10.2	42.0	47.8

LOAN AND TRUST COMPANIES.

City.	Gold.	Silver.	Total specie.	Currency.	Checks.	Total.	Gold.	Silver.	Specie.	Currency.	Checks.
							P. ct.	*P. ct.*	*P. ct.*	*P. ct.*	*P. ct.*
Chicago	$205	$38	$243	$9,641	$7,653	$17,537	1.2	.2	1.4	55.0	43.6
New York	1,405	2,558	3,963	139,244	829,473	972,680	.1	.3	.4	14.3	85.3
St. Louis	370	667	1,037	15,398	63,841	80,276	.5	.8	1.3	19.2	79.5
Albany	------	229	229	7,258	11,218	18,705	------	1.2	1.2	38.8	60.0
Baltimore	------	------	------	6	382	388	------	------	------	1.5	98.5
Boston	450	6,742	7,192	178,700	458,194	644,086	------	1.0	1.1	27.7	71.1
Brooklyn	1,712	2,071	3,783	81,447	331,267	416,497	.4	.5	.9	19.6	79.5
Philadelphia	6,022	5,004	11,026	119,486	417,741	548,253	1.1	.9	2.0	21.8	76.2
Pittsburg	1,501	1,685	3,186	16,234	77,401	96,821	1.6	1.7	3.3	16.8	79.9
Washington	------	------	------	10,100	19,044	29,144	------	------	------	34.6	65.4
Total	11,665	18,994	30,659	577,514	2,216,214	2,824,387	.5	.6	1.0	20.4	78.6

STOCK SAVINGS BANKS.

							P. ct.	P. ct.	P. ct.	P. ct.	P. ct.
Chicago	$140	$243	$383	$5,958	$4,020	$10,361	1.3	2.3	3.6	57.5	38.9
Cincinnati	10	7	17	109	1,271	1,397	.7	.5	1.2	7.8	91.0
Detroit	571	1,218	1,789	22,114	40,559	64,462	.9	1.9	2.8	34.3	62.9
Louisville	15	17	32	120	71	223	6.7	7.6	14.3	53.8	31.9
New Orleans	-------	58	58	826	68	952	-----	6.1	6.1	86.8	7.1
Washington	-------	55	55	781	819	1,655	-----	3.3	3.3	47.2	49.5
Total	736	1,598	2,334	29,908	46,808	79,050	.9	2.0	2.9	37.8	59.3

MUTUAL SAVINGS BANKS.

							P. ct.	P. ct.	P. ct.	P. ct.	P. ct.
New York	-------	-------	-------	---------	$220	$220	-----	-----	-------	------	100.0
Brooklyn	$1,025	$98	$1,123	$8,669	148	9,940	10.5	1.0	11.5	87.0	1.5
Total	1,025	98	1,123	8,669	368	10,160	10.1	1.0	11.1	85.3	3.6

AGGREGATE RETAIL DEPOSITS.

							P. ct.	P. ct.	P. ct.	P. ct.	P. ct.
New York	$29,165	$55,791	$84,956	$1,208,009	$8,286,547	$9,579,512	0.3	0.6	0.9	12.6	86.5
Chicago	35,632	24,114	59,746	651,057	2,598,321	3,309,124	1.1	.7	1.8	19.7	78.5
St. Louis	14,053	11,882	25,935	275,030	751,227	1,052,192	1.3	1.1	2.5	26.2	71.4
Boston	793	10,793	11,586	332,800	2,165,290	2,509,676	-----	.4	.4	13.4	86.2
Philadelphia	27,556	19,730	47,286	492,941	1,451,016	1,991,243	1.4	1.0	2.4	24.8	72.8
Total	107,199	122,310	229,509	2,959,837	15,252,401	18,441,747	.6	.7	1.3	16.1	82.7
Other reserve cities	73,525	116,162	189,687	1,462,709	4,097,271	5,749,667	1.3	2.0	3.3	25.4	71.3
Grand total	180,724	238,472	419,196	4,422,546	19,349,672	24,191,414	.7	1.0	1.7	18.3	80.0

Country without reserve cities.—If we take the returns for the rest of the country without these reserve cities, we find that the retail deposits aggregate $36,255,308, of which $24,929,620, or 68.7 per cent, is in checks. We see, therefore, that the percentage of checks in the retail deposits outside of the reserve cities was pretty high.

If we examine the returns of agricultural States we find the same thing true. The following table shows the retail deposits in five States, less the deposits in cities of more than 25,000 in 1902–3, according to Census Bulletin No. 20. The percentage runs from 68.5 in Texas to 78.5 in Nebraska and the average for retail deposits is 72.8. Other States, like North Dakota and South Dakota, in which there are no cities of this size, show a similar state of affairs. This goes to show what bankers in agricultural districts say—that the farmers are using checks very largely. Indeed, there is a great change in this respect since the hard times of 1890–1896. Farmers who then had no surplus now have bank accounts, and there has been a notable increase in deposit banking and therefore in payments by means of checks.

A striking illustration of the large use of checks in an agricultural community was found by the writer in the summer on the Green Bay peninsula in Wisconsin. In reply to questions about the methods of doing business, he was shown some checks of local creameries and was told that of payments aggregating about $65,000, for milk and cream, by one of these in two years, only 2 or 3 per cent was in money and that the receipts showed about the same proportion. The business of the other two creameries was done in the same way. The postmaster, from whom the information was obtained, added that money was so scarce that he was in the habit of "cashing" the warrants of rural carriers with local checks to use the warrants for remittance to the money-order department of the post-office instead of money. The returns of retail deposits of the banks at Sturgeon Bay, the banking center, appear to validate this information. They show 95.9 per cent of checks.

TABLE VII.—*Retail deposits returned by all classes of banks of certain States, less those from cities of more than 25,000 in 1902–3 according to Census Bulletin No. 20.*

State.	Gold.	Silver.	Total specie.	Currency.	Checks.	Total.	Gold.	Silver.	Specie.	Currency.	Checks.
							P. ct.	*P. ct.*	*P. ct.*	*P. ct.*	*P. ct.*
Illinois	$23,728	$54,270	$77,998	$381,170	$1,091,972	$1,551,140	1.5	3.5	5.0	24.5	70.5
Iowa	10,779	36,912	47,691	177,151	681,599	906,441	1.2	4.1	5.3	19.5	75.2
Kansas	11,234	31,614	42,848	144,532	544,926	732,306	1.5	4.3	5.8	19.7	74.4
Nebraska	5,022	22,484	27,506	133,494	586,202	747,202	.7	3.0	3.7	18.0	78.5
Texas	10,512	59,698	70,210	230,919	655,963	957,092	1.1	6.2	7.3	24.1	68.5
Total	61,275	204,978	266,253	1,067,266	3,560,662	4,894,181	1.3	4.2	5.4	21.8	72.8

RETURNS FROM INDUSTRIAL CENTERS.

It has been remarked that the wage-earners, especially manual laborers, probably use checks to a very small extent. If we examine the returns from industrial cities like Lawrence, Fall River, Lowell, and Brockton, Mass.; Paterson, N. J.; and Pawtucket, R. I., we find that the proportion of checks in retail deposits in those places is well up with the average of the general tables. Taking the returns from the national banks alone, Lawrence shows a percentage of 63 in total deposits of $72,198; Fall River 80.7 per cent of checks in deposits of $110,589; Lowell 69 per cent in deposits of $79,567; Brockton shows 46.4 per cent of checks in a total of $26,407; Paterson shows 52.6 per cent in a total of $78,373.

These percentages are high for cities where the number of wage-earners is so large. We must remember, however, that it is the proportion of purchases thus paid for that we are considering, and not the number of people who purchase. Again, each place is the center of a large district and the deposits of the merchants represent thousands of dollars of sales to people outside of the cities proper. Moreover, one fact brought out by the returns may be significant of the use of checks by wage-earners themselves. The mutual savings banks are commonly regarded as the banks of the poor man, particularly the wage-earner. But the mutual savings banks in Lawrence show 41.9 per cent of their total receipts, on the day in question, in checks. Those of Lowell had 44 per cent in checks. But these high percentages are due in each case to the high ratio in one bank. On the other hand, of the deposits in the mutual savings banks of Fall River, only 4 per cent were in checks. Each of these deposits aggregated less than $8,000.

The highest percentage of checks in the deposits of the mutual savings banks almost drives us to one of two conclusions: Either the mutual savings banks are not, *par excellence*, the banks of the working man, or else the working man uses checks to a large degree.

Evidence of pay rolls.—The following table of wage payments for the week ending March 13 were furnished by the banks in reply to the question asking them to send in the amount of pay rolls made in cash and in checks respectively for the said week. The tables are given in detail by banks and States for several reasons. They are given by States in order that any possible connection between the payment of wages and the industrial character of the State may be seen. They are given by banks partly for the same reason and partly to get some light on the question whether any particular class of banks is resorted to more than another for this purpose.

TABLE VIII.—*Wage pay rolls for week ended March 13, 1909, made up by national banks, state banks, private banks, loan and trust companies, stock savings banks, and mutual savings banks.*

NATIONAL BANKS.

States.	Pay rolls in—		Cash.	Checks.
	Cash.	Checks.		
			Per cent.	*Per cent.*
Alabama	$461,387	$54,537	89.4	10.6
Arizona	23,600	50,400	31.9	68.1
Arkansas	62,935	44,653	58.5	41.5
California	1,194,439	1,349,702	47.0	53.0
Colorado	517,848	845,367	38.0	62.0
Connecticut	2,148,363	75,845	96.6	3.4

TABLE VIII.—*Wage payrolls for week ended March 13, 1909, made up by national banks, state banks, private banks, loan and trust companies, stock savings banks, and mutual savings banks*—Continued.

NATIONAL BANKS—Continued.

States.	Pay rolls in—		Cash.	Checks.
	Cash.	Checks.		
			Per cent.	*Per cent.*
Delaware	$154,041	$69,413	69.0	31.0
District of Columbia	244,719	100,963	70.8	29.2
Florida	568,017	70,372	89.0	11.0
Georgia	610,362	1,011,268	37.6	62.4
Idaho	17,220	73,124	19.0	81.0
Illinois	4,638,999	2,688,921	63.2	16.8
Indiana	1,877,634	524,327	78.2	21.8
Iowa	455,689	430,930	51.4	48.6
Kansas	279,924	545,427	33.9	66.1
Kentucky	561,024	226,059	71.2	28.8
Louisiana	331,701	156,280	68.0	32.0
Maine	460,990	122,974	78.9	21.1
Maryland	1,891,974	383,851	83.1	16.9
Massachusetts	8,760,233	194,016	97.8	2.2
Michigan	948,423	605,054	61.0	39.0
Minnesota	901,567	1,426,398	38.8	61.2
Mississippi	81,258	55,796	59.1	40.9
Missouri	1,764,586	1,280,827	57.9	42.1
Montana	19,872	394,395	4.8	95.2
Nebraska	326,672	557,479	36.9	63.1
Nevada	12,250	155,150	7.3	92.7
New Hampshire	506,614	58,505	89.6	10.4
New Jersey	2,363,092	557,118	80.9	19.1
New Mexico	27,370	128,100	17.6	82.4
New York	10,253,924	2,319,666	81.7	18.3
North Carolina	202,881	67,632	75.0	25.0
North Dakota	20,051	57,956	25.7	74.3
Ohio	5,785,622	1,927,537	75.0	25.0
Oklahoma	173,730	442,566	28.2	71.8
Oregon	61,777	445,022	12.2	87.8
Pennsylvania	14,932,534	1,695,112	89.8	10.2
Rhode Island	502,531	5,509	98.9	1.1
South Carolina	201,018	6,110	97.0	3.0
South Dakota	17,420	179,806	8.8	91.2
Tennessee	558,546	94,993	85.5	14.5
Texas	860,736	837,886	50.7	49.3
Utah	108,248	290,370	27.1	72.9
Vermont	219,041	30,664	87.7	12.3
Virginia	804,425	161,096	83.3	16.7
Washington	171,481	750,775	18.6	81.4

TABLE VIII.—*Wage pay rolls for week ended March 13, 1909, made up by national banks, state banks, private banks, loan and trust companies, stock savings banks, and mutual savings banks*—Continued.

NATIONAL BANKS—Continued.

States.	Pay rolls in—		Cash.	Checks.
	Cash.	Checks.		
			Per cent.	*Per cent.*
West Virginia	$332,036	$208,217	61.5	38.5
Wisconsin	710,272	1,045,686	40.5	59.5
Wyoming	63,570	52,678	54.7	45.3
Total	68,192,646	24,856,532	73.3	26.7

STATE BANKS.

States.	Cash.	Checks.	Cash.	Checks.
			Per cent.	*Per cent.*
Alabama	$230,345	$61,973	78.8	21.2
Arizona	51,679	199,252	20.7	79.3
Arkansas	97,216	100,870	49.1	50.9
California	693,352	842,833	45.1	54.9
Colorado	27,650	34,425	44.5	55.5
Connecticut	231,348	5,500	97.7	2.3
Delaware	2,722	50	98.2	1.8
District of Columbia	9,500	1,258	88.3	11.7
Florida	48,910	19,386	71.6	28.4
Georgia	125,104	54,395	69.7	30.3
Idaho	12,735	65,068	16.4	83.6
Illinois	2,411,845	2,561,476	48.5	51.5
Indiana	182,668	236,131	43.6	56.4
Iowa	216,462	355,535	37.9	62.1
Kansas	110,157	243,321	31.2	68.8
Kentucky	231,410	105,895	68.4	31.6
Louisiana	506,373	105,053	82.8	17.2
Maine	39,411	34,560	53.3	46.7
Maryland	47,701	38,723	55.2	44.8
Massachusetts	144,979	7,318	95.2	4.8
Michigan	801,559	564,001	58.7	41.3
Minnesota	146,467	428,863	25.5	74.5
Mississippi	59,150	44,518	57.1	42.9
Missouri	554,536	703,618	44.1	55.9
Montana	30,950	959,028	3.1	96.9
Nebraska	20,861	201,467	9.4	90.6
Nevada	86,700	206,050	29.6	70.4
New Hampshire	11,874	924	92.8	7.2
New Jersey	188,878	11,290	94.4	5.6
New Mexico	2,600	3,300	44.1	55.9
New York	5,687,395	884,994	86.5	13.5
North Carolina	94,387	42,978	68.7	31.3

TABLE VIII.—*Wage pay rolls for week ended March 13, 1909, made up by national banks, state banks, private banks, loan and trust companies, stock savings banks, and mutual savings banks*—Continued.

STATE BANKS—Continued.

States.	Pay rolls in—		Cash.	Checks.
	Cash.	Checks.		
			Per cent.	*Per cent.*
North Dakota	$11,882	$51,326	18.8	81.2
Ohio	845,127	426,654	66.5	33.5
Oklahoma	49,586	135,465	26.8	73.2
Oregon	73,445	160,355	31.4	68.6
Pennsylvania	1,126,659	697,085	61.7	38.3
Rhode Island	927,836	1,417	99.8	.2
South Carolina	108,000	21,270	83.5	16.5
South Dakota	23,933	198,163	10.8	89.2
Tennessee	162,066	243,674	40.0	60.0
Texas	99,084	196,353	33.6	66.4
Utah	26,872	49,593	35.2	64.8
Vermont	16,152	2,200	88.0	12.0
Virginia	136,316	53,737	71.7	28.3
Washington	170,900	619,050	21.6	78.4
West Virginia	139,951	104,392	57.3	42.7
Wisconsin	316,469	475,182	40.0	60.0
Wyoming	14,550	4,550	76.2	23.8
Total	18,369,746	12,564,519	61.0	39.0

PRIVATE BANKS.

			Per cent.	*Per cent.*
Alabama	$1,560	$250	86.2	13.8
Arkansas	3,500	----------	100.0	----------
California	1,400	5,100	21.5	78.5
Colorado	3,125	16,550	15.9	84.1
Connecticut	10,000	55	99.5	.5
Florida	1,914	1,475	56.5	43.5
Georgia	2,306	2,290	50.2	49.8
Illinois	112,850	334,974	25.2	74.8
Indiana	75,238	49,058	60.5	39.5
Iowa	27,229	213,707	11.3	88.7
Kansas	1,795	2,082	46.3	53.7
Maryland	30	----------	100.0	----------
Massachusetts	19,000	----------	100.0	----------
Michigan	34,497	15,079	69.6	30.4
Minnesota	1,470	4,000	26.9	73.1
Mississippi	475	1,650	22.4	77.6
Missouri	3,830	4,851	44.1	55.9
Montana	500	2,000	20.0	80.0

TABLE VIII.—*Wage payrolls for week ended March 13, 1909, made up by national banks, state banks, private banks, loan and trust companies, stock savings banks, and mutual savings banks*—Continued.

PRIVATE BANKS—Continued.

States.	Pay rolls in— Cash.	Pay rolls in— Checks.	Cash.	Checks.
			Per cent.	*Per cent.*
Nebraska	$75		100.0	
New York	57,848	$10,493	84.6	15.4
Ohio	57,573	28,798	66.6	33.4
Oregon	728	5,343	12.0	88.0
Pennsylvania	25,156	7,552	76.8	23.2
South Dakota	535	450	54.3	45.7
Texas	12,293	31,438	28.1	71.9
Utah	200	500	33.0	67.0
Vermont	268		100.0	
Virginia	5,783	1,421	80.3	19.7
Washington	300	3,000	9.1	90.9
Wisconsin	801		100.0	
Total	462,279	742,116	38.4	61.6

LOAN AND TRUST COMPANIES.

States.	Pay rolls in— Cash.	Pay rolls in— Checks.	Cash.	Checks.
			Per cent.	*Per cent.*
Arkansas	$12,400	$41,095	23.2	76.8
California	16,979		100.0	
Colorado	1,750	31,500	5.3	94.7
Connecticut	150,030	2,900	98.1	1.9
Delaware	16,700	3,300	83.5	16.5
District of Columbia	20,231	28,076	41.9	58.1
Idaho		2,500		100.0
Indiana	24,944	45,922	35.2	64.8
Maine	151,318	46,662	76.5	23.5
Maryland	19,534	300	98.5	1.5
Massachusetts	1,173,233	77,323	93.8	6.2
Minnesota	2,000	7,957	20.1	79.9
Missouri	544,480	323,655	62.7	37.3
New Hampshire	17,000	1,500	91.9	8.1
New Jersey	739,405	157,071	82.5	17.5
New York	1,608,669	261,211	80.6	19.4
North Carolina	52,096	10,189	83.6	16.4
Ohio	85,224	26,000	76.6	23.4
Pennsylvania	1,344,127	311,003	81.2	18.8
Rhode Island	567,202	9,054	98.5	1.5
Tennessee	25	26	49.0	51.0
Vermont	29,864	2,602	92.0	8.0

TABLE VIII.—*Wage payrolls for week ended March 13, 1909, made up by national banks, state banks, private banks, loan and trust companies, stock savings banks, and mutual savings banks*—Continued.

LOAN AND TRUST COMPANIES—Continued.

States.	Pay rolls in—		Cash.	Checks.
	Cash.	Checks.		
			Per cent.	*Per cent.*
Washington	$5,000	$20,000	20.0	80.0
West Virginia	500	200	71.5	28.5
Total	6,582,711	1,410,046	82.4	17.6

STOCK SAVINGS BANKS.

			Per cent.	*Per cent.*
California	$39,079	$155,525	19.2	80.8
District of Columbia	4,705	400	92.2	7.8
Georgia	125	150	45.5	54.5
Idaho		2,000		100.0
Illinois	283,638	303,454	48.3	51.7
Iowa	96,444	493,661	16.3	83.7
Kentucky	1,000		100.0	
Maryland	1,350	607	69.0	31.0
Michigan	71,306	52,794	57.5	42.5
New Hampshire	21,000		100.0	
North Carolina	1,000	2,000	33.3	66.7
Ohio	8,886	6,223	58.8	41.2
Pennsylvania	31,547	1,700	94.9	5.1
Tennessee	25,719	1,622	94.1	5.9
Texas		250		100.0
Vermont	1,135	1,545	42.4	57.6
Virginia	4,630		100.0	
Washington		400		100.0
West Virginia	2,300		100.0	
Total	593,864	1,022,331	36.7	63.3

MUTUAL SAVINGS BANKS.

			Per cent.	*Per cent.*
Connecticut	$250		100.0	
Maine	1,850	$250	88.1	11.9
Maryland	25		100.0	
Massachusetts	136		100.0	
South Carolina	2,390	80	96.8	3.2
Total	4,651	330	93.4	6.6

It will be seen from the tables of the returns of 4,306 national banks which furnished this information, that pay rolls amounting to $68,192,646 were made up in cash and $24,856,532 in checks. The percentages are 73.3 and 26.7, respectively. The largest percentage of checks, 95.2, was in Montana, and it will be noticed that the percentages run highest in the States of Arizona, Colorado, Idaho, Kansas, Minnesota, Montana, Nevada, New Mexico, North Dakota, Oklahoma, Oregon, South Dakota, Utah, and Washington. These are, in general, agricultural States. The industrial States of Connecticut, Massachusetts, New Jersey, Pennsylvania, and Rhode Island show a very small proportion of wage payments by checks. South Carolina seems peculiar in having only 3 per cent in checks, as against Georgia with 62.4 and North Carolina with 25.

The returns of the state banks show pay rolls aggregating $18,369,746 in cash and $12,564,519 in checks, the former being 61 per cent and the latter 39 per cent. The amount paid in checks through the state banks is half that shown by the national banks, while the amount paid in cash is about one-fourth. In the state bank returns the check percentages run highest in Arizona, Idaho, Iowa, Kansas, Minnesota, Montana, Nebraska, Nevada, North Dakota, Oklahoma, Oregon, South Dakota, Texas, and Washington. Again we see the agricultural States to the front. The lowest percentages are shown by the industrial States, as in the preceding group—Connecticut, Delaware, Massachusetts, New Hampshire, New Jersey, and Rhode Island. The last-named State shows only 0.2

per cent of its pay rolls in checks; New Hampshire has 7.2 per cent, and the other States classed here as industrial come in between.

Turning to the pay rolls made by the private banks, the aggregate is small, being little over $1,000,000. Of the whole amount, however, 61.6 per cent was in checks. The highest percentages are in California, Colorado, Illinois, Iowa, Minnesota, Mississippi, Montana, Oregon, Texas, and Washington. We find the agricultural States again with the largest percentages.

Similar figures for the loan and trust companies show that of the aggregate of about $8,000,000 in pay rolls 17.6 per cent was in checks. The highest percentage was in Colorado, if we ignore the returns of one bank in Idaho, all paid by checks. Minnesota shows about 80 per cent and Washington also has 80.

Similar figures for the stock savings banks show $1,500,000 in pay rolls, with Idaho, Texas, and Washington showing three small pay rolls all in checks, while Kentucky, New Hampshire, Virginia, and West Virginia show four altogether in cash. The returns of the mutual savings banks are trifling.

We have, then, an aggregate of pay rolls for the week ending March 13 of $134,811,771, of which 30 per cent was in checks and 70 per cent in cash. It should be said that some of these pay rolls were not actually made up. In many places wages are paid monthly, and in a good many such instances the banks stated that fact and returned one-fourth of the month's pay roll, indicating, however, how it was made up.

Of course there is no way of knowing how many people are represented in this wage payment, for doubtless salaries of officers are included as well as wages. The figures show, however, that a large number of the wage-earners of the country are accustomed to receive payment by check, and that this custom predominates in agricultural rather than in industrial sections of the country. This is in keeping with the showing made by all the other tables that the proportion of checks in country payments is high. The showing made by the table is evidence of the fact that large numbers of wage-earners at any rate receive checks, whether they draw them or not. If they receive them, they must cash them. In some cases, unquestionably, the pay check will be deposited to the account of the recipient and he will draw his own checks. In the large majority of cases, however, the probability is that these checks are turned into the stores or cashed at the banks. There is some reason to think that in some places they are largely cashed in saloons. Nevertheless, they swell the volume of business done by checks to the extent to which they are used in paying bills, and to the degree that they promote the use of bank accounts and checks by the wage-earners themselves. There is no way of making any allowance for these items.

The common belief is that wage-earners do not use checks in making payments to any extent worth mentioning. This is probably true if by wage-earners is meant the manual laborers. People in clerical positions, with no larger income than many manual laborers, are users of checks to a degree as large proportionally as wealthy people. The manual laborer is in another class in this respect. He is usually paid by the week, or, at any rate, by the month. Some States, indeed, now require weekly payments. In so far as they do the amount which each person receives is smaller than if the wage period were longer. The wages received, therefore, are usually too small to be the basis of a bank account. The banks, it is urged, do not want such accounts. This statement, however, must be taken with many grains of allowance, especially in the smaller places. Many banks in small places are glad to get all accounts, however small.

We must remember that the volume of expenditures of wage-earners, in the sense of manual laborers, is, after all, not so large a proportion of the total expenditure of the country as would drag down the percentage of business done by checks to a very great extent.

Moreover, the use of pay checks makes a contribution of some amount, even from the wage-earning class, to the percentage of checks in doing business. If 30,000,000 individual wage-earners had spent $1 a day in addition to the amount of our retail bank returns, and had spent it all in money, the total retail deposits would have been $90,000,000, approximately the sum obtained after allowance for returns of nonreporting banks. With the amount of checks deposited remaining as in the tables, the checks would still be 50 per cent of the payments.

Returns from merchants.—When the investigation of the deposits of retail tradesmen was under way in 1894, the writer requested friends in different parts of the country to secure for him some information directly from merchants in retail trade concerning the proportion of their receipts in checks from day to day. The information was meager, and it came too late to be of use to the Comptroller in 1894. It was included, however, in the report of 1896 and will be found there in detail. The information thus received has been made the basis of some criticism of the report of 1896 and used as evidence that a large proportion of the people pay their retail purchases with checks, despite the showing of the bank deposits. For that reason it seems worth while to discuss the value of the evidence received at that time and to add a little more to it now. In the criticism based on this information emphasis has been put on the returns which were lowest and but little attention paid to those which tallied fairly with the general percentage shown in the bank reports; and so far as the writer knows no attempt has ever been made by the critics to reconcile differences or to give a reasonable explanation for assuming that the lowest returns were the proper ones to choose as typical.

The first place mentioned in the discussion of 1896 from which this kind of evidence was secured was New Brunswick, N. J. Of four stores there from which reports were received, three, whose patronage was general, received a trifle over 51 per cent in checks in payment of a total trade of somewhat over $10,000. A fourth grocery store there received 1.6 per cent, but its trade for the whole month was less than $1,000—that is, less than one-tenth of the trade of the other three. But the important matter is not the proportion of purchasers who pay by check, but the proportion of the volume of purchases paid for by check. The average percentage of the four groceries, however, is 47.5, which is almost exactly the figure of the bank returns for the city of New Brunswick in 1896. Two grocers and two fuel dealers in Lewiston, Me., received during the month of September, 1894, 10 per cent and 25.4 per cent, respectively. There is reason to think that the average of these, 17 per cent, was low.

Undue emphasis has been placed on certain returns from Iowa City, Iowa. The returns were for the trade of one day, a Saturday, November 24, and showed that the percentage of checks received "varied from 2 in the case of grocers to 30 in the case of furniture dealers, butchers, and dealers in flour and feed." The returns are given in detail in the report of 1896. To one who is familiar with the trading customs of the Middle West there is nothing at all surprising in this showing, and it does not invalidate so fully as some critics have thought the average proportion of checks in the retail bank returns of Iowa City at that time, which was 74 per cent. Saturday is the day when the smaller purchasers do their trading. The larger purchasers avoid the rush of Saturday trade in cities of this kind and buy in the quiet days of the week. No attention has been paid, however, in criticisms of these Iowa City returns to the percentage of checks shown in the running accounts. Attention has been called to the cash sales only. The running accounts of the returns received directly from merchants and which we are discussing show 33 per cent of checks in Iowa City, 44 in Davenport, 31 in Winterset, while the percentage of checks in the cash sales were 8.7 and 7, respectively. But the running accounts outweigh the cash sales of the day many times. Therefore even the lowest showing for the proportion of checks in payments to merchants in these places at this time would be much larger than the 14 of which so much may be made if one is trying to prove a point rather than to describe the situation or find conclusions based on all the facts.

The table giving the returns from Iowa City and the other two places mentioned was inserted by the writer in his report just as it was received. It will be seen from an inspection of that table, as given in the Comptroller's report for 1896, that the cash and running accounts together show the average of 14 per cent in checks. The writer has always questioned whether in making this average the cash sales and the running accounts were properly weighted according to their volumes.

Similar remarks will apply to Lawrence, Kans. The percentage shown by the direct replies of merchants in 1894 was low. As a matter of fact, however, it is probably demonstrable that as Lawrence, Kans., is a university town, it is one in which the habit of paying by check is well developed.

The direct data of 1894 were supplemented in 1896 with information representing the accounts of about 40 retail traders for a month each. The figures were in substantial harmony with the general returns of the banks.

A large number of returns direct from merchants of the character of their receipts from day to day for a week or a month would be very valuable in such an inquiry. However, the writer doubts whether they would change the general conclusion as to the proportion of checks used in retail trades if proper allowance is made for errors in the bank returns, as was done in 1896. It would not seem worth while, therefore, in the present investigation to go extensively into this phase of the matter, especially when the labor entailed in the analysis of the 12,000 bank reports was as much as could be undertaken in the limited time at the writer's disposal before the report had to be made. A few test cases, however, have again been sought and are here listed. All these cases are in Illinois, although not in the same place.

Returns from merchants.—Case 1: A retail furniture store on one day took in $634, of which $10 was in money; the rest was in checks. On another day it took in $265, of which only $10 was in money. The average receipts of this store from month to month show not much more than 10 per cent in money. It is situated in a city of a little less than 25,000. Like all stores in such places in this part of the country, it has a large farmers' trade.

Case 2: A retail butcher reports to the writer $105 in money in a total of $540.

Case 3: One of the largest retail stores in the city of Chicago reports for the month of June, 52.9 per cent of its receipts in checks. This is one of the stores which are thronged every Saturday by purchasers of all classes.

Case 4: A confectioner; the writer supposed that here would be a kind of business in which checks would probably not appear at all. The proprietor told him that from 5 to 10 per cent of his cash sales[a] daily were paid for in checks and that about 50 per cent of his "charged" sales were paid for with checks. The "charged" sales were three-fourths of the total sales for the month, so that the proportion of checks in his total month's receipts would run about 40 per cent.

Case 5: A retail baker; here again the writer was of the opinion, *a priori*, that there would be few checks in the month's receipts. As he stood and watched people buying "a 5-cent loaf," "10 cents' worth of cookies," "half a dozen rolls," for half an hour at a time on several occasions, before he put the question to the proprietor, his belief was strengthened. To his surprise, the proprietor of the bakery told him that while none of his cash sales were paid for by check, 80 per cent of his "charged" sales were so paid for and that they amounted to about 50 per cent of his business. This would give approximately 40 per cent, in his case, of checks in his total payments.

Case 6: The writer then went into a barber shop thinking that here he certainly would find the place where checks were unknown. However, as he entered the door the first thing in sight was a large array of the shaving mugs of customers. The proprietor said that he received about 15 per cent of his month's receipts in checks.

Case 7: This was for one of the largest retail general stores in the city of Chicago, in which one can buy anything

[a] A "cash sale" is a sale paid for at the time of purchase, whether the payment be made with check or money.

from a case of pins to a piano or a diamond. Its patronage is drawn mainly from the middle class of wage-earners. It reports: "We figure about 15 per cent of payments for retail purchases are paid by checks." In this case no statement of the volume of business was given, nor of the length of time for which the statement is made.

Case 8: "Notion store" in a small city. In this store, of a total of $3,750 received in a certain period of time, 1½ per cent was in checks. This is one of the stores sometimes called in different parts of the country "five and ten cent stores."

Case 9: A grocer in the same city with the furniture store first mentioned. This store is known as a strictly first-class grocery store, and professes to sell "no cheap goods," in the sense of poor goods. Its reputation is of the best. The proprietor told the writer that on an average, month in and month out, probably more than 60 per cent of his receipts were in checks. Of course there are days when no checks come in for cash sales. There are other days when they are received pretty heavily. On the Friday on which the writer happened to call on the proprietor there were no checks in the cash sales, but 70 per cent of the sales were charged, and of these 85 per cent, he said, are usually paid in checks. So that his average of probably more than 60 per cent was sustained by these figures.

Case 10: A druggist; the drug business, again, is one which a person would expect the money payments to predominate. The writer called on three druggists. One gave the actual figures of his business for a certain period and was able to tell what percentage of this was received in the form of credit paper, since he, like some other business men, keeps track of every check he receives. It appeared that 62 and a fraction per cent of his receipts for a year were in checks.

Case 11: Another druggist [a] whose store is of the same general character, reported a very small percentage of checks in his receipts—not more than 10, he thought. This was his "best guess."

Case 12: The third druggist reported as his "best guess" a figure between the two others, about 25 per cent.

Case 13: Another large store in Chicago doing a business of many millions a year, and catering in the main to the middle class of people. Their checks and money orders for the month of May were 17.7 per cent of their receipts and in June 15.1 per cent.

Case 14: It was urged on the writer by some disputants that the street car companies and the steam railroads would certainly show a very small percentage of checks in their receipts. Of course this is true because of their regulations against receiving checks and because the fare is such, especially on the street car, as to preclude the use of checks. However, the writer decided to test the matter and secured figures from a station agent on an important railroad in one of the smaller towns. Of course his statement showed at once that while the passenger receipts were practically all cash, the receipts for freight payments showed a large percentage of checks. Checks are not

[a] It should be said that although called drug stores, these stores, in addition to their drug business, sell a miscellaneous assortment of articles, since they are located in a country town.

received at the passenger offices except as a matter of accommodation to well-known patrons. Perhaps not more than 5 per cent of the passenger receipts at this station are in checks, and they are taken, as has been noted, as a matter of accommodation. This practice, however, is much more general than one might at first think. The total receipts and the percentage of receipts in cash at this station on freight account were obtained for each of five days and showed 80.2, 95.3, 94.9, 89.1, 96.1, and 92.1, respectively, of checks.

Case 15: A retail clothier reports that of the amount of his cash sales about 35 per cent is paid with checks and of his "charged" sales about 90 per cent. His "charged" sales are about three-fourths of his total sales. This would make the proportion of checks in his total sales probably a little over 75 per cent. The business is principally ready-made clothing and gentlemen's furnishings.

Case 16: A department store in a town of 20,000 in Illinois, reports that about 18 per cent of the receipts for sales (not including checks cashed) is in checks. This proportion is an average of actual receipts for three months in the spring. The patronage of the store is largely wage-earners.

Case 17: This was for a department store in the same city of about the same grade and catering to the same general class of people. The proportion of checks in its total receipts for a week was 43.

Case 18: This store deals principally in ladies' furnishings, although some men's furnishings are also sold, as well as lace curtains and other articles of that kind for house furnishing. The proportion of checks in a week's receipts in August for cash sales alone was 69. In addition are to be counted the checks in payment of "charged" sales which were 23 per cent of the total business. About 90 per cent of the charged sales were paid with checks, so that the percentage of checks in all payments is about 73.

Case 19: A considerable percentage of the checks deposited by this firm—a great department store—are checks which they have cashed for customers. The proportion of checks deposited to total receipts averages 62 per cent for a month. The following extract from a letter received from the firm explains the conditions: "We cash a great many teachers' and other city employees' checks, a very small proportion of which applies to payments of accounts or for merchandise. We also cash a great many checks for our customers, as it frequently is much more convenient than going to a bank for their funds. It is also customary for a great many employees of manufacturing concerns, who are paid by check to cash same in our establishment. Again many cash customers will make a purchase of a few dollars and draw a check for a larger amount, when they desire some currency. As we have a great many cashiers all over the house, and each one receives checks, it is impossible when they come to the counting room for us to determine whether they have been applied in whole or part upon purchases.

"I presume that the above conditions prevail to a very much larger extent in our retail establishment than in a majority of other concerns. You will readily see from the points enumerated that the amount of checks we receive and deposit bears no relation in any way to the volume of business done, as a very large amount of the checks would be considered as 'accommodation banking.'

"The proportion of currency in our bank deposits is comparatively small, as our heavy pay rolls are paid from currency receipts, also all other necessary currency disbursements."

Case 20: Another great department store in Chicago, whose yearly business reaches into the millions, reports: "We have taken several months as a basis for the information which you desire, and find that the percentage of checks to our total receipts is 46.45."

Case 21: A retail shoe store in a small city in Illinois. The receipts of several months, approximating $30,000, showed 34 per cent in checks.

WHAT THE DEPOSITS SHOW.

What, now, do the figures tell us? They certainly show what the merchants deposited and what, therefore, they received. They must include the money and the checks received in payment of sales of goods, in so far as expenses have not been paid in the meantime from these receipts, plus any pay checks which have been taken in settlement of purchases, but in excess of the value of the purchase, so that "change" for the balance was given the customer.

We have seen, however, that the pay checks and expenses paid are in all probability negligible quantities for the day in question. The retail deposits on this occasion may therefore be taken as fairly representing the receipts of the merchants for sales, plus some amount of checks cashed as a matter of accommodation. Except for this amount, the deposits represent therefore the payments for purchases. Some running accounts are doubtless included, but there is no reason for thinking that the proportion of checks in the payments of these running accounts was less than the average shown by the tables. Doubtless a good many merchants did not "bank" their receipts. Let us assume, however, although the assumption seems extravagant, that 20,000,000 wage-earners in industrial pursuits and domestic and personal service spent, each, 60 cents on the day in question, all in money, and that only half of this found its way into our statistics. This would give us $6,000,000 to be added to the cash side. If, in addition, we "guess" at 10 per cent as the proportion of the whole, which on this "nonsettlement" day were for running accounts, we may make allowances as follows:

	Deductions.		Checks.	Total.
	Checks.	Total.		
Total returns			$44,279,292	$60,446,722
Deduct checks cashed:				
10 per cent of all checks	$4,427,929	$4,427,929		
10 per cent of total, for payments on account, in ratio of tables (73 per cent)	4,412,614	6,044,672	8,840,543	10,472,601
Remainder			35,438,749	49,974,121
Add to total, money received but not "banked"				6,000,000
Modified returns, with allowances for deductions and cash not "banked"			35,438,749	55,974,121

This gives us 63 per cent of checks. If we perform a similar operation on the corrected totals, that is, the returns increased by the amounts allowed for the banks which did not report, first deducting the $6,000,000 money not "banked" from the corrected check totals, we find an average of 60 per cent of checks.

ESTIMATES FROM EXPENDITURE AND POPULATION.

We may make an estimate of the average total retail expenditure of the country for purposes of comparison with the retail deposits returned by the banks in this inquiry.

According to Bulletin No. 77, July, 1908, of the United States Bureau of Labor, the average food cost per workingman's family in 1907, allowing for advances in prices from the figures of 1901 which were taken as a base, was $374.75. Allowing 10 per cent advance[a] since the figures were published, the average food cost would be $412. This expenditure for food is about 43 per cent of the total expenditure. This gives $958 as the average annual expenditure of each workingman's family, or, for an average family of five, a per capita daily expenditure of about 52 cents. Let us take this as the average for those in the manufacturing industries, in which about 12,000,000 people are employed, representing, perhaps, 36,000,000 of our population. This is on the assumption that half are married and that the average family numbers five persons. Thus we get for total daily expenditure for this class $18,720,000.

[a] There has been little or no advance. But the point is to be sure not to *underestimate* the expenditure of those economic classes who use money more largely than checks.

Other classes doubtless are spending more than this. The professional classes, the farmers, and many of those in what is called "personal and domestic service," spent more than these did. Suppose the average amount is 80 cents, representing an annual income of about $1,500; then the total daily expenditure of the other classes would be about $43,000,000, giving a total of about $60,000,000, estimating the population at 90,000,000. When we consider the advance in wages and salaries and the large amounts spent by the wealthy, this amount appears too small, and it probably is so.

The report of the Interstate Commerce Commission for 1907 gives 1,672,074 as the number of railway employees in the year ending June 30, 1907. The aggregate amount of compensation received by these was $1,072,386,427. This is an average yearly wage of $641, which is considerably higher than for manufactures. Of the whole number of employees, however, the general officers, other officers, general office clerks, station agents, enginemen, and conductors receive a high enough wage and belong to the general class of people who use checks to justify us in supposing that a considerable proportion of them keep bank accounts and pay with checks. Far the larger proportion of these employees receive over $2 a day.

About 50 per cent of the people engaged in transportation, as well as in manufacturing, are reported by the census of 1900 as married. Undoubtedly more than one member of each family is working, so that the aggregate family income is considerably more than is shown by the earnings of any one individual. Women in manufactures receive on an average about $300 a year, while the men receive about $500. If one man and one woman in the same family are working, we would have, therefore, an aggregate family income of from $800 to $1,000, which is approximately the amount previously estimated.

The matter of using checks is largely determined by the social class of the individual. As has been remarked before, a clerk with an income of $1,000 or $1,200 would probably have a bank account and check against it, when a laborer would not. The same is true in a measure of teachers, stenographers, private secretaries, and most of the other people employed in this kind of personal service. The same is true, too, to a much greater extent of the professional classes and the so-called wealthy class. Now, those who use checks doubtless make far the largest part—possibly 90 per cent—of their payments therewith. Their per capita expenditure undoubtedly exceeds that of the wage-earning class. How much we do not know, but we might guess that it would be more than double. If, then, we consider the aggregate of the expenditures of those people in trade and the manufacturing industries and in transportation who are in the habit of using checks, together with those of the various classes just mentioned, concerning whose practice there is little doubt, there seems little ground for not believing that the larger proportion of the expenditure of the community is made by means of checks. This is the conclusion to which our tables also point.

Another way of going at the problem may perhaps be based on the character of the population. In the inquiry of 1896 there was a discussion of the probable percentage of checks used by negroes and the foreign population. An inspection of the table of occupations of negroes in 1900 shows that the number engaged in occupations in which they would be likely to use checks is very small. The whole number at that date was 8,000,000, and of these less than 80,000 were engaged in business pursuits in which checks would ordinarily be used. That there must be some use of checks by this great population we are bound to conclude, not only because some of them are engaged, as just said, in occupations in which checks are ordinarily used, but also because no inconsiderable number of them have amassed fair amounts of wealth. Ten years ago there were 156,372 negroes who owned their own farms, and about 30,000 more who were part owners.

In the discussion of this subject in 1896, 5 per cent was the average assigned in the negro population as compared with other divisions of the people in the use of checks. This must be weighted by their probable per capita expenditure in computing the general average. As to the foreign population, practically none of them, in their home countries, have been used to deposit banking, and are therefore unacquainted with payments by check. In 1896 it was found that among the foreign population along Milwaukee avenue, in Chicago, one retail grocer got 15.5 per cent of his proceeds for the month in checks, one butcher 10 per cent, a coal dealer 12 per cent, one clothier 9 per cent, one dry-goods merchant 19 per cent, one furniture dealer 18 per cent. We may perhaps assume, therefore, that 15 per cent of the payments of this population are made by means of checks, for we must remember that the foreigner learns very rapidly.

The native white population, aside from the wage-earners, undoubtedly are users of checks to a very great extent. Payment by check is, of course, the custom among people of large incomes, and probably also with all classes of people with an income of $1,200 or more, in all occupations excepting manual labor. The writer believes that it will be found true that of two men, each with an income of $1,200 a year, the one making his as bookkeeper or by other clerical service, and the other by manual labor, the former will very likely have a bank account and pay his bills to a large extent with checks, while the latter will pay with money.

We must remember, however, that what we are trying to get is the average volume of purchases paid for with credit documents. We are not trying to find the number of people who use checks. If one person pays out as much as ten others and pays all his bills with checks, the percentage of business payments made with checks would be 50, although the number of people would be 11, only one of whom used checks. A good deal of the misapprehension as to the extent of the use of checks in business payments arises from not keeping clearly in mind the distinction between the proportion of people who use checks and the proportion of business done with checks. It is the latter that we are discussing.

The returns of the present inquiry certainly do not support the views of critics who assert that the figure assigned from the investigation of 1896 as the fair one to represent the proportion of retail payments made with credit paper was too large. That figure was 50 per cent. A careful consideration of the present data leads the writer to believe that the ratio then assigned was nearly correct, and that 60 would be nearer the truth to-day.

THE WHOLESALE RETURNS.

We come now to a discussion of the returns of the deposits of wholesale dealers. In this term, as in the case of retail dealers, there is likely to be some indefiniteness. A merchant or firm may do both wholesale and retail business, and a bank may not be able to distinguish his deposits as retail and wholesale. Occasionally such cases occurred, but not many were specifically mentioned and the whole number was few. There can not be more than the most trifling error, if any, in the returns, due to this cause.

There was doubtless, also, some question in the minds of a good many of the correspondents as to the propriety of including certain kinds of business firms under the term "wholesale dealers," such as lumbermen and commission merchants. These latter, however, so far as could be determined, were all classed with the wholesale dealers. Businesses like the lumber business were probably classed under "all others" in most cases. If any depositors in this or similar kinds of business were classed with wholesale dealers, the presence of their deposits would introduce no error into the returns because their methods of payment are doubtless the same as those of wholesale dealers.

The error due to a bank's ignorance of the business of its patrons would be much smaller in the case of wholesale dealers than in the case of retail traders. A wholesale merchant's account is large enough to make the bank sufficiently interested to know about it. He undoubtedly is an occasional, if not a frequent, borrower, and his business therefore would be known to his banker. So far, then, as concerns the character of the returns, they may be taken as reflecting pretty accurately the method of payments of the wholesale merchants.

We must remember, however, that wholesale trade, after all, is a relative term, if we have regard to its magnitude in an individual case. A man may class himself as a wholesale merchant, and yet sell goods in such quantities as would be regarded as small by a wholesale merchant in the same line, perhaps, in a neighboring city.

The classification depends, as in the case of retail merchants, not so much on the amount sold as on the class of customers. If the merchant sells, not directly to consumers, but to retail merchants or others who are to sell again to the consumer, he may properly be classed as a wholesale dealer.

Corrections for nonreplying banks.—As in the case of the retail dealers, we might make some allowance for banks which did not reply. This can not be in proportion to the nonreplying banks, because a very large part of the banks which did not send returns are the smaller state and private banks. However, it is hardly worth while to go to the trouble of making such a correction, for the evidence is overwhelming that wherever wholesale business is done in the country the method of payment used is preponderatingly by means of checks. The percentage of checks in payments derived from three-fourths of the deposits, or even one-half of the deposits, of wholesale merchants in the banks in the country would doubtless be practically the same as that which would be obtained if we had an exact statement of the entire sum of the deposits. Following are the tables of deposits of wholesale dealers by banks:

TABLE IX.—*Wholesale deposits in national banks, state banks, private banks, loan and trust companies, stock savings banks, and mutual savings banks.*

NATIONAL BANKS.

State.	Gold.	Silver.	Total specie.	Currency.	Checks.	Total.	Gold.	Silver.	Specie.	Currency.	Checks.
							P. ct.	*P. ct.*	*P. ct.*	*P. ct.*	*P. ct.*
Alabama	$1,252	$3,819	$5,071	$23,402	$232,196	$260,669	0.4	1.4	1.9	8.9	89.0
Arizona	3,610	1,214	4,824	3,949	21,367	30,140	12.0	4.0	16.0	13.1	70.9
Arkansas	335	1,152	1,487	4,278	178,035	183,800	.2	.6	.8	2.3	96.8
California	115,716	14,141	129,857	17,612	2,511,788	2,659,257	4.3	.5	4.8	.7	94.4
Colorado	14,539	2,487	17,026	18,175	458,763	493,964	2.9	.5	3.4	3.7	92.9
Connecticut	297	3,425	3,722	59,609	980,142	1,043,473	------	.3	.3	5.7	94.0
Delaware	20	438	458	6,413	69,273	76,144	------	.6	.6	8.4	91.0
District of Columbia	30	2,520	2,550	30,763	127,926	161,239	------	1.6	1.6	19.0	79.3
Florida	315	4,107	4,422	15,082	395,196	414,700	------	1.0	1.0	3.6	95.3
Georgia	1,835	10,518	12,353	43,974	669,012	725,339	.2	1.4	1.6	6.1	92.3
Idaho	1,240	178	1,418	1,140	56,434	58,992	2.1	.3	2.1	1.9	95.7
Illinois	12,883	11,365	24,248	185,022	10,557,437	10,766,707	.1	.1	.2	1.7	98.1
Indiana	16,720	12,954	29,674	92,330	1,511,772	1,633,776	1.0	.8	1.8	5.7	92.5
Iowa	7,883	2,970	10,853	14,081	582,909	607,843	1.3	.5	1.8	2.3	95.9
Kansas	2,085	3,017	5,102	14,408	1,114,094	1,133,604	.2	.3	.5	1.2	98.3
Kentucky	4,102	4,690	8,792	23,629	1,126,024	1,158,445	.4	.4	.8	2.0	97.1
Louisiana	70	2,643	2,713	14,587	618,344	635,644	------	.4	.4	2.3	97.2
Maine	30	419	449	13,476	276,138	290,063	------	------	.2	4.6	95.
Maryland	152	5,272	5,424	77,702	1,260,795	1,343,921	------	.4	.4	5.8	93.8
Massachusetts	437	9,187	9,624	221,161	10,532,745	10,763,530	------	.1	.1	2.1	97.8
Michigan	3,282	4,054	7,336	44,899	853,194	905,429	.3	.4	.8	4.9	94.3

Minnesota	9,190	3,953	13,143	34,181	3,634,198	3,681,522	.3	.1	.4	.9	98.8
Mississippi	795	1,848	2,643	6,704	125,180	134,527	.6	1.4	2.0	5.0	92.9
Missouri	4,805	8,813	13,618	52,110	3,713,179	3,778,907	.1	.2	.4	1.4	98.2
Montana	1,290	391	1,681	3,743	168,093	173,517	.7	.2	.9	2.2	96.8
Nebraska	2,515	1,175	3,690	11,432	2,011,974	2,027,096	.1	------	.2	.6	99.2
Nevada	985	380	1,365	183	9,249	10,797	9.1	3.5	12.6	1.7	85.7
New Hampshire	90	1,499	1,589	12,751	212,746	227,086	------	.7	.7	5.6	93.7
New Jersey	4,757	3,663	8,420	119,872	2,531,954	2,660,246	.2	.1	.3	4.5	95.2
New Mexico	475	153	628	1,527	31,360	33,515	1.4	.5	1.9	4.6	93.5
New York	10,370	13,383	23,753	376,581	32,109,078	32,509,412	------	------	.1	1.2	98.7
North Carolina	1,105	6,745	7,850	21,374	278,374	307,598	.4	2.2	2.6	6.9	90.5
North Dakota	125	279	404	1,711	47,664	49,779	.3	.6	.8	3.5	95.7
Ohio	32,091	16,113	48,204	173,359	3,983,007	4,204,570	.8	.4	1.2	4.1	94.7
Oklahoma	930	1,991	2,921	8,220	204,771	215,912	.4	.9	1.3	3.8	94.4
Oregon	10,095	3,046	13,141	1,499	349,625	364,265	2.7	.8	3.5	.4	96.1
Pennsylvania	33,632	29,395	63,027	393,420	10,043,293	10,499,740	.3	.3	.6	3.8	95.6
Rhode Island	45	1,150	1,195	24,625	484,182	510,002	------	.2	.2	4.9	94.9
South Carolina	20	1,598	1,618	7,332	120,158	129,108	------	1.2	1.2	5.7	93.1
South Dakota	460	444	904	2,282	31,540	34,726	1.3	1.3	2.6	6.6	90.8
Tennessee	530	2,695	3,225	28,463	873,912	905,600	.1	.2	.3	3.1	96.6
Texas	6,837	15,778	22,615	62,763	1,475,365	1,560,743	.4	1.1	1.5	4.0	94.5
Utah	1,670	984	2,654	932	70,228	73,814	2.3	1.3	3.6	1.3	95.1
Vermont	--------	164	164	4,183	152,467	156,814	------	.1	.1	2.4	97.5
Virginia	1,982	4,130	6,112	41,266	871,543	918,921	.2	.5	.7	4.5	94.8
Washington	19,830	1,940	21,770	9,069	332,685	363,524	5.5	.5	6.0	2.5	91.5
West Virginia	405	673	1,078	7,888	175,413	184,379	.2	.4	.6	4.2	95.1
Wisconsin	5,380	2,901	8,281	27,913	1,287,141	1,323,335	.4	.2	.6	2.1	97.3
Wyoming	100	7	107	1,140	10,392	11,639	.9	.1	1.0	9.8	89.2
Total	337,342	225,861	563,203	2,362,215	99,472,355	102,397,773	.3	.2	.5	2.3	97.2

TABLE IX.—*Wholesale deposits in national banks, state banks, private banks, loan and trust companies, stock savings banks, and mutual savings banks*—Continued.

STATE BANKS.

State.	Gold.	Silver.	Total specie.	Currency.	Checks.	Total.	Gold.	Silver	Specie.	Currency.	Checks.
							P. ct.	*P. ct.*	*P. ct.*	*P. ct.*	*P. ct.*
Alabama	$237	$1,325	$1,562	$6,166	$89,294	$97,022	0.24	1.4	1.6	6.3	92.1
Arizona	745	--------	745	1,183	3,549	5,477	13.6	------	13.6	21.6	64.8
Arkansas	190	547	737	2,549	42,585	45,871	.4	1.2	1.6	5.6	92.8
California	69,475	8,453	77,928	7,572	1,610,848	1,696,348	4.1	.5	4.6	.4	95.0
Colorado	100	50	150	760	1,933	2,843	3.5	1.7	5.2	26.7	68.1
Connecticut	15	341	356	10,797	68,545	79,698	------	.4	.4	13.5	86.1
Delaware	--------	--------	--------	18	610	628	------	------	--------	3.0	97.0
District of Columbia	--------	124	124	2,334	1,978	4,436	------	2.8	2.8	52.6	44.6
Florida	40	383	423	2,380	20,065	22,868	.2	1.7	1.9	10.4	87.7
Georgia	185	1,363	1,548	4,091	104,800	110,439	.2	1.2	1.4	3.7	94.9
Idaho	65	64	129	75	21,512	21,716	.3	.3	.6	.3	99.1
Illinois	11,583	9,336	20,919	167,582	2,703,540	2,892,041	.4	.3	.7	5.7	93.6
Indiana	400	1,024	1,424	5,947	57,391	64,762	.6	1.6	2.2	9.2	88.6
Iowa	115	185	300	2,341	226,661	229,302	------	------	.1	1.0	98.9
Kansas	415	1,016	1,431	3,939	103,651	109,021	.4	.9	1.3	3.6	95.1
Kentucky	2,150	868	3,018	11,189	401,287	415,494	.5	.2	.7	2.7	96.6
Louisiana	90	17,539	17,629	71,802	496,577	586,008	------	3.0	3.0	12.3	84.7
Maine	--------	180	180	3,537	27,502	31,219	------	.6	.6	11.3	88.1
Maryland	--------	33	33	379	4,016	4,428	------	1.0	1.0	8.5	90.6
Michigan	1,640	1,193	2,833	15,799	389,014	407,646	.4	.3	.7	3.9	95.3
Minnesota	1,840	1,316	3,156	8,118	122,677	133,951	1.3	1.0	2.3	6.1	91.6
Mississippi	55	947	1,002	2,711	36,573	40 286	.1	2.4	2.5	6.7	90.7

Missouri	2.728	2,490	5.218	40,918	751,308	797,444	.4	.3	.7	5.1	94.2
Montana	1,770	277	2.047	1,568	46,194	49,809	3.6	.5	4.1	3.2	92.7
Nebraska	230	244	474	2,022	23,750	26,246	.9	1.0	1.8	7.2	90.6
Nevada	1,190	287	1,477	69	1,818	3,364	35.4	8.5	43.9	2.1	54.0
New Hampshire				148	6,356	6,504				2.3	97.7
New Jersey		57	57	7,108	24,972	32,137		.2	.2	22.1	77.7
New Mexico					1,211	1,211					100.0
New York	7,699	10,355	18,054	297,705	4,009,756	4,325,515	.2	.2	.4	6.9	92.8
North Carolina	55	668	723	2,398	12,761	15,882	.4	4.2	4.6	15.1	80.3
North Dakota		125	125	181	18,569	18,875		.7	.7	.9	98.3
Ohio	12,166	4,183	16,349	45,335	499,027	560,711	2.2	.7	2.9	8.1	88.9
Oklahoma	2,795	10,570	13,365	63,736	127,237	204,338	1.3	5.2	6.5	31.2	62.3
Oregon	6,840	533	7,373	670	269,432	277,475	2.4	.2	2.6	.2	97.2
Pennsylvania	6,513	3,733	10,246	60,442	426,807	497,495	1.3	.8	2.1	12.1	85.8
Rhode Island	10	201	211	2,000	3,791	6,002	.2	3.4	3.6	33.3	63.1
South Carolina	5	1,170	1,175	1,956	46,303	49,434		2.4	2.4	4.0	93.6
South Dakota		17	17	206	15,063	15,286		.1	.1	1.4	98.5
Tennessee	1,005	2,009	3,014	9,694	216,705	229,413	.4	.8	1.2	4.2	94.6
Texas	110	163	273	1,893	39,308	41,474	.3	.4	.7	4.7	94.6
Utah	1,065	276	1,341	603	39,943	41,887	2.5	.7	3.2	1.4	95.4
Vermont					3,676	3,676					100.0
Virginia	102	674	776	5,701	87,543	94,020	.1	.7	.8	6.1	93.1
Washington	2,920	185	3,105	5,640	232,509	241,254	1.2	.1	1.3	2.3	96.4
West Virginia	1,215	828	2,043	15,327	161,044	178,414	.7	.5	1.2	8.6	90.2
Wisconsin	3,025	1,480	4,505	16,213	437,004	457,722	.7	.3	1.0	3.5	95.5
Wyoming					797	797					100.0
Total	140,783	86,812	227,595	912,802	14,037,492	15,177,889	.9	.6	1.5	6.1	92.4

TABLE IX.—*Wholesale deposits in national banks, state banks, private banks, loan and trust companies, stock savings banks, and mutual savings banks*—Continued.

PRIVATE BANKS.

State.	Gold.	Silver.	Total specie.	Currency.	Checks.	Total.	Gold.	Silver.	Specie.	Currency.	Checks.
							P. ct.	*P. ct.*	*P. ct.*	*P. ct.*	*P. ct.*
Colorado					$2,625	$2,625					100.0
Florida					142	142					100.0
Georgia					6,702	6,702					100.0
Illinois	$545	$252	$797	$6,682	57,988	65,467	0.9	0.2	1.1	10.2	88.7
Indiana	40	50	90	376	9,626	10,092	.4	.5	.9	3.7	95.4
Iowa		11	11		1,670	1,681		.7	.7		99.3
Massachusetts					850	850					100.0
Michigan				311	13,580	13,891				2.2	97.7
Missouri					7,710	7,710					100.0
New York	5	86	91	520	12,331	12,942		.7	.7	4.0	95.2
Ohio	520	373	893	1,849	26,793	29,535	1.7	1.3	3.0	6.2	90.8
Oregon	25	4	29	20		49	51.0	8.2	59.2	40.8	
Pennsylvania				160	4,682	4,842				3.3	96.7
Texas	110	800	910	6,373	28,465	35,748	.3	2.2	2.5	17.9	79.6
Virginia				15,843	21,947	37,790				41.9	58.1
Washington					300	300					100.0
Total	1,245	1,576	2,821	32,134	195,411	230,366	.5	.7	1.2	14.0	84.8

LOAN AND TRUST COMPANIES.

							P. ct.	P. ct.	P. ct.	P. ct.	P. ct.
Arkansas	$5	$266	$271	$489	$1,183	$1,943	0.3	13.7	14.0	25.1	60.9
California	400	75	475	-----	1,503	1,978	20.2	3.8	24.0	-----	75.9
Connecticut	25	455	480	10,128	84,818	95,426	-----	.5	.5	10.6	88.9
Delaware	-----	575	575	61	17,983	18,619	-----	3.0	3.0	.3	96.7
Illinois	440	321	761	7,994	232,119	240,874	.2	.1	.3	3.3	96.3
Indiana	820	233	1,053	1,036	7,574	9,663	8.5	2.4	10.9	10.7	78.4
Maine	10	66	76	2,441	61,190	63,707	-----	.1	.1	3.8	96.0
Maryland	-----	-----	-----	-----	8,591	8,591	-----	-----	-----	-----	100.0
Massachusetts	330	3,385	3,715	55,280	1,894,452	1,953,447	-----	.2	.2	2.7	97.1
Missouri	150	661	811	4,494	196,467	201,772	.1	.3	.4	2.2	97.4
New Hampshire	-----	8	8	103	8,595	8,706	-----	.1	.1	1.2	98.7
New Jersey	135	776	911	18,521	271,303	290,735	-----	.3	.3	6.4	93.2
New York	1,220	2,790	4,010	119,678	2,546,579	2,670,267	-----	.1	.1	4.5	95.4
North Carolina	125	1,284	1,409	2,823	77,923	82,155	.2	1.5	1.7	3.4	94.9
Ohio	300	628	928	1,306	2,052	4,286	7.1	14.9	22.0	30.2	47.8
Pennsylvania	4,671	5,435	10,106	75,198	669,371	754,675	.6	.7	1.3	10.0	88.7
Rhode Island	10	1,015	1,025	20,945	339,956	361,926	-----	.3	.3	5.8	93.9
Vermont	10	80	90	930	12,703	13,723	-----	.6	.6	6.8	92.6
Total	8,651	18,053	26,704	321,427	6,434,362	6,782,493	.1	.3	.4	4.7	94.9

STOCK SAVINGS BANKS.

							P. ct.	P. ct.	P. ct.	P. ct.	P. ct.
California	-----	-----	-----	-----	$617	$617	-----	-----	-----	-----	100.0
District of Columbia	-----	-----	-----	$200	-----	200	-----	-----	-----	100.0	-----
Georgia	-----	$10	$10	116	616	742	-----	1.4	1.4	15.6	83.0
Illinois	$10	47	57	1,155	12,289	13,501	0.1	.3	.4	8.6	91.0
Iowa	520	293	813	3,560	94,559	98,932	.5	.3	.8	3.6	95.6

TABLE IX.—*Wholesale deposits in national banks, state banks, private banks, loan and trust companies, stock savings banks, and mutual savings banks*—Continued.

STOCK SAVINGS BANKS—Continued.

State.	Gold.	Silver.	Total specie.	Currency.	Checks.	Total.	Gold.	Silver.	Specie.	Currency.	Checks.
							P. ct.	*P. ct.*	*P. ct.*	*P. ct.*	*P. ct.*
Maryland				$134	$1,130	1,264				10.6	89.4
Michigan	$342	$243	$585	8,198	93,291	102,074	0.3	0.2	0.6	8.0	91.4
New Hampshire		15	15	80	273	368		4.0	4.0	21.7	74.2
Ohio	40		40	240	4,650	4,930	.8		.8	4.8	94.4
Pennsylvania	460		460	783	3,121	4,364	10.6		10.6	17.9	71.5
Tennessee	5	105	110	242	2,786	3,138	.1	3.4	3.5	7.7	88.8
Virginia				63	25	88				71.6	28.4
West Virginia	45	35	80	295	1,045	1,420	3.2	2.5	5.7	20.8	73.5
Total	1,422	748	2,170	15,066	214,402	231,638	.6	.3	.9	6.5	92.6

MUTUAL SAVINGS BANKS.

State.	Gold.	Silver.	Total specie.	Currency.	Checks.	Total.	Gold.	Silver.	Specie.	Currency.	Checks.
							P. ct.	*P. ct.*	*P. ct.*	*P. ct.*	*P. ct.*
New Jersey				$620	$138	$758				81.8	18.2
New York				946	1,500	2,446				38.7	61.3
Pennsylvania		$1	$1	27	371	399				6.8	93.2
Total		1	1	1,593	2,009	3,603				44.0	56.0

TABLE X.—*Aggregate wholesale deposits, all banks, by States.*

Locality.	Gold.	Silver.	Total specie.	Currency.	Checks.	Total.	Gold.	Silver.	Specie.	Currency.	Checks.
							P. ct.	*P. ct.*	*P. ct.*	*P. ct.*	*P. ct.*
Alabama	$1,489	$5,144	$6,633	$29,568	$321,490	$357,691	0.5	1.4	1.9	8.3	89.8
Arizona	4,355	1,214	5,569	5,132	24,916	35,617	12.1	3.3	15.4	14.6	70.0
Arkansas	530	1,965	2,495	7,316	221,803	231,614	.2	.9	1.1	3.2	95.7
California	185,591	22,669	208,260	25,184	4,124,756	4,358,200	4.2	.6	4.8	.6	94.6
Colorado	14,639	2,537	17,176	18,935	463,321	499,432	2.9	.5	3.4	3.7	92.9
Connecticut	337	4,221	4,558	80,534	1,133,505	1,218,597	------	.2	.3	6.6	93.0
Delaware	20	1,013	1,033	6,492	87,866	95,391	------	1.8	1.9	6.8	92.3
District of Columbia	30	2,644	2,674	33,297	129,904	165,875	------	1.5	1.6	20.2	78.2
Florida	355	4,490	4,845	17,462	415,403	437,710	------	1.1	1.2	3.9	94.9
Georgia	2,020	11,891	13,911	48,181	781,130	843,222	.2	1.4	1.6	5.7	92.7
Idaho	1,305	242	1,547	1,215	77,946	80,708	1.6	.3	1.9	1.5	96.6
Illinois	25,461	21,321	46,782	368,435	13,563,373	13,978,590	.2	.1	.3	2.7	97.0
Indiana	17,980	14,261	32,241	99,689	1,586,363	1,718,293	1.1	.8	1.9	5.8	92.3
Iowa	8,518	3,459	11,977	19,982	905,799	937,758	.9	.4	1.3	2.2	96.5
Kansas	2,500	4,033	6,533	18,347	1,217,745	1,242,625	.2	.3	.5	1.3	98.2
Kentucky	6,252	5,558	11,810	34,818	1,527,311	1,573,939	.4	.3	.7	2.1	97.2
Louisiana	160	20,182	20,342	86,389	1,114,921	1,221,652	------	1.5	1.6	7.0	91.4
Maine	40	665	705	19,454	364,830	384,989	------	.1	.2	4.9	94.9
Maryland	152	5,305	5,457	78,215	1,274,532	1,358,204	------	.3	.4	5.8	93.8
Massachusetts	767	12,572	13,339	276,441	12,428,047	12,717,827	------	------	.1	2.1	97.8
Michigan	5,264	5,490	10,754	69,207	1,349,079	1,429,040	.4	.4	.8	4.8	94.4
Minnesota	11,030	5,269	16,299	42,299	3,756,875	3,815,473	.3	.1	.4	1.1	98.5
Mississipp	850	2,795	3,645	9,415	161,753	174,813	.5	1.6	2.1	5.5	92.4
Missouri	7,683	11,964	19,647	97,522	4,668,664	4,785,833	.1	.2	.3	2.0	97.7

TABLE X.—*Aggregate wholesale deposits, all banks, by States*—Continued.

Locality.	Gold.	Silver.	Total specie.	Currency.	Checks.	Total.	Gold.	Silver.	Specie.	Currency.	Checks.
							P. ct.	*P. ct.*	*P. ct.*	*P. ct.*	*P. ct.*
Montana	$3,060	$668	$3,728	$5,311	$214,287	$223,326	1.3	0.3	1.6	2.3	96.1
Nebraska	2,745	1,419	4,164	13,454	2,035.724	2,053,342	.1	------	.2	.6	99.2
Nevada	2,175	667	2,842	252	11,067	14,161	15.4	4.7	20.1	1.8	78.1
New Hampshire	90	1,522	1,612	13,082	227,970	242,664	------	.5	.6	5.3	94.1
New Jersey	4,892	4,496	9,388	146,121	2,828,367	2,983,876	.2	.1	.3	4.9	94.8
New Mexico	475	153	628	1,527	32,571	34,726	1.3	.4	1.7	4.4	93.9
New York	19,294	26,614	45,908	795,430	38,679,244	39,520,582	------	------	.1	2.1	97.8
North Carolina	1,285	8,697	9,982	26,595	369,058	405,635	.3	2.1	2.4	6.5	91.1
North Dakota	125	404	529	1,892	66,233	68,654	.2	.5	.7	2.8	96.5
Ohio	45,117	21,297	66,414	222,089	4,515,529	4,804,032	1.0	.4	1.4	4.7	93.9
Oklahoma	3,725	12,561	16,286	71,956	332,008	420,250	.8	2.9	3.7	17.1	79.2
Oregon	16,960	3,583	20,543	2,189	619,057	641,789	2.7	.5	3.2	.3	96.5
Pennsylvania	45,276	38,564	83,840	530,030	11,147,645	11,761,515	.5	.4	.9	4.5	94.6
Rhode Island	65	2,366	2,431	47,570	827,929	877,930	------	.2	.3	5.4	94.3
South Carolina	25	2,768	2,793	9,288	166,461	178,542	------	1.4	1.5	5.1	93.4
South Dakota	460	461	921	2,488	46,603	50,012	.9	1.0	1.9	5.0	93.1
Tennessee	1,540	4,809	6,349	38,399	1,093,403	1,138,151	.2	.4	.6	3.5	95.9
Texas	7,057	16,741	23,798	71,029	1,543,138	1,637,965	.5	1.0	1.5	4.3	94.1
Utah	2,735	1,260	3,995	1,535	110,171	115,701	2.4	1.1	3.5	1.3	95.2
Vermont	10	244	254	5,113	168,846	174,213	------	------	.1	2.9	97.0
Virginia	2,084	4,804	6,888	62,873	981,058	1,050,819	.2	.3	.5	6.0	93.5
Washington	22,750	2,125	24,875	14,709	565,494	605,078	3.8	.4	4.2	2.4	93.4
West Virginia	1,665	1,536	3,201	23,510	337,502	364,213	.5	.4	.9	6.4	92.7

Wisconsin	8,405	4,381	12,786	44,126	1,724,145	1,781,057	.4	.3	.7	2.5	96.8
Wyoming	100	7	107	1,140	11,189	12,436	.8		.8	9.0	90.2
Total	489,443	333,051	822,494	3,645,237	120,356,031	124,823,762	.4	.3	.7	2.9	96.4

TABLE XI.—*Aggregate wholesale deposits, all banks, by banks.*

	Gold.	Silver	Total specie.	Currency.	Checks.	Total.	Gold.	Silver	Specie.	Currency.	Checks.
							P. ct.	*P. ct.*	*P. ct.*	*P. ct.*	*P. ct.*
National banks	$337,342	$225,861	$563,203	$2,362,215	$99,472,355	$102,397,773	0.3	0.2	1.5	6.0	92.4
State banks	140,783	86,812	227,595	912,802	14,037,492	15,177,889	.9	.6	1.5	5.9	92.6
Private banks	1,245	1,576	2,821	32,134	195,411	230,366	.5	.7	1.2	14.0	84.8
Loan and trust companies	8,651	18,053	26,704	321,427	6,434,362	6,782,493	.1	.3	.4	4.7	94.9
Stock savings banks	1,422	748	2,170	15,066	214,402	231,638	.6	.3	.9	6.5	92.6
Mutual savings banks		1	1	1,593	2,009	3,603				44.2	55.8
Total	489,443	333,051	822,494	3,645,237	120,356,033	124,823,762	.4	.3	.7	2.9	96.4

DISCUSSION OF TABLES.

The wholesale deposits of the national banks.—The deposits of wholesale dealers returned by the 5,452 national banks aggregated $102,397,773, of which 97.2 per cent were in checks and other credit documents. The currency aggregated $2,362,215, or 2.3 per cent; and the specie $563,203, or about one-half of 1 per cent, two-fifths being silver and three-fifths gold. In this table, as in all the others, in figuring the percentages, the small amounts of gold, silver, and currency have been favored in keeping or throwing away fractions of 1 per cent.

The highest percentage shown by the returns is 99.2 in Nebraska; Minnesota has 98.8, New York shows 98.7, Kansas 98.3, Vermont 97.5, Missouri 98.2, Wisconsin 97.3, Illinois 98.1, Massachusetts 97.8, Pennsylvania 95.6. The States which show the largest volume of deposits are New York, Illinois, Massachusetts, and Pennsylvania. The lowest percentage shown by any of the States is that of Arizona, 70.9. The total deposits there were $30,140. The District of Columbia, with total deposits of $161,239, has 79.3 per cent of checks. Nevada, with aggregate deposits of $10,797, gives a return of 85.7; Wyoming with $11,639 has 89.2 per cent; Alabama with $260,669, shows 89 per cent. No other State shows less than 90 per cent.

In 44 States the percentage of checks in deposits is over 90; in 24 States it is over 95.

The wholesale deposits of the state banks.—The 4,288 state banks from which replies were received returned wholesale deposits amounting to $15,177,889. Of this amount 92.4

per cent, or $14,037,492, were in checks. The currency, $912,802, was 6.1 per cent of the aggregate. The specie, $227,595, was about 1.5 per cent, and gold formed about three-fifths of it.

In three instances the percentage of checks shown in the returns is 100. These are the deposits of New Mexico, Vermont, and Wyoming. The volume of deposits in each case, however, is so trifling that no significance attaches to this fact. Otherwise, the percentages run very like those of the national banks. Aside from the three cases of 100 per cent just mentioned, the highest percentage returned is 99.1 from Idaho. Iowa has 98.9, North Dakota 98.3, Oregon 97.2, South Dakota 98.5, and New York 92.8.

Omitting the three cases of 100 per cent already mentioned, as not being significant, 14 States show a percentage of 95 or more, and 30 of 90 or more. The lowest percentage is that of the District of Columbia, 44.6; but, as remarked before, the total deposits are a little over $4,000, and therefore trifling. Nevada has 54 per cent, but here again the deposits are only $3,000. The state banks are evidently not used throughout the country by wholesale dealers to so great an extent as the national banks. Nevertheless the proportion of checks in the deposits runs very much the same.

The wholesale deposits of the private banks.—The wholesale returns of private banks were trifling, being in the aggregate only $230,366. More than half the returns come from four states, Ohio, Virginia, Texas, and Illinois. Therefore they are not significant.

The wholesale deposits of the loan and trust companies.—The aggregate of these was $6,780,000, 94.9 per cent being in checks. There were only ten States in which the amount of deposits was large enough to be worthy of consideration for our purpose. New York leads with deposits of $2,670,267, and 95 per cent of them in checks. Massachusetts comes second with $1,953,447 and 97 per cent in checks. Of the States with deposits of more than $50,000, the highest percentage, 97.4, is afforded by Missouri, from deposits of $201,000. The lowest, 88.7, is Pennsylvania, whose total deposits of this class are $754,000.

Nothing need be said about the wholesale deposits of the savings banks, because the number of banks and the amount involved are both unimportant. Moreover, as has been already remarked, the accounts of the mutual savings banks in no case have any bearing upon our present inquiry.

The aggregate wholesale deposits.—Tables X and XI give the aggregate wholesale deposits in all reporting banks by states and by classes of banks, respectively. The total is $124,823,762, of which 96.4 per cent is in checks. The highest percentage is that of Nebraska, 99.2. New York has 97.8, and so is fourth in the list, Kansas, Minnesota, and Nebraska all showing larger percentages. Massachusetts shows the same as New York.

The percentage of checks shown in the table of wholesale deposits by banks is approximately the same for the national banks, the state banks, the loan and trust companies, and the stock savings bank. The loan and trust companies show the highest percentage. The private banks show 84.8 per cent of their wholesale deposits in checks. The percentage for mutual savings banks is not significant.

RETURNS OF WHOLESALE DEPOSITS IN REPRESENTATIVE RESERVE CITIES AND BY GEOGRAPHICAL DIVISIONS.

There is no reason for so detailed an examination of the wholesale returns as was thought necessary in the case of the retail deposits. Nevertheless the data are presented in corresponding tables to show the similarity of practice in different parts of the country. It will be seen that, despite the fact that so large a part of the business shown by the returns was done in these cities, the proportion of payments made by check is not materially different from that of the rest of the country. Nor is the proportion for the country at large, without the reserve cities, modified much by omitting the reserve cities. There is a change of about 3 per cent—from about 97 to 94.

Reserve cities—Wholesale deposits of national banks.—It will be seen that of the deposits returned by the national banks for representative reserve cities, 98.2 per cent was in the form of credit documents. Remembering what has been said about the preponderating influence of the national banks as compared with other commercial banks, the significance of this high figure is emphasized. Of wholesale deposits of sixty-five odd millions returned by the national banks for these reserve cities, nearly 29 were in New York, and the percentage of checks and other credit instruments in the deposits of that city was 99.4. Boston shows 98.6, Cincinnati 96.8, and Chicago and St. Louis each have 98.4. Thirteen of the 24 cities show 95 per cent of checks or over in their wholesale deposits. Brooklyn's figure is low because, of course, of the fact that it is a suburb of New York, and its business is mostly done in that city.

Reserve cities—Wholesale deposits of state banks.—The amount in this case is insignificant, being a little less than $8,000,000. Of this whole amount over $6,000,000 are in the deposits of the three central reserve cities. The percentage of Chicago, 93.8, in this case is highest; New York shows 92.9, St. Louis 92.6. The amounts involved in the other cases are small.

Reserve cities—Wholesale deposits of other banks.—The details for the other banks show no peculiarities, excepting that the amounts involved are much smaller and the percentages run somewhat lower. Here, again, we see that these banks, aside from the loan and trust companies, play a relatively small part in the volume of the commercial life of the country when contrasted with the national banks. The tables show the distribution of the deposits among the various classes of banks.

Reserve cities—Aggregate wholesale deposits.—The table of aggregate wholesale deposits for the reserve cities shows that the percentages run highest for the five cities of New York, Boston, St. Louis, Chicago, and Philadelphia, in the order named. The average for the five is 98.1 per cent and for the whole country 97.4.

TABLE XII.—*Wholesale deposits at representative reserve cities in national banks, state banks, private banks, loan and trust companies, stock savings banks, and mutual savings banks.*

NATIONAL BANKS.

City.	Gold.	Silver.	Total specie.	Currency.	Checks.	Total.	Gold.	Silver.	Specie.	Currency.	Checks
							P. ct.	*P. ct.*	*P. ct.*	*P. ct.*	*P. ct.*
Chicago	$7,388	$6,029	$13,417	$142,769	$9,685,992	$9,842,178	0.1		0.1	1.4	98.4
New York	3,862	4,247	8,109	172,956	28,584,519	28,765,584				.6	99.4
St. Louis	1,185	3,261	4,446	26,403	1,942,183	1,973,032	.1	.2	.3	1.3	98.4
Total	12,435	13,537	25,972	342,128	40,212,694	40,580,794			.1	.9	99.0
Albany	120	499	619	15,493	153,951	170,063	.1	.3	.4	9.1	90.5
Baltimore	152	4,835	4,987	69,101	1,182,848	1,256,936		.4	.4	5.5	94.1
Boston	107	2,558	2,665	111,100	8,240,360	8,354,125				1.4	98.6
Brooklyn	190	837	1,027	31,631	185,661	218,319	.1	.4	.5	14.5	85.0
Cincinnati	3,875	3,203	7,078	37,697	1,373,473	1,418,248	.3	.2	.5	2.7	96.8
Cleveland	7,520	1,943	9,463	36,504	1,057,104	1,103,071	.7	.2	.9	3.3	95.8
Columbus	2,821	2,394	5,215	15,835	228,491	249,541	1.1	1.0	2.1	6.3	91.6
Dallas	810	2,450	3,260	8,344	296,668	308,272	.3	.8	1.1	2.7	96.2
Detroit	1,375	1,814	3,189	16,357	348,167	367,713	.4	.5	.9	4.4	94.7
Fort Worth	50	1,040	1,090	4,606	147,166	152,862		.7	.7	3.0	96.3
Galveston	20	425	445	1,445	15,762	17,652	.1	2.4	2.5	8.2	89.3
Houston	220	1,091	1,311	4,040	308,145	313,496	.1	.3	.4	1.3	98.3
Indianapolis	8,095	5,244	13,339	42,006	685,246	740,591	1.1	.7	1.8	5.7	92.5
Louisville	2,810	2,211	5,021	11,564	820,919	837,504	.3	.3	.6	1.4	98.0
New Orleans	70	1,200	1,270	12,636	486,265	500,171		.3	.3	2.5	97.2
Philadelphia	8,255	8,301	16,556	150,346	4,988,046	5,154,948	.2	.2	.4	2.9	96.7

TABLE XII.—*Wholesale deposits at representative reserve cities in national banks, state banks, private banks, loan and trust companies, stock savings banks, and mutual savings banks*—Continued.

NATIONAL BANKS—Continued.

City.	Gold.	Silver.	Total specie.	Currency.	Checks.	Total.	Gold.	Silver.	Specie.	Currency.	Checks.
							P. ct.	*P. ct.*	*P. ct.*	*P. ct.*	*P. ct.*
Pittsburg	$7,712	$4,378	12,090	$79,720	$2,968,194	$3,060,004	0.2	0.2	0.4	2.6	97.0
San Antonio	60	1,881	1,941	6,005	94,077	102,023	.1	1.8	1.9	5.9	92.2
Savannah	------	172	172	880	13,192	14,244	------	1.2	1.2	6.2	92.6
Waco	10	868	878	2,849	48,456	52,183	------	1.6	1.6	5.4	93.0
Washington	30	2,520	2,550	30,763	127,926	161,239	------	1.6	1.6	19.0	79.3
Total	56,737	63,401	120,138	1,031,050	63,982,811	65,133,999	.1	.1	.2	1.6	98.2

STATE BANKS.

City.	Gold.	Silver.	Total specie.	Currency.	Checks.	Total.	Gold.	Silver.	Specie.	Currency.	Checks.
							P. ct.	*P. ct.*	*P. ct.*	*P. ct.*	*P. ct.*
Chicago	$7,468	$5,692	$13,160	$149,093	$2,459,719	$2,621,972	------	------	0.5	5.7	93.8
New York	4,622	7,810	12,432	227,012	3,128,279	3,367,723	0.2	0.2	.4	6.7	92.9
St. Louis	1,903	930	2,833	24,115	343,185	370,133	.6	.3	.9	6.5	92.6
Total	13,993	14,432	28,425	400,220	5,931,183	6,359,828	------	------	.5	6.3	93.2
Albany	5	35	40	2,454	10,901	13,395	------	.3	.3	18.3	81.4
Brooklyn	355	1,249	1,604	28,330	196,013	225,947	.2	.6	.8	12.5	86.7
Cincinnati	1,617	985	2,602	14,151	95,458	112,211	1.4	.9	2.3	12.6	85.1
Cleveland	2,935	1,083	4,018	13,180	96,410	113,608	2.6	1.0	3.6	11.6	84.8
Columbus	35	123	158	598	65,644	66,400	.1	.4	.3	.9	98.8
Detroit	------	1	1	103	9,261	9,365	------	------	------	1.1	98.9
Houston	110	163	273	1,893	38,390	40,556	.3	.4	.7	4.7	94.6

Louisville	2,020	419	2,439	8,599	213,518	224,556	.9	.2	1.1	3.9	95.0
New Orleans	90	7,201	7,291	25,401	442,140	474,832	------	1.5	1.5	5.4	93.1
Philadelphia	260	664	924	14,132	62,443	77,499	.3	.9	1.2	18.2	80.6
Pittsburg	1,852	976	2,828	10,642	119,716	133,186	1.4	.7	2.1	8.0	89.9
Savannah	25	619	644	1,501	31,871	34,016	.1	1.8	1.9	4.4	93.7
Washington	--------	124	124	2,334	1,978	4,436	------	2.8	2.8	52.6	44.6
Total	23,297	28,074	51,371	523,538	7,314,926	7,889,835	.3	.3	.6	6.3	93.1
PRIVATE BANKS.											
							P. ct.	P. ct.	P. ct.	P. ct.	P. ct.
Chicago	$350	$39	$389	$1,888	$13,638	$15,915	2.2	0.2	2.4	11.9	85.7
Galveston	110	800	910	1,373	7,967	10,250	1.1	7.8	8.9	13.4	77.7
San Antonio	--------	--------	--------	5,000	20,000	25,000	------	------	--------	20.0	80.0
Total	460	839	1,299	8,261	41,605	51,165	.9	1.6	2.5	16.1	81.4
LOAN AND TRUST COMPANIES.											
							P. ct.	P. ct.	P. ct.	P. ct.	P. ct.
Chicago	$345	$168	$513	$7,112	$208,396	$216,021	0.1	0.1	0.2	3.3	96.5
New York	570	1,348	1,918	81,253	2,233,272	2,316,443	------	------	--------	3.5	96.5
St. Louis	60	138	198	2,400	38,889	41,487	.2	.3	.5	5.8	93.7
Albany	--------	59	59	2,142	3,812	6,013	------	1.0	1.0	35.6	63.4
Baltimore	--------	--------	--------	----------	8,591	8,591	------	------	--------	--------	100.0
Boston	105	2,175	2,280	34,103	1,672,333	1,708,716	------	.2	.2	1.8	97.9
Brooklyn	420	869	1,289	27,509	120,571	149,369	.3	.6	.9	18.4	80.7
Philadelphia	1,486	2,098	3,584	36,012	382,151	421,747	.4	.5	.9	8.5	90.6
Pittsburg	635	1,209	1,844	10,362	63,158	75,364	.9	1.6	2.5	13.7	83.8
Total	3,621	8,064	11,685	200,893	4,731,173	4,943,751	------	.1	.2	4.0	95.8

TABLE XII.—*Wholesale deposits at representative reserve cities in national banks, state banks, private banks, loan and trust companies, stock savings banks, and mutual savings banks*—Continued.

STOCK SAVINGS BANKS.

City.	Gold.	Silver.	Total specie.	Currency.	Checks.	Total.	Gold.	Silver.	Specie.	Currency.	Checks.
							P. ct.	*P. ct.*	*P. ct.*	*P. ct.*	*P. ct.*
Chicago	$10	$28	$38	$1,107	$5,833	$6,978	0.2	0.4	0.6	15.8	83.6
Cincinnati				120	392	512				23.5	76.5
Detroit	342	241	583	8,034	84,321	92,938	.4	.3	.7	8.6	90.7
Washington				200		200				100.0	
Total	352	269	621	9,461	90,546	100,628	.3	.3	.6	9.4	90.0

MUTUAL SAVINGS BANKS.

City.	Gold.	Silver.	Total specie.	Currency.	Checks.	Total.	Gold.	Silver.	Specie.	Currency.	Checks.
							P. ct.	*P. ct.*	*P. ct.*	*P. ct.*	*P. ct.*
New York					$500	$500					100.0
Brooklyn				$946	1,000	1,946				48.5	51.5
Total				946	1,500	2,446				38.7	61.3

AGGREGATE WHOLESALE DEPOSITS AT REPRESENTATIVE RESERVE CITIES.

							P. ct.	P. ct.	P. ct.	P. ct.	P. ct.
New York	$9,054	$13,405	$22,459	$481,221	$33,946,570	$34,450,250	------	------	------	1.4	98.6
Chicago	15,561	11,956	27,517	301,969	12,373,578	12,703,064	0.1	0.1	0.2	2.5	97.3
St. Louis	3,148	4,329	7,477	52,918	2,324,257	2,384,652	.1	.2	.3	2.2	97.5
Boston	212	4,733	4,945	145,203	9,912,693	10,062,841	------	------	------	1.5	98.5
Philadelphia	10,001	11,063	21,064	200,490	5,432,640	5,654,194	.2	.2	.4	3.5	96.1
Total	37,976	45,486	83,462	1,181,801	63,989,738	65,255,001	------	.1	.1	1.8	98.1
Other reserve cities	46,491	55,161	101,652	592,348	12,180,823	12,866,823	.3	.4	.8	4.6	94.6
Grand total	84,467	100,647	185,114	1,774,149	76,170,561	78,121,824	.1	.1	.2	2.3	97.4

Wholesale deposits by geographical divisions.—The returns for the different geographical divisions of the country show no substantial difference in the proportion of checks in total deposits. The percentages of the national banks again run a trifle higher and involve much larger sums. The loan and trust companies, with the exception of the Western Division and the South Central Division, also average high. In the case of each of the divisions mentioned, however, the amount of deposits returned was trifling, so that neither of these figures is worth consideration. The tables follow.

TABLE XIII.—*Wholesale deposits by geographical divisions in national banks, state banks, private banks, loan and trust companies, stock savings banks, and mutual savings banks.*

NATIONAL BANKS.

Geographical divisions.	Gold.	Silver.	Total specie.	Currency.	Checks.	Total.	Gold.	Silver.	Specie.	Currency.	Checks.
							P. ct.	*P. ct.*	*P. ct.*	*P. ct.*	*P. ct.*
North Atlantic Division	$49,658	$62,285	$111,943	$1,225,678	$57,322,745	$58,660,366	0.1	0.1	0.2	2.0	97.8
South Atlantic Division	5,864	36,001	41,865	251,794	3,967,690	4,261,349	.2	.8	1.0	5.9	93.1
North Central Division	97,419	68,038	165,457	653,728	29,328,109	30,147,294	.3	.2	.5	2.2	97.3
South Central Division	14,851	34,616	49,467	172,046	4,833,827	5,055,340	.3	.7	1.0	3.4	95.6
Western Division	169,550	24,921	194,471	58,969	4,019,984	4,273,424	4.0	.6	4.6	1.4	94.0
Total	337,342	225,861	563,203	2,362,215	99,472,355	102,397,773	.3	.2	.5	2.3	97.2

STATE BANKS.

Geographical divisions.	Gold.	Silver.	Total specie.	Currency.	Checks.	Total.	Gold.	Silver.	Specie.	Currency.	Checks.
							P. ct.	*P. ct.*	*P. ct.*	*P. ct.*	*P. ct.*
North Atlantic Division	$14,237	$14,867	$29,104	$381,737	$4,571,405	$4,982,246	0.3	0.3	0.6	7.0	92.4
South Atlantic Division	1,602	5,243	6,845	34,584	439,120	480,549	.3	1.1	1.4	7.2	91.4
North Central Division	34,142	22,609	56,751	308,601	5,347,655	5,713,007	.6	.4	1.0	5.4	93.6
South Central Division	6,632	33,968	40,600	169,740	1,449,566	1,659,906	.6	2.0	2.6	10.1	87.3
Western Division	84,170	10,125	94,295	18,140	2,229,746	2,342,181	3.6	.4	4.0	.8	95.2
Total	140,783	86,812	227,595	912,802	14,037,492	15,177,889	.9	.5	1.5	5.8	92.7

TABLE XIII.—*Wholesale deposits by geographical divisions in national banks, state banks, private banks, loan and trust companies, stock savings banks, and mutual savings banks*—Continued.

PRIVATE BANKS.

Geographical divisions.	Gold.	Silver.	Total specie.	Currency.	Checks.	Total.	Gold.	Silver.	Specie.	Currency.	Checks.
							P. ct.	*P. ct.*	*P. ct.*	*P. ct.*	*P. ct.*
North Atlantic Division	$5	$86	$91	$680	$17,863	$18,634	4.0	0.5	0.5	3.7	95.8
South Atlantic Division	-------	-------	-------	15,843	28,791	44,634	-------	-------	-------	35.5	64.5
North Central Division	1,105	686	1,791	9,218	117,367	128,376	.9	.5	1.4	7.2	91.4
South Central Division	110	800	910	6,373	28,465	35,748	.3	2.2	2.5	17.9	79.6
Western Division	25	4	29	20	2,925	2,974	.8	.1	.9	.7	98.4
Total	1,245	1,576	2,821	32,134	195,411	230,366	.5	.7	1.2	14.0	84.8

LOAN AND TRUST COMPANIES.

Geographical divisions.	Gold.	Silver.	Total specie.	Currency.	Checks.	Total.	Gold.	Silver.	Specie.	Currency.	Checks.
							P. ct.	*P. ct.*	*P. ct.*	*P. ct.*	*P. ct.*
North Atlantic Division	$6,411	$14,010	$20,421	$303,224	$5,888,967	$6,212,612	0.1	0.2	0.3	4.9	94.8
South Atlantic Division	125	1,859	1,984	2,884	104,497	109,365	.2	1.7	1.9	2.6	95.5
North Central Division	1,710	1,843	3,553	14,830	438,212	456,595	.4	.4	.8	3.2	96.0
South Central Division	5	266	271	489	1,183	1,943	.3	13.7	14.0	25.1	60.9
Western Division	400	75	475	-------	1,503	1,978	20.2	3.8	24.0	-------	75.9
Total	8,651	18,053	26,704	321,427	6,434,362	6,782,493	.1	.3	.4	4.7	94.9

STOCK SAVINGS BANKS.

							P. ct.	P. ct.	P. ct.	P. ct.	P. ct.
North Atlantic Division	$460	$15	$475	$863	$3,394	$4,732	9.7	0.3	10.0	18.3	71.7
South Atlantic Division	45	45	90	808	2,816	3,714	1.2	1.2	2.4	21.8	75.8
North Central Division	912	583	1,495	13,153	204,789	219,437	.4	.3	.7	6.0	93.3
South Central Division	5	105	110	242	2,786	3,138	.1	3.4	3.5	7.7	88.8
Western Division	------	------	------	------	617	617	------	------	------	------	100.0
Total	1,422	748	2,170	15,066	214,402	231,638	.6	.3	.9	6.5	92.6

MUTUAL SAVINGS BANKS.

							P. ct.	P. ct.	P. ct.	P. ct.	P. ct.
North Atlantic Division	------	$1	$1	$1,593	$2,009	$3,603	------	------	------	44.4	55.6

Conclusion as to wholesale deposits.—There is no reason to think that the percentage of checks represented in the deposits of the wholesale dealers of the various classes of banks is not typical. The average percentage in the total wholesale deposits of $124,823,762 is 96.3. The percentage does not differ materially in the small cities from what is shown in the returns of the banks of the large cities. If we eliminate from the deposits of the five States of Illinois, Iowa, Kansas, Nebraska, and Texas the returns from banks in cities of more than 25,000, as was done in the case of the retail deposits, we find, as the following table shows, that there is no important change.

TABLE XIV.—*Wholesale deposits returned for certain States, less those in cities of over 25,000.*

State	Gold.	Silver.	Total specie.	Currency.	Checks.	Total.	Gold.	Silver.	Specie.	Currency.	Checks.
							P. ct.	*P. ct.*	*P. ct.*	*P. ct.*	*P. ct.*
Illinois	$5,165	$5,855	$11,020	$33.726	$560,873	$605,619	0.8	0.9	1.8	5.5	92.7
Iowa	1,080	1,367	2.447	8,788	487.255	498,490	.2	.3	.5	1.8	97.7
Kansas	1,455	2,333	3,788	12,697	377,815	394.300	.3	.6	.9	3.2	95.9
Nebraska	395	395	790	3,129	123,528	127,447	.3	.3	.6	2.5	97.3
Texas	5,677	8,891	14,568	38,323	614,963	667,854	.9	1.3	2.2	5.7	92.0
Total	13,772	18,841	32,613	96,663	2,164,434	2,293,710	.6	.8	1.4	4.2	94.4

Moreover, the percentages for North and South Dakota, in which there are no cities of the size mentioned, range among the highest. There are no important sources of error; hence no allowances to be made for corrections. Further, there is no variation of importance in the percentages shown by the different classes of banks, excepting of course the mutual savings banks, which are of no significance for the present purpose. The general conclusion is, therefore, that no reason exists for not accepting 96 as the percentage which fairly represents the proportion of wholesale business of the country done by checks on the day in question.

THE "ALL OTHERS" CLASS OF DEPOSITS.

What constitutes the class of "all others" deposits in the bank returns? The intention was to have these figures represent the deposits of all accounts excepting those of retail and wholesale merchants and of other banks. This seems to be the interpretation put upon the question by nearly all the banks that sent in replies. However, some were in doubt whether to include the accounts of other banks and bankers and gave figures from both points of view, while some doubtless included the deposits made to the credit of other banks. Some of the blanks returned were accompanied with letters explaining the character of the "all others" class in the bank concerned. To supplement this information and prevent as far as possible any mistake about the inclusion of the accounts of other banks, the writer asked a dozen or so of the correspondents to explain what kind of accounts were included in this class. Except in one case, the answers were that bank accounts were not included and that the list would be too long and too miscellaneous to give. However, the following were instanced: Museums, publishers, railroads, livery, printers, machinists, travelers, hotels, insurance, treasurers of organizations, real estate, pool rooms, laundry, professional men, brokers, stock and bond financial corporation accounts, church and charitable accounts, public funds, students and college professors, women, "those who have no specific business," and all other individual accounts. Of course many other classes are included. The list is a very miscellaneous one, representing pretty nearly all classes in the community. Doubtless the deposits of corporations and other business firms constituted a large part of the deposits of this class made on the day in question.

Allowances and corrections to be made in the figures of the "all others" class of deposits.—It is urged by critics that in this class there must be a great many duplications of checks already counted. It is difficult to see how this is possible. The retail merchant has deposited his receipts, the wholesale merchant has deposited his receipts, and since the accounts of other banks are nearly all excluded from the third class, it is difficult to see how there can be much duplication.

The first obvious thing to do is to add to the returns received an amount to allow for the deposits of banks that did not reply. In the opinion of the writer it is not important to do this for this class of deposits any more than it is for the wholesale deposits. The character of the returns is too nearly uniform, and the percentage of the credit documents everywhere ranges about the same. The indications are that the percentage of credit documents in any reasonable proportion of the total returns will be as accurate as a percentage derived from the total itself. It has been urged that the banks which do not reply to such inquiries are the small banks in the agricultural districts and that in their deposits we would expect naturally a larger proportion of money. The figures show, however, that this claim is not well founded. The proportion of credit paper in the deposits of the banks of the agricultural portions of the country ranges higher, if anything, than in the cities, so far as concerns the retail trade and, inferentially, individual deposits. Moreover, it is a mere assumption that the nonreporting banks are mainly the small banks in the country districts. A great many city banks also did not report. However, even if we were to admit the point and were to add the total deposits of the nonreporting banks on the day in question, and class them all on the money rather than the credit side of our account, it is doubtful whether the proportion of credit paper in the total receipts would be materially changed.

It is in this third class of deposits that we find the accounts of the broker and the speculator. What shall we do with these? In discussing this subject, Francis A. Walker once said:[a] "Was I not justified in saying that a very large part of the credit transactions, the amount of which is so freely adduced to show the comparative insignificance of the cash transactions, are, with respect to

[a] Discussions in Economics and Statistics, I: 204.

that object, purely fictitious? Those who roll as sweet morsels under their tongues such gigantic figures as thirty and forty thousand millions a year, in speaking of the work of a single clearing house, are really deceived if they think that these sums represent either transactions that would have taken place did not the clearing-house mill stand ready to take the grist, or transactions the non-existence of which would impair production and legitimate trade."

The remark of Mr. Walker is true, but not pertinent. Very likely the vast volume of these transactions would not take place in the absence of our credit system, or if it were less efficient. It is true, too, doubtless, that the blotting out of many of these transactions would not impair what Mr. Walker calls "legitimate trade." A large proportion of deposits in this "all others" class undoubtedly represents speculative transactions, all of which, or practically all of which, are settled with credit paper, and most of which the business of the country might well get on without. This, however, is no reason for omitting them from consideration in the inquiry in hand. To say that they are not a part of legitimate trade and therefore should be omitted, is beside the point. The important question is whether they constitute a part of the demand for a medium of exchange. The "legitimacy" is not in question. It would be just as reasonable to omit from our money column the deposits of people who make their living by gambling with cards, or at horse races, or in other illegitimate ways, as to omit the "speculative" or "fictitious" transactions in the credit column of the bank returns. These transactions call for money for reserve purposes if not for direct payment; therefore they constitute one of the factors in the demand for money. For that reason they should be included.

If, however, the whole volume of "speculative" transactions on the day in question should be eliminated, all of it being regarded as represented in the figures of our deposits by checks, the proportion of checks in the remaining deposits would evidently still be over 90 per cent. For, surely, of the $502,800,000 of "all others" deposits not more than half were probably speculative in their character. If, therefore, we subtract $250,000,000 from the total, and also subtract $250,000,000 from the check account, we have remaining $232,000,000 odd of checks in a total of $252,000,000 of deposits, which is 92.1 per cent.

The returns of "all other depositors" from the national banks.—The aggregate deposits of the "all others" class returned by the national banks is $407,268,393, of which 96.8 per cent, or $394,157,077, was in checks. Of the whole amount, nearly $230,000,000 were returned by the banks of New York, and 99 per cent of their deposits was in credit paper. Massachusetts had $34,000,000 of deposits, of which 97.1 per cent were in credit paper. Pennsylvania had $32,000,000 of deposits, with 92.4 per cent of checks. Illinois had $25,000,000 of deposits, with a percentage of 96.3 in checks. California shows $7,000,000 of deposits, of which 94.8 per cent were in checks. Missouri, with $15,000,000 of deposits, had 97.4 per cent in checks; and the Ohio returns show nearly $8,000,000 of deposits, with 90.3 per cent in checks. The highest percentage is that of New York, the 99 already mentioned; the lowest is that of Rhode Island, which shows 81.5, with aggregate deposits of $338,328. Ten States show a percentage of 95 or more in checks, and 28 States show a percentage of 90 or more.

The all other deposits of state banks.—The aggregate deposits of this class in the returns of the state banks was $62,172,815, or less than one-sixth of the figures given by the national banks. Of this amount, 94.1 per cent, or $58,512,025, were in checks. The largest deposits of this class in the state banks of any State were those of New York, aggregating a little over $34,600,000, with a percentage of 98 in checks. Illinois shows nearly $7,000,000 of deposits of this class in the state banks, with 89.9 per cent as the proportion of checks. The lowest percentage returned was 47.8 for the District of Columbia, with total deposits of $28,994. The returns of three States show a percentage of checks of 95 or more; 17 States show 90 or more. The averages as a rule run a trifle lower than those of the national banks, but the difference is not great and the amounts involved are considerably smaller.

All other deposits of the private banks.—The aggregate of these was $2,198,677, and of this amount $1,878,319, or 85.4 per cent, was in checks. Omitting the returns of the two States of Idaho and Wisconsin, in which the total deposits were in checks, but insignificant in amount, we find that the highest percentage of checks was in Massachusetts. This was caused by the returns of a firm of peculiar character, rather stock jobbing than banking, and the deposits were the money of customers held for investment. It is therefore not a fair case. Having regard only to those States in which the aggregate deposits of this class exceeded $50,000, we find Illinois in the lead with deposits of over $1,000,000, with 90 per cent in checks. The next largest is Indiana, with a little over $200,000 and 85 per cent in checks. Iowa has $250,000, with 94 per cent in checks; Ohio, with $186,000, has 66 per cent in checks; Pennsylvania, with $58,000, has 50 per cent; and Texas, with $70,000, has 83 per cent. The relatively inferior part played by the private banks in the commercial transactions of the country is strikingly emphasized by this table.

All other deposits of loan and trust companies.—The sum of these was $27,650,000, and 93.6 per cent of this amount was deposited in the form of checks. Nearly half of the total amount is credited to New York State, the amount being $12,576,000. Massachusetts has a little over $5,000,000; Pennsylvania has $2,871,000; New Jersey, $1,749,000; Missouri, $1,534,000. Illinois is the only other State whose banks of this kind show more than $500,000 of these deposits. Omitting the cases in which a high percentage of checks was derived from very small returns, we find that New York leads with 96.6 per cent of checks; that Maryland is second with 95.8 per cent, and Massachusetts third with 95.5 per cent

All other deposits of the savings banks.—These amounted to $3,523,449, of which $1,170,097, or 33 per cent, were in checks. Of the whole amount, two millions are to be credited to the stock savings banks and about one and one-half millions to the mutual savings banks. The stock savings banks by themselves gave an average of 83.9 per cent in checks. Omitting again two unimportant cases in which the percentage of checks deposited was 100, we find that the percentages in stock savings banks range from 95.8 in Pennsylvania, with $367,000 of deposits, to 25.6 in Alabama, with $481,000 deposits. Michigan shows 76 per cent, with $113,000 deposits; Illinois, 77.8, with $116,000; California, 76.3, with $439,000. Ohio, with $60,000 deposits has 64 per cent in checks.

In the case of the mutual savings banks, including under this name all savings banks of a cooperative character, we find the percentage of checks in "all others" deposits, which, of course, are the general deposits, running much lower than for the commercial banks. The average is 31.8 per cent of total deposits of $1,509,818. It is remarkable that the percentage should be so high for these banks, which, it has been commonly supposed, are the banks of the laboring classes. Some of the deposits may have been made by out-of-town customers with money orders or drafts, but it is doubtful whether this amount could be very much on the day in question. Massachusetts, which is par excellence the mutual savings bank State, received on March 16, in the banks which reported, $235,661, of which 38 per cent was deposited in the form of checks. New York State, on the other hand, with its trustee savings banks, which are essentially of the same class, received $776,561, of which one-fourth, or 25 per cent, was in checks. The comparison strengthens the suspicion which some students of the subject have had for some time—that the savings banks of Massachusetts are used pretty largely by people not of the laboring class. A similar inference may apparently be drawn from Connecticut's figures of $84,420 of deposits with 35 per cent of checks. The aggregate returns of all classes in these banks is $1,509,818, of which $480,640, or 31.8 per cent, are in checks. Such a showing as this does not strengthen the argument against postal savings banks.

The percentage of the figures of the stock savings banks shows pretty clearly that they, at any rate, are not the banks of the wage-earners.

Conclusions as to the percentage of checks in all others deposits.—The total deposits of this class are $502,817,194, of which 95.9 per cent were in checks. Of this whole amount $499,000,000 were held by the national and state banks and loan and trust companies, and $481,-500,000 of their holdings were deposited in the form of checks and other credit instruments. This is 96.5 per cent. The deposits of these institutions, therefore, dominate the percentage by their proportion of checks, which is only six-tenths of 1 per cent above the average. We have seen that to this class of deposits, if anywhere in our returns, we must look for duplications and for all so-called speculative and gambling transactions which some people would throw out. We have seen further, however, that most of the banks which replied to the circular were careful to omit from this class their deposits of banks and bankers. Some such deposits were undoubtedly included.

The duplication of checks, however, is not as great as would have been the case if all the banks had included these. No reason appears for thinking that the percentage of checks in the deposits of this class does not fairly represent the methods of payment ordinarily followed by those whose accounts made up these deposits, and we may fairly take the average of 95 as representing this class. The tables follow, arranged as for the other classes of deposits:

TABLE XV.—*All other deposits in national banks, state banks, private banks, loan and trust companies, stock savings banks, and mutual savings banks.*

NATIONAL BANKS.

State.	Gold.	Silver.	Total specie.	Currency.	Checks.	Total.	Gold.	Silver.	Specie.	Currency.	Checks.
							P. ct.	*P. ct.*	*P. ct.*	*P. ct.*	*P. ct.*
Alabama	$3,075	$13,569	$16,644	$73,846	$662,430	$752,920	0.4	1.8	2.2	9.7	87.9
Arizona	5,086	1,090	6,176	6,778	171,000	183,954	2.7	.6	3.3	3.7	93.0
Arkansas	1,300	3,946	5,246	22,695	175,571	203,512	.6	1.9	2.5	11.2	86.3
California	253,050	37,216	290,266	84,297	6,774,286	7,148,849	3.5	.5	4.0	1.2	94.8
Colorado	46,321	16,314	62,635	81,433	1,359,843	1,503,911	3.1	1.1	4.2	5.4	90.4
Connecticut	1,644	14,038	15,682	166,949	1,774,420	1,957,051	.1	.6	.8	8.6	90.6
Delaware	112	2,294	2,406	30,930	150,037	183,373	------	1.3	1.3	16.9	82.0
District of Columbia	159	5,734	5,893	167,672	884,727	1,058,292	------	.5	.5	15.9	83.6
Florida	335	6,583	6,918	48,521	684,015	739,454	------	.9	.9	6.6	92.5
Georgia	3,832	19,212	23,044	111,399	950,729	1,085,172	.3	1.8	2.1	10.2	87.6
Idaho	9,730	21,609	31,339	23,955	330,223	385,517	2.5	5.6	8.1	6.2	85.6
Illinois	40,292	60,757	101,049	814,457	24,463,043	25,378,549	.1	.2	.4	3.2	96.3
Indiana	39,771	33,509	73,280	269,876	2,031,593	2,374,749	1.7	1.4	3.1	11.3	85.6
Iowa	10,995	11,934	22,929	105,110	2,859,671	2,987,710	.4	.4	.8	3.5	95.7
Kansas	17,310	19,684	36,994	83,252	1,518,757	1,639,003	1.1	1.2	2.3	5.1	92.6
Kentucky	8,503	16,541	25,044	84,103	990,678	1,099,825	8.0	1.5	2.3	7.6	90.1
Louisiana	280	3,703	3,983	49,300	1,503,958	1,557,241	------	.2	.3	3.2	96.5
Maine	267	4,461	4,728	71,721	555,960	632,409	------	.7	.7	11.3	88.0
Maryland	3,772	8,657	12,429	279,978	2,543,549	2,835,956	.1	.3	.4	9.9	89.6
Massachusetts	2,973	41,541	44,514	951,231	33,315,620	34,311,365	------	.1	.1	2.8	97.1
Michigan	12,128	28,335	40,463	195,352	1,623,198	1,859,013	.7	1.5	2.2	10.5	87.3
Minnesota	58,707	22,280	80,987	206,524	4,296,970	4,584,481	1.3	.5	1.8	4.5	93.7

Mississippi	250	3,002	3,252	13,919	158,830	176,001	.1	1.7	1.9	7.9	90.2
Missouri	27,935	40,362	68,297	335,544	15,033,195	15,437,036	.1	.3	.4	2.2	97.4
Montana	10,874	3,303	14,177	33,525	666,562	714,264	1.5	.5	2.0	4.7	93.3
Nebraska	7,846	11,515	19,361	78,138	4,982,831	5,080,330	.1	.2	.4	1.5	98.1
Nevada	5,100	529	5,629	3,617	143,589	152,835	3.3	.3	3.7	2.4	93.9
New Hampshire	340	3,332	3,672	44,493	490,389	538,554	.1	.6	.7	8.3	91.0
New Jersey	11,315	21,150	32,465	510,829	2,709,433	3,252,727	.4	.6	1.0	15.7	83.3
New Mexico	2,010	1,476	3,486	13,479	88,841	105,806	1.9	1.4	3.3	12.8	83.9
New York	46,839	49,301	96,140	2,333,948	227,284,309	229,714,397	------	------	--------	1.0	99.0
North Carolina	637	8,276	8,913	51,156	440,846	500,915	.1	1.7	1.8	10.2	88.0
North Dakota	205	1,850	2,055	29,432	393,641	425,128	------	.5	.5	6.9	92.6
Ohio	117,070	54,981	172,051	590,892	7,123,266	7,886,209	1.5	.7	2.2	7.5	90.3
Oklahoma	1,434	8,179	9,613	51,213	530,562	591,388	.2	1.4	1.6	9.7	89.7
Oregon	45,916	4,233	50,149	12,309	1,174,304	1,236,762	3.7	.3	4.0	1.0	95.0
Pennsylvania	296,062	122,912	418,974	2,034,732	29,834,031	32,287,737	.9	.4	1.3	6.3	92.4
Rhode Island	170	1,606	1,776	60,712	275,840	338,328	------	.5	.6	17.9	81.5
South Carolina	50	5,698	5,748	26,064	149,563	181,375	------	3.1	3.1	14.4	82.5
South Dakota	920	3,232	4,152	50,306	355,576	410,034	.2	.8	1.0	12.3	86.7
Tennessee	5,444	19,835	25,279	127,823	905,588	1,058,690	.5	1.9	2.4	12.1	85.5
Texas	8,333	32,537	40,870	235,587	3,330,323	3,606,780	.2	.9	1.1	6.5	92.4
Utah	9,180	2,869	12,049	8,023	396,258	416,330	2.2	.7	2.9	1.9	95.2
Vermont	510	2,602	3,112	27,565	223,763	254,440	.2	1.0	1.2	10.8	88.0
Virginia	5,915	12,618	18,533	136,721	1,853,078	2,008,332	.3	.6	.9	6.8	92.3
Washington	64,280	28,270	92,550	63,812	1,492,566	1,648,928	3.9	1.7	5.6	3.9	90.5
West Virginia	6,099	6,505	12,604	61,416	295,824	369,844	1.6	1.8	3.4	16.6	80.0
Wisconsin	23,063	18,702	41,765	150,147	4,114,635	4,306,547	.6	.4	1.0	3.5	95.5
Wyoming	8,870	1,101	9,971	7,243	89,156	106,370	8.4	1.0	9.4	6.8	83.8
Total	1,226,309	862,983	2,089,292	11,022,024	394,157,077	407,268,393	.3	.2	.5	2.7	96.8

TABLE XV.—*All other deposits in national banks, state banks, private banks, loan and trust companies, stock savings banks, and mutual savings banks*—Continued.

STATE BANKS.

State.	Gold.	Silver.	Total specie.	Currency.	Checks.	Total.	Gold.	Sil-ver.	Specie.	Cur-rency.	Checks.
							P ct	*P ct*	*P ct.*	*P ct*	*P ct.*
Alabama	$2,140	$4,601	$6,741	$24,400	$237,402	$268,543	0.8	1.7	2.5	9.1	88.4
Arizona	5,470	1,729	7,199	13,272	62,863	83,334	6.5	2.1	8.6	16.0	75.4
Arkansas	2,540	6,506	9,046	84,266	138,618	231,930	1.1	2.8	3.9	36.3	59.8
California	190,804	29,919	220,723	22,644	2,354,370	2,597,737	7.4	1.2	8.5	.9	90.5
Colorado	3,625	747	4,372	3,431	84,280	92,083	3.9	.8	4.7	3.7	91.5
Connecticut	30	1,489	1,519	18,445	941,834	961,798	------	.1	.1	2.0	97.9
Delaware	----------	215	215	3,364	355,621	359,200	------	------	------	.9	99.1
District of Columbia	60	509	569	14,563	13,862	28,994	.2	1.8	2.0	50.3	47.8
Florida	220	1,363	1,583	5,438	43,894	50,915	.4	2.7	3.1	10.7	86.2
Georgia	680	5,198	5,878	41,170	562,430	609,478	.1	.9	1.0	6.7	92.3
Idaho	2,695	2,876	5,571	14,374	118,502	138,447	1.9	2.1	4.0	10.5	85.5
Illinois	28,946	35,635	64,581	632,916	6,196,159	6,893,656	.4	.5	.9	9.2	89.9
Indiana	4,840	5,877	10,717	53,237	413,808	477,762	1.0	1.2	2.2	11.2	86.5
Iowa	4,105	3,636	7,741	48,861	794,425	851,027	.5	.4	.9	5.7	93.4
Kansas	3,797	8,115	11,912	61,076	1,034,373	1,107,361	.3	.7	1.0	5.6	90.1
Kentucky	4,374	9,939	14,313	45,417	574,363	634,093	.7	1.6	2.3	7.2	90.5
Louisiana	907	20,350	21,257	64,139	582,310	667,706	.1	3.1	3.2	9.6	87.2
Maine	65	236	301	10,721	46,589	57,611	.1	.4	.5	18.6	80.9
Maryland	----------	988	988	15,370	47,662	64,020	------	1.5	1.5	24.0	74.4
Michigan	4,856	7,424	12,280	102,558	540,395	655,233	.7	1.1	1.8	15.7	82.5
Minnesota	8,165	5,831	13,996	65,740	695,163	774,899	1.1	.7	1.8	8.5	89.7
Mississippi	165	5,975	6,140	18,044	115,724	139,908	.1	4.2	4.3	13.0	82.7

Missouri	6,012	22,645	28,657	125,324	1,842,741	1,996,722	.3	1.1	1.4	6.3	92.3
Montana	4,833	1,827	6,660	9,612	127,268	143,540	3.4	1.3	4.6	6.7	88.7
Nebraska	1,945	5,945	7,890	138,640	764,481	911,011	.2	.7	.9	15.2	83.9
Nevada	17,368	504	17,872	360	101,279	119,511	14.7	.4	15.1	.3	84.6
New Hampshire	----------	49	49	1,806	9,817	11,672	------	.4	.4	15.5	84.1
New Jersey	139	617	756	30,602	190,830	222,188	.1	.2	.3	13.7	86.0
New Mexico	3	85	88	130	3,185	3,403	.1	2.5	2.6	3.8	93.6
New York	67,037	18,631	85,668	605,667	33,981,697	34,673,032	.2	------	.2	1.8	98.0
North Carolina	245	1,520	1,765	11,985	75,185	88,935	.3	1.7	2.0	13.4	84.6
North Dakota	1,458	1,852	3,310	19,739	209,596	232,645	.5	.7	1.2	8.5	90.3
Ohio	14,030	17,383	31,413	145,732	918,712	1,095,857	1.3	1.6	2.9	13.4	83.6
Oklahoma	465	3,889	4,354	25,037	247,966	277,357	.1	1.4	1.5	9.0	89.5
Oregon	39,645	5,754	45,399	10,039	1,015,356	1,070,794	3.7	6.5	4.2	1.9	94.9
Pennsylvania	7,216	9,288	16,504	148,101	510,178	674,783	1.1	1.4	2.4	22.0	75.6
Rhode Island	----------	134	134	4,309	5,917	10,360	------	1.3	1.3	41.6	57.1
South Carolina	270	3,634	3,904	13,244	71,879	89,027	.3	4.1	4.4	14.8	80.8
South Dakota	960	2,802	3,762	26,688	324,016	354,466	.3	.8	.1	7.5	91.4
Tennessee	465	2,429	2,894	17,119	312,460	332,473	.1	.7	.8	5.1	94.1
Texas	145	1,092	1,237	11,082	70,127	82,446	.2	1.3	1.5	13.4	85.1
Utah	5,895	2,411	8,306	5,784	229,764	243,854	2.4	1.0	3.4	2.4	94.2
Vermont	----------	229	229	3,065	6,960	10,254	------	2.2	2.2	29.9	67.9
Virginia	841	3,365	4,206	38,358	151,516	194,080	.5	1.7	2.2	19.6	78.2
Washington	26,619	3,244	29,863	18,296	426,702	474,861	5.6	.7	6.3	3.8	89.9
West Virginia	492	2,204	2,696	15,614	137,504	155,814	.3	1.4	1.7	10.1	88.2
Wisconsin	20,852	8,641	29,493	102,935	785,514	917,942	2.3	.9	3.2	11.2	85.6
Wyoming	10	331	341	2,984	36,728	40,053	------	.8	.8	7.5	91.7
Total	485,429	279,663	765,092	2,895,698	58,512,025	62,172,815	.8	.4	1.2	4.7	94.1

TABLE XV.—*All other deposits in national banks, state banks, private banks, loan and trust companies, stock savings banks, and mutual savings banks.*

PRIVATE BANKS.

State.	Gold.	Silver.	Total specie.	Currency.	Checks.	Total.	Gold.	Silver.	Specie.	Currency.	Checks.
							P. ct.	P. ct.	P. ct.	P. ct.	P. ct.
Alabama		$4	$4	$30	$161	$195		2.0	2.0	15.4	82.6
Arkansas	$235	717	952	972	6,489	8,413	2.8	8.5	11.3	11.6	77.1
California	835	74	909	226	4,956	6,091	13.8	.1	14.9	3.7	81.4
Colorado	730	1,338	2,068	5,882	33,910	41,860	1.7	3.2	4.9	14.1	81.0
Connecticut		13	13	2,295	10,719	13,027		.1	.1	17.6	82.3
Florida	10	361	371	1,135	4,690	6,196	.2	5.8	6.0	18.3	75.7
Georgia		126	126	1,420	3,284	4,830		2.6	2.6	29.4	68.0
Idaho					1,754	1,754					100.0
Illinois	3,426	7,474	10,900	102,877	1,035,736	1,149,513	.3	.7	.9	8.9	90.1
Indiana	2,990	3,054	6,044	23,867	178,239	208,150	1.4	1.5	2.9	11.5	85.6
Iowa	285	1,771	2,056	13,063	241,822	256,941	.1	.7	.8	5.1	94.1
Kansas		111	111	483	6,625	7,219		1.5	1.5	6.7	91.8
Maryland				172	711	883				19.5	80.5
Massachusetts				20	6,498	6,518				.3	99.7
Michigan	305	1,070	1,375	16,160	19,012	36,547	.8	2.9	3.7	44.2	52.1
Minnesota				260	2,386	2,646				10.0	90.0
Mississippi		4	4	21	40	65		6.2	6.2	32.3	61.5
Missouri	420	348	768	4,629	23,353	28,750	1.5	1.2	2.7	16.1	81.2
Montana	40	4	44	438	4,222	4 704	.8	.1	.9	9.4	89.7
Nebraska		146	146	1,028	7,773	8,947		1.6	1.6	11.5	86.9
Nevada	380	11	391	60	2,668	3,119	12.2	.3	12.5	1.9	85.5
New York	55	202	257	11,843	19,838	31,938	.1	.6	.8	37.1	62.1
North Carolina				100	128	228				43.8	56.2

Ohio	650	1,375	2,025	59,978	124,144	186,147	.3	.7	1.0	32.3	66.7
Oklahoma	----------	17	17	80	280	377	------	4.5	4.5	21.2	74.3
Oregon	1,135	115	1,250	206	6,457	7,913	14.4	1.5	15.9	2.6	81.5
Pennsylvania	5,550	2,984	8,534	20,424	29,650	58,608	9.5	5.1	14.6	34.8	50.6
South Dakota	----------	32	32	404	31,271	31,707	------	.1	.1	1.4	98.5
Texas	1,005	2,242	3,247	8,358	59,170	70,775	1.4	3.2	4.6	11.8	83.6
Utah	35	15	50	104	1,702	1,856	1.9	.8	2.7	5.6	91.7
Virginia	----------	--------	----------	1,141	721	1,862	------	------	--------	61.3	38.7
Washington	15	5	20	150	3,788	3,958	.4	.1	.5	3.8	95.7
Wisconsin	----------	--------	----------	----------	4,092	4,092	------	------	--------	-------	100.0
Wyoming	----------	63	63	755	2,030	2,848	------	2.2	2.2	26.5	71.3
Total	18,101	23,676	41,777	278,581	1,878,319	2,198,677	.8	1.1	1.9	12.7	85.4

LOAN AND TRUST COMPANIES.

							P. ct.	P. ct.	P. ct.	P. ct.	P. ct.
Arkansas	----------	$111	$111	$3,903	$8,656	$12,670	------	0.9	0.9	30.8	68.2
California	$1,063	94	1,157	----------	5,239	6,396	16.6	1.5	18.1	-------	81.9
Colorado	200	209	409	2,257	42,941	45,607	.4	.4	.8	4.9	94.2
Connecticut	32	850	882	24,610	140,491	165,983	------	.5	.5	14.8	84.6
Delaware	15	466	481	8,642	19,419	28,542	------	1.6	1.7	30.3	68.0
District of Columbia	255	1,157	1,412	81,338	284,748	367,498	.1	.3	.4	22.2	77.4
Idaho	250	221	471	764	10,049	11,284	2.2	1.9	4.2	6.8	89.0
Illinois	1,435	860	2,295	64,953	458,240	525,488	.3	.1	.4	12.3	87.3
Indiana	3,517	2,426	5,943	40,501	126,392	172,836	2.0	1.4	3.4	23.4	73.1
Iowa	90	18	108	3,819	----------	3,927	2.3	.5	2.8	97.2	--------
Kansas	----------	42	42	15	7,050	7,107	------	.6	.6	.2	99.2
Maine	15	1,180	1,195	16,436	206,443	224,074	------	.5	.5	7.3	92.2
Maryland	----------	30	30	3,910	92,225	96,165	------	------	--------	4.1	95.8
Massachusetts	2,807	5,926	8,733	236,876	6,439,856	5,685,465	------	.1	.2	4.3	95.5
Minnesota	1,025	106	1,131	1,842	10,829	13,802	7.4	.7	8.2	13.4	78.4

TABLE XV.—*All other deposits in national banks, state banks, private banks, loan and trust companies, stock savings banks, and mutual savings banks*—Continued.

LOAN AND TRUST COMPANIES—Continued.

State.	Gold.	Silver.	Total specie.	Currency.	Checks.	Total.	Gold.	Silver.	Specie.	Currency.	Checks.
							P. ct.	P. ct.	P. ct.	P. ct.	P. ct.
Missouri	3,165	17,168	20,333	139,437	1,374,909	1,534,679	0.2	1.1	1.3	9.1	89.6
New Hampshire		42	42	395	802	1,239		3.4	3.4	31.9	64.7
New Jersey	2,494	5,999	8,493	200,870	1,540,300	1,749,663	.2	.3	.5	11.5	88.0
New York	4,756	8,827	13,583	390,540	12,172,823	12,576,946			.1	3.1	96.6
North Carolina	30	1,139	1,169	2,374	27,819	31,362	.1	3.6	3.7	7.6	88.6
Ohio	240	253	493	2,684	12,245	15,422	1.6	1.6	3.2	17.4	79.4
Pennsylvania	17,869	30,362	48,231	355,226	2,468,140	2,871,597	.6	1.1	1.7	12.4	85.9
Rhode Island	180	4,095	4,275	56,590	397,218	458,083		1.0	1.0	12.4	86.6
South Carolina		32	32	101	2,196	2,329		1.4	1.4	4.3	94.3
Tennessee		6	6	85		91		6.6	6.6	93.4	
Vermont	933	228	1,161	3,813	11,576	16,550	5.6	1.4	7.0	23.1	69.9
Virginia				40	559	599				6.7	93.3
Washington	500	100	600	1,000	6,000	7,600	6.5	1.3	7.8	13.2	79.0
West Virginia		92	92	957	19,807	20,856		.4	.4	4.6	95.0
Total	40,871	82,039	122,910	1,643,978	25,886,972	27,653,860	.1	.3	.4	6.0	93.6

STOCK SAVINGS BANKS.

State.	Gold.	Silver.	Total specie.	Currency.	Checks.	Total.	Gold.	Silver.	Specie.	Currency.	Checks.
Alabama		$25	$25	$333	$123	$481		5.0	5.0	69.3	25.6
Arkansas		19	19			19		100.0	100.0		
California	$74,135	7,175	81,310	22,794	335,091	439,195	16.9	1.6	18.5	5.2	76.3
Colorado				85	5,178	5,263				1.6	98.4

District of Columbia	5	1,231	1,236	31,582	14,624	47,442		2.6	2.6	66.5	30.9
Florida		138	138	715	2,732	3,585		3.8	3.8	19.9	76.3
Georgia		38	38	346	536	920		4.1	4.1	37.6	58.2
Idaho	5	13	18	60	320	398	1.3	3.3	4.5	15.1	80.4
Illinois	440	2,421	2,861	22,837	90,556	116,254	.4	2.1	2.5	19.7	77.8
Indiana		17	17	52	40	109		15.6	15.6	47.7	36.7
Iowa	4,810	7,883	12,693	46,418	642,566	701,677	.7	1.1	1.8	6.6	91.5
Kansas					2,507	2,507					100.0
Kentucky	305	185	490	4,276	14,111	18,877	1.6	1.0	2.6	22.7	74.7
Louisiana	10	29	39	1,421	13,346	14,806	.1	.3	.4	9.6	90.1
Maryland		100	100	1,945	4,590	6,635		1.6	1.6	29.3	69.1
Michigan	582	1,114	1,696	25,411	86,151	113,258	.5	.9	1.5	22.5	76.0
Minnesota		11	11	337	7	355		3.0	3.0	95.2	1.8
Mississippi		98	98	127	2,907	3,132		3.1	3.1	4.0	92.9
Missouri		2	2	5	1,101	1,108		.2	.2	.4	99.4
Nebraska	185	1,439	1,624	4,096	8,516	14,236	1.3	10.0	11.4	28.8	59.8
New Hampshire	40	186	226	1,180	2,370	3,776	1.1	4.9	6.0	31.3	62.7
New Mexico				617		617				100.0	
North Carolina	25	312	337	2,457	19,945	22,739	.1	1.4	1.5	10.7	87.8
Ohio	3,840	1,230	5,070	16,274	38,716	60,060	6.4	2.0	8.4	27.1	64.5
Pennsylvania	675	450	1,125	14,370	351,536	367,031	.2	.1	.3	3.9	95.8
South Dakota	10	15	25	200	900	1,125	.9	1.4	2.3	17.7	80.0
Tennessee	140	1,087	1,227	7,763	22,082	31,072	.4	3.5	3.9	25.0	71.1
Texas					1,447	1,447					100.0
Utah	2,035	142	2,177	1,141	5,352	8,670	23.4	1.6	25.0	13.2	61.8
Vermont		3	3	1,225	1,546	2,774		.1	.1	44.1	55.8
Virginia		40	40	1,520	19,391	20,951		.2	.2	7.3	92.5
West Virginia	55	7	62	1,880	1,170	3,112	1.8	.2	2.0	60.4	37.6
Total	87,297	25,410	112,707	211,467	1,689,457	2,013,631	4.3	1.3	5.6	10.5	83.9

TABLE XV.—*All other deposits in national banks, state banks, private banks, loan and trust companies, stock savings banks, and mutual savings banks*—Continued.

MUTUAL SAVINGS BANKS.

State.	Gold.	Silver.	Total specie.	Currency.	Checks.	Total.	Gold.	Silver.	Specie.	Currency.	Checks.
							P. ct.	*P. ct.*	*P. ct.*	*P. ct.*	*P. ct.*
California	$29,540	$186	$29,726	$1,404	$11,498	$42,628	69.3	0.4	69.8	3.3	26.9
Connecticut	1,032	829	1,861	53,105	29,454	84,420	1.2	1.0	2.3	62.9	34.8
Delaware	10	3	13	509	135	657	1.5	.5	2.0	77.5	20.5
Indiana	1,045	379	1,424	4,959	25,787	32,170	3.3	1.2	4.4	15.4	80.2
Maine	77	370	447	14,601	14,466	29,514	.3	1.2	1.5	49.5	49.0
Maryland	675	81	756	16,105	23,253	40,114	1.7	------	1.9	40.2	57.9
Massachusetts	1,852	1,610	3,462	142,892	89,307	235,661	.8	.7	1.5	60.5	38.0
Minnesota	775	509	1,284	10,408	7,154	18,846	4.1	2.7	6.8	55.3	37.9
New Hampshire	85	74	159	6,822	8,887	15,868	.5	.5	1.0	42.9	56.0
New Jersey	565	99	664	52,304	24,175	77,143	.8	.1	.9	67.8	31.3
New York	5,645	1,743	7,388	570,333	198,840	776,561	.7	.2	.9	73.5	25.6
Pennsylvania	4,127	362	4,489	76,663	28,215	109,367	3.8	.3	4.1	70.1	25.8
Rhode Island	3,997	217	4,214	17,435	7,943	29,592	13.5	.7	14.2	58.9	26.9
Vermont	15	89	104	5,647	11,526	17,277	.1	.5	.6	32.7	66.7
Total	49,440	6,551	55,991	973,187	480,640	1,509,818	3.3	.4	3.7	64.5	31.8

TABLE XVI.—*Aggregate all other deposits, by States.*

Locality.	Gold.	Silver.	Total specie.	Currency.	Checks.	Total.	Gold.	Silver.	Specie.	Currency.	Checks.
							P. ct.	*P. ct.*	*P. ct.*	*P. ct.*	*P. ct.*
Alabama	$5,215	$18,199	$23,414	$98,609	$900,116	$1,022,139	0.5	1.7	2.2	9.6	88.2
Arizona	10,556	2,819	13,375	20,050	233,863	267,288	4.0	1.1	5.1	7.5	87.4
Arkansas	4,075	11,299	15,374	111,836	329,334	456,544	.9	2.5	3.4	24.4	72.2
California	549,427	74,664	624,091	131,365	9,485,440	10,240,896	5.4	.7	6.1	1.3	92.6
Colorado	50,876	18,608	69,484	93,088	1,526,152	1,688,724	3.0	1.1	4.1	5.4	90.5
Connecticut	2,738	17,219	19,957	265,404	2,896,918	3,182,279	.1	.6	.7	8.4	90.9
Delaware	137	2,978	3,115	43,445	525,212	571,772	.1	.5	.6	7.6	91.8
District of Columbia	479	8,631	9,110	295,155	1,197,961	1,502,226	------	.6	.6	19.7	79.7
Florida	565	8,445	9,010	55,809	735,331	800,150	.1	1.0	1.1	6.9	92.0
Georgia	4,512	24,574	29,086	154,335	1,516,979	1,700,400	.3	1.4	1.7	9.1	89.2
Idaho	12,680	24,719	37,399	39,153	460,848	537,400	2.5	4.5	7.0	7.3	85.7
Illinois	74,539	107,147	181,686	1,638,040	32,243,734	34,063,460	.2	.4	.6	4.8	94.5
Indiana	52,163	45,262	97,425	392,492	2,775,859	3,265,776	1.5	1.4	2.9	12.0	85.1
Iowa	20,285	25,242	45,527	217,271	4,538,484	4,801,282	.4	.5	.9	4.5	94.6
Kansas	21,107	27,952	49,059	144,826	2,569,312	2,763,197	.7	1.0	1.7	5.2	93.1
Kentucky	13,182	26,665	39,847	133,796	1,579,152	1,752,795	.6	1.5	2.3	7.5	90.2
Louisiana	1,197	24,082	25,279	114,860	2,099,614	2,239,753	------	1.1	1.1	5.2	93.7
Maine	424	6,247	6,671	113,479	823,458	943,608	.1	.6	.7	12.1	87.2
Maryland	4,447	9,856	14,303	317,480	2,711,990	3,043,773	.1	.3	.4	10.4	89.2
Massachusetts	7,632	49,077	56,709	1,336,019	39,851,281	41,239,009	------	.1	.1	3.2	96.7
Michigan	17,871	37,943	55,814	339,481	2,268,756	2,664,051	.7	1.4	2.1	12.7	85.2
Minnesota	68,672	28,737	97,409	285,111	5,012,509	5,395,029	1.3	.5	1.8	5.3	92.9
Mississippi	415	9,079	9,494	32,111	277,501	319,106	.1	2.8	2.9	10.1	87.0
Missouri	37,532	80,525	118,057	604,939	18,275,299	18,998,295	.2	.4	.6	3.2	96.2

TABLE XVI.—*Aggregate all other deposits, by States*—Continued.

Locality.	Gold.	Silver.	Total specie.	Currency.	Checks.	Total.	Gold.	Silver.	Specie.	Currency.	Checks.
							P. ct.	*P. ct.*	*P. ct.*	*P. ct.*	*P. ct.*
Montana	$15,747	$5,134	$20,881	$43,575	$798,052	$862,508	1.5	.6	2.4	5.2	92.4
Nebraska	9,976	19,045	29,021	221,902	5,763,601	6,014,524	.1	.3	.4	3.7	95.9
Nevada	22,848	1,044	23,892	4,037	247,536	275,465	8.3	.4	8.7	1.1	90.2
New Hampshire	465	3,683	4,148	54,696	512,265	571,109	.1	.6	.7	9.5	89.8
New Jersey	14,513	27,865	42,378	794,605	4,464,738	5,301,721	.3	.5	.8	15.0	84.2
New Mexico	2,013	1,561	3,574	14,226	92,026	109,826	1.8	1.4	3.2	13.1	83.7
New York	124,332	78,704	203,036	3,912,331	273,657,507	277,772,874	.4	.2	.6	1.2	98.2
North Carolina	937	11,247	12,184	68,072	563,923	644,179	.2	1.7	1.9	10.6	87.5
North Dakota	1,663	3,702	5,365	49,171	603,237	657,773	.2	.6	.8	7.4	91.8
Ohio	135,830	75,222	211,052	815,560	8,217,083	9,243,695	1.5	.9	2.4	8.9	88.7
Oklahoma	1,899	12,085	13,984	76,330	778,808	869,122	.2	1.4	1.6	8.8	89.6
Oregon	86,696	10,102	96,798	22,554	2,196,117	2,315,469	3.7	.4	4.1	.9	95.0
Pennsylvania	331,499	166,358	497,857	2,649,516	33,221,750	36,369,123	.9	.4	1.3	7.2	91.5
Rhode Island	4,347	6,052	10,399	139,046	686,918	836,363	.5	.7	1.2	16.7	82.1
South Carolina	320	9,364	9,684	39,409	223,638	272,731	.2	3.4	3.6	14.4	82.0
South Dakota	1,890	6,081	7,971	77,598	711,763	797,332	.3	.7	1.0	9.7	89.3
Tennessee	6,049	23,357	29,406	152,790	1,240,130	1,422,326	.4	1.7	2.1	10.6	87.3
Texas	9,483	35,871	45,354	255,027	3,461,067	3,761,448	.2	1.0	1.2	6.7	92.1
Utah	17,145	5,437	22,582	15,052	633,076	670,710	2.5	.8	3.3	2.3	94.4
Vermont	1,458	3,151	4,609	41,315	255,371	301,295	.5	1.0	1.5	13.7	84.8
Virginia	6,756	16,023	22,779	177,780	2,025,265	2,225,824	.3	.7	1.0	7.9	91.1
Washington	91,414	31,619	123,033	83,258	1,929 056	2,135,347	4.3	1.4	5.7	3.8	90.5
West Virginia	6,646	8,808	15,454	79,867	454,305	549,626	1.2	1.6	2.8	14.5	82.7

Wisconsin	43,915	27,343	71,258	253,082	4,904,241	5,228,581	.9	.5	1.4	4.8	93.4
Wyoming	8,880	1,495	10,375	10,982	127,914	149,271	5.9	1.0	6.9	7.3	85.8
Total	1,907,447	1,280,322	3,187,769	17,024,935	482,604,490	502,817,194	.4	.3	.7	3.4	95.9

TABLE XVII.—*Aggregate all other deposits, by banks.*

	Gold	Silver.	Total specie	Currency.	Checks.	Total.	Gold.	Silver.	Specie.	Currency.	Checks.
							P. ct.	*P. ct.*	*P. ct*	*P. ct*	*P. ct.*
National banks	$1,226,309	$862,983	$2,089,292	$11,022,024	$394,157,077	$407,268,393	0.3	0.2	0.5	2.7	96.8
State banks	485,428	279,664	765,092	2,895,698	58,512,025	62,172,815	.8	.4	1.2	4.6	94.2
Private banks	18,101	23,676	41,777	278,581	1,878,319	2,198,677	.8	1.1	1.9	12.7	85.4
Loan and trust companies	40,871	82,039	122,910	1,643,978	25,886,972	27,653,860	.2	.3	.5	6.2	93.3
Stock savings banks	87,297	25,410	112,707	211,467	1,689,457	2,013,631	4.3	1.3	5.6	10.5	83.9
Mutual savings banks	49,440	6,551	55,991	973,187	480,640	1,509 818	3.3	.4	3.7	64.5	31.8
Total	1,907,446	1,280,323	3,187,769	17,024,935	482,604,490	502,817,194	.4	.3	.7	3.4	95.9

TABLE XVIII.—*All other deposits at representative reserve cities in national banks, state banks, private banks, loan and trust companies, stock savings banks, and mutual savings banks.*

NATIONAL BANKS.

City.	Gold.	Silver.	Total specie.	Currency.	Checks.	Total.	Gold.	Silver.	Specie.	Currency.	Checks.
							P. ct.	*P. ct.*	*P. ct.*	*P. ct.*	*P. ct.*
Chicago	$24,014	$24,402	$48,416	$568,252	$21,814,240	$22,430,908	0.1	0.1	0.2	2.5	97.3
New York	3,902	12,285	16,187	1,037,563	152,369,726	153,423,476				.7	99.3
St. Louis	6,355	24,281	30,636	192,792	9,522,966	9,746,394	.1	.3	.4	2.0	97.6
Total	34,271	60,968	95,239	1,798,607	183,706,932	185,600,778	.2	.3	.5	9.7	98.8
Albany	595	3,481	4,076	71,240	875,468	950,784	.1	.4	.5	7.5	92.0
Baltimore	1,442	5,926	7,368	222,619	2,026,738	2,256,725	.1	.2	.3	9.9	89.8
Boston	1,195	9,082	10,277	582,491	30,736,969	31,329,737				1.9	98.1
Brooklyn	750	954	1,704	117,901	912,945	1,032,550		.1	.1	11.4	88.5
Cincinnati	10,310	8,981	19,291	115,014	2,276,782	2,411,087	.4	.4	.8	4.8	94.4
Cleveland	54,128	11,637	65,765	157,123	2,051,918	2,274,806	2.4	.5	2.9	6.9	90.2
Columbus	14,770	3,832	18,602	44,736	816,247	879,585	1.7	.4	2.1	5.1	92.8
Dallas	915	3,087	4,002	27,239	234,769	266,010	.3	1.2	1.5	10.2	88.3
Detroit	4,106	2,898	7,004	90,269	651,139	748,412	.5	.4	.9	12.1	87.0
Fort Worth	160	1,549	1,709	30,236	727,072	759,017		.2	.2	4.0	95.8
Galveston	155	579	734	5,210	184,267	190,211	.1	.3	.4	2.7	96.9
Houston	725	2,643	3,368	30,111	521,648	555,127	.1	.5	.6	5.4	94.0
Indianapolis	9,355	8,916	18,271	70,393	746,902	835,566	1.1	1.1	2.2	8.4	89.4
Louisville	6,600	2,841	9,441	29,382	521,969	560,792	1.2	.5	1.7	5.2	93.1
New Orleans	160	1,483	1,643	23,741	1,294,470	1,319,854		.1	.1	1.8	98.1
Philadelphia	55,616	44,548	100,164	1,001,607	19,697,902	20,799,673	.3	.2	.5	4.8	94.7
Pittsburg	207,656	28,876	236,532	401,053	5,770,629	6,408,214	3.2	.4	3.6	6.3	90.1
San Antonio	385	1,755	2,140	13,186	238,645	253,971	.1	.7	.8	5.2	94.0

Savannah	------	1,074	1,074	4,972	16,175	22,221	------	4.8	4.8	22.4	72.8
Waco	35	382	417	4,581	59,625	64,623	.1	.6	.7	7.1	92.2
Washington	159	5,734	5,893	167,672	884,727	1,058,292	------	.5	.5	15.9	83.6
Total	403,488	211,226	614,714	5,009,383	254,953,938	260,578,035	.2	.1	.3	1.9	97.8
STATE BANKS.											
Chicago	$21,530	$24,166	$45,696	$517,841	$4,949,818	$5,513,355	------	------	0.8	9.4	89.8
New York	63,300	12,675	75,975	457,906	33,049,123	33,583,004	0.2	------	.2	1.4	98.4
St. Louis	2,765	672	3,437	30,512	263,202	297,151	.9	0.2	1.1	10.4	88.5
Total	87,595	37,513	125,108	1,006,259	38,262,143	39,393,510	------	------	------	------	------
Albany	5	25	30	1,469	4,213	5,712	.1	.4	.5	25.8	73.7
Baltimore	------	701	701	8,000	15,120	23,821	------	2.9	2.9	33.6	63.5
Brooklyn	655	468	1,123	46,207	159,877	207,207	.3	.2	.5	22.5	77.0
Cincinnati	1,092	473	1,565	17,446	40,473	59,484	1.9	.8	2.7	29.3	68.0
Cleveland	2,525	1,448	3,973	39,877	125,728	169,578	1.5	.9	2.4	23.5	74.1
Columbus	2,050	4,058	6,108	13,066	89,552	108,726	1.9	3.7	5.6	12.1	82.3
Detroit	10	17	27	298	181	506	2.0	3.4	5.4	58.9	35.7
Houston	30	534	564	6,623	46,068	53,255	.1	1.0	1.1	12.4	86.5
Indianapolis	695	26	721	1,840	5,956	8,517	8.2	.3	8.5	21.6	69.9
Louisville	1,090	4,175	5,265	10,565	254,578	270,408	.4	1.5	1.9	3.9	94.2
New Orleans	762	13,624	14,386	43,473	528,319	586,178	.1	2.4	2.5	7.4	90.1
Philadelphia	85	165	250	6,997	33,817	41,064	.2	.4	.6	17.1	82.3
Pittsburg	1,785	2,045	3,830	33,035	167,240	204,105	.9	1.0	1.9	16.2	81.9
Savannah	25	623	648	3,363	40,797	44,808	.1	1.4	1.5	7.5	91.0
Washington	60	509	569	14,563	13,862	28,994	.2	1.8	2.0	50.3	47.8
Total	98,464	66,404	164,868	1,253,081	39,787,924	41,205,873	.2	.2	.4	3.0	96.6

TABLE XVIII.—*All other deposits at representative reserve cities in national banks, state banks, private banks, loan and trust companies, stock savings banks, and mutual savings banks*—Continued.

PRIVATE BANKS.

City.	Gold.	Silver.	Total specie.	Currency.	Checks.	Total.	Gold	Silver.	Specie.	Currency.	Checks.
							P. ct.	*P. ct.*	*P. ct.*	*P. ct.*	*P. ct.*
Chicago	$407	$985	$1,392	$13,432	$449,579	$464,403	0.1	0.2	0.3	2.9	96.8
New York				233	1,751	1,984				11.8	88.2
Galveston	5	544	549	1,855	26,516	28,920		1.9	1.9	6.4	91.7
San Antonio	1,000	1,500	2,500	4,000	11,500	18,000	5.6	8.3	13.9	22.2	63.9
Total	1,412	3,029	4,441	19,520	489,346	513,307	.3	.6	.9	3.8	95.3

LOAN AND TRUST COMPANIES.

City.	Gold.	Silver.	Total specie.	Currency.	Checks.	Total.	Gold	Silver.	Specie.	Currency.	Checks.
							P. ct.	*P. ct.*	*P. ct.*	*P. ct.*	*P. ct.*
Chicago	$1,335	$810	$2,145	$63,303	$386,172	$451,620	0.3	0.2	0.5	14.0	85.5
New York	1,431	4,035	5,466	166,706	11,152,565	11,324,737				1.5	98.5
St. Louis	2,385	15,582	17,967	117,522	1,174,080	1,309,569	.2	1.2	1.4	9.0	89.6
Total	5,151	20,427	25,578	347,531	12,712,817	13,085,926					
Albany	5	337	342	3,322	4,761	8,425	.1	4.0	4.1	39.4	56.5
Baltimore		7	7	2,334	89,816	92,157				2.5	97.5
Boston	1,017	2,602	3,619	177,854	6,033,493	6,214,966				2.9	97.1
Brooklyn	850	1,363	2,213	99,563	643,376	745,152	.1	.2	.3	13.4	86.3
Indianapolis	1,805	296	2,101	7,188	7,818	17,107	10.6	1.7	12.3	42.0	45.7
Philadelphia	6,905	7,335	14,240	220,036	1,965,204	2,199,480	.3	.3	.6	10.0	89.4

Pittsburg	762	1,385	2,147	15,353	42,559	60,059	1.3	2.3	3.6	25.6	70.8
Washington	255	1,157	1,412	81,338	284,748	367,498	.1	.3	.4	22.2	77.4
Total	16,750	34,909	51,659	954,519	21,784,592	22,790,770	------	.1	.2	4.2	95.5
STOCK SAVINGS BANKS.											
							P. ct.	*P. ct.*	*P. ct.*	*P. ct.*	*P. ct.*
Chicago	$145	$2,169	$2,314	$20,974	$66,492	$89,780	0.2	2.4	2.6	23.4	74.0
Cincinnati	55	35	90	1,408	1,483	2,981	1.8	1.2	3.0	47.2	49.8
Cleveland	------	------	------	776	922	1,698	------	------	------	45.7	54.3
Detroit	377	563	940	18,285	69,262	88,487	.4	.6	1.0	20.7	78.3
Louisville	305	185	490	4,276	14,111	18,877	1.6	1.0	2.6	22.6	74.8
New Orleans	10	29	39	1,115	13,346	14,500	.1	.2	.3	7.7	92.0
Pittsburg	665	445	1,110	13,320	348,833	363,263	.2	.1	.3	3.7	96.0
Washington	5	1,231	1,236	31,582	14,624	47,442	------	2.6	2.6	66.5	30.9
Total	1,562	4,657	6,219	91,736	529,073	627,028	.3	.7	1.0	14.6	84.4
MUTUAL SAVINGS BANKS.											
							P. ct.	*P. ct.*	*P. ct.*	*P. ct.*	*P. ct.*
New York	$2,337	$477	$2,814	$360,012	$88,847	$451,673	0.5	0.1	0.6	79.7	19.7
Albany	70	4	74	11,227	7,914	19,215	.4	------	.4	58.5	41.1
Baltimore	675	75	750	15,631	19,281	35,662	1.9	.2	3.1	43.8	54.1
Boston	532	165	697	58,532	21,440	80,669	.6	.2	.8	72.6	26.6
Brooklyn	1,429	140	1,569	101,616	30,542	133,727	1.1	.1	1.2	76.0	22.8
Philadelphia	3,552	311	3,863	67,431	20,530	91,824	3.9	.3	4.2	73.4	22.4
Pittsburg	480	35	515	8,095	6,998	15,608	3.1	.2	3.3	51.9	44.8
Total	9,075	1,207	10,282	622,544	195,552	828,378	1.1	.1	1.2	75.2	23.6

TABLE XVIII.—*All other deposits at representative reserve cities in national banks, state banks, private banks, loan and trust companies, stock savings banks, and mutual savings banks*—Continued.

AGGREGATE ALL OTHER DEPOSITS.

City.	Gold.	Silver.	Total specie.	Currency.	Checks.	Total.	Gold.	Silver.	Specie.	Currency.	Checks.
							P. ct.	*P. ct*	*P. ct*	*P. ct.*	*P. ct.*
New York	$70,970	$29,472	$100,442	$2,022,420	$196,662,012	$198,784,874	------	------	--------	1.0	98.9
Chicago	47,431	52,532	99,963	1,183,802	27,666,301	28,950,066	0.1	0.1	0.2	4.1	95.7
St. Louis	11,505	40,535	52,040	340,826	10,960,248	11,353,114	.1	.3	.4	3.0	96.6
Boston	2,744	11,849	14,593	818,877	36,791,902	37,625,372	------	------	--------	2.1	97.9
Philadelphia	66,158	52,359	118,517	1,296,071	21,717,453	23,132,041	.3	.2	.5	5.6	93.9
Total	198,808	186,747	385,555	5,661,996	293,797,916	299,845,467	------	------	.1	1.9	98.0
Other reserve cities	331,943	134,685	466,628	2,298,787	23,932,509	26,697,924	1.2	.5	1.7	8.6	89.7
Grand total	530,751	321,432	852,183	7,960,783	317,730,425	326,543,391	.1	.1	.2	2.4	97.4

The following table shows the "all other deposits" in the agricultural districts of certain States, as already noted:

TABLE XIX.—*Aggregate all other deposits, all banks reporting from certain States, less cities of more than 25,000 inhabitants.*

	Gold.	Silver	Total specie.	Currency.	Checks.	Total.	Gold.	Silver.	Specie.	Currency.	Checks.
							P. ct.	*P. ct.*	*P. ct.*	*P. ct.*	*P. ct.*
Illinois	$17,756	$41,144	$58,900	$365,847	$3,573,868	$3,998,615	0.4	1.0	1.5	9.2	89.3
Iowa	10,715	18,811	29,526	162,355	2,765,418	2,957,299	.4	.6	1.0	5.5	93.4
Kansas	16,927	24,184	41,111	120,323	2,224,599	2,386,033	.7	1.0	1.7	5.1	93.2
Nebraska	3,207	13,127	16,334	178,675	1,672,188	1,867,197	.2	.7	.9	9.6	89.5
Texas	6,298	24,203	30,501	140,781	1,494,855	1,666,137					
Total	54,903	121,469	176,372	967,981	11,730,928	12,875,281	.4	.9	1.4	7.6	90.9

TABLE XX.—*All other deposits, by geographical divisions, in national banks, state banks, private banks, loan and trust companies, stock savings banks, and mutual savings banks.*

NATIONAL BANKS.

Geographical division.	Gold.	Silver.	Total specie.	Currency.	Checks.	Total.	Gold.	Silver.	Specie.	Currency.	Checks.
							P. ct.	*P. ct.*	*P. ct.*	*P. ct.*	*P. ct.*
N Atlantic Div	$358,506	$248,394	$606,900	$6,053,676	$295,631,179	$302,291,755	0.1	0.1	0.2	2.0	97.8
S. Atlantic Div	20,911	75,577	96,488	913,857	7,952,368	8,962,713	.2	.9	1.1	10.1	88.8
N. Central Div	356,242	307,141	663,383	2,909,030	68,796,376	72,368,789	.5	.4	.9	4.0	95.1
S. Central Div	28,619	101,312	129,931	658,486	8,257,940	9,046,357	.3	1.1	1.4	7.3	91.3
Western Div	460,417	118,010	578,427	338,471	12,686,628	13,603,526	3.4	.9	4.3	2.5	93.2
Total	1,224,695	850,434	2,075,129	10,873,520	393,324,491	406,273,140	.3	.2	.5	2.7	96.8

TABLE XX.—*All other deposits, by geographical divisions, in national banks, state banks, private banks, loan and trust companies, stock savings banks, and mutual savings banks*—Continued.

STATE BANKS.

Geographical division.	Gold.	Silver.	Total specie.	Currency.	Checks.	Total.	Gold.	Silver.	Specie.	Currency.	Checks.
							P. ct.	*P. ct.*	*P. ct.*	*P. ct.*	*P. ct.*
N. Atlantic Div	$74,487	$30,673	$105,160	$822,716	$35,693,822	$36,621,698	0.2	0.1	0.3	2.2	97.5
S. Atlantic Div	2,808	18,996	21,804	159,106	1,459,553	1,640,463	.2	1.2	1.4	9.7	88.9
N. Central Div	99,965	125,787	225,752	1,523,446	14,519,383	16,268,581	.6	.8	1.4	9.4	89.2
S. Central Div	11,201	54,781	65,982	289,504	2,278,970	2,634,456	.4	2.1	2.5	11.0	86.5
Western Div	296,967	49,427	346,394	100,926	4,560,297	5,007,617	5.9	1.0	6.9	2.0	91.1
Total	485,428	279,664	765,092	2,895,698	58,512,025	62,172,815	.8	.4	1.2	4.7	94.2

PRIVATE BANKS.

Geographical division.	Gold.	Silver.	Total specie.	Currency.	Checks.	Total.	Gold.	Silver.	Specie.	Currency.	Checks.
							P. ct.	*P. ct.*	*P. ct.*	*P. ct.*	*P. ct.*
N. Atlantic Div	$605	$3,199	$3,804	$34,582	$66,705	$105,091	0.6	3.0	3.6	32.8	63.6
S. Atlantic Div	10	487	497	3,968	9,534	13,999	.1	3.5	3.6	28.3	68.1
N. Central Div	8,076	15,381	23,457	222,749	1,674,453	1,920,659	.4	.8	1.2	11.6	87.2
S. Central Div	1,240	2,984	4,224	9,461	66,140	79,825	1.6	3.7	5.3	11.9	82.8
Western Div	3,170	1,625	4,795	7,821	61,487	74,103	4.3	2.2	6.5	10.6	82.9
Total	13,101	23,676	36,777	278,581	1,878,319	2,193,677	.6	1.1	1.7	12.7	85.6

LOAN AND TRUST COMPANIES.

							P. ct.	P. ct.	P. ct.	P. ct.	P. ct.
N. Atlantic Div	$29,086	$57,509	$86,595	$1,285,356	$23,377,649	$24,747,600	0.1	0.3	0.3	5.2	94.5
S. Atlantic Div	300	2,916	3,216	97,362	446,773	547,351	.1	.5	.6	17.8	81.6
N. Central Div	9,472	20,873	30,345	253,251	1,989,665	2,273,261	.4	.9	1.3	11.2	87.5
S. Central Div	------	117	117	3,988	8,656	12,761	------	.9	.9	31.3	67.8
Western Div	2,013	624	2,637	4,021	64,229	70,887	2.9	.9	3.8	5.7	90.5
Total	40,871	82,039	122,910	1,643,978	25,886,972	27,653,860	.2	.3	.5	6.0	93.5

STOCK SAVINGS BANKS.

							P. ct.	P. ct.	P. ct.	P. ct.	P. ct.
N. Atlantic Div	$715	$639	$1,354	$16,775	$355,452	$373,581	0.2	0.2	0.4	4.5	95.1
S. Atlantic Div	85	1,866	1,951	40,445	62,988	105,384	.1	1.8	1.9	38.4	59.7
N. Central Div	9,867	14,132	23,999	115,630	871,060	1,010,689	1.0	1.4	2.4	11.4	86.2
S. Central Div	455	1,443	1,898	13,920	54,016	69,834	.7	2.1	2.8	19.9	77.3
Western Div	76,175	7,330	83,505	24,697	345,941	454,143	16.8	1.6	18.4	5.4	76.2
Total	87,297	25,410	112,707	211,467	1,689,457	2,013,631	4.3	1.3	5.6	10.5	83.9

MUTUAL SAVINGS BANKS.

							P. ct.	P. ct.	P. ct.	P. ct.	P. ct.
N. Atlantic Div	$17,395	$5,393	$22,788	$939,802	$412,813	$1,375,403	1.3	0.4	1.7	68.3	30.0
S. Atlantic Div	685	84	769	16,614	23,388	40,771	1.7	.2	1.9	40.8	57.3
N. Central Div	1,820	888	2,708	15,367	32,941	51,016	3.6	1.7	5.3	30.1	64.6
Western Div	29,540	186	29,726	1,404	11,498	42,628	69.3	.4	69.8	3.3	26.9
Total	49,440	6,551	55,991	973,187	480,640	1,509,818	3.3	.4	3.7	64.5	31.8

STUDY OF THE AGGREGATE FIGURES.

If we add the various kinds of receipts of all classes of dealers in all kinds of banks which reported, we get a grand total of $688,087,678. Of this vast sum $647,239,813 were deposited in the form of checks and other credit documents; this is 94 per cent. The corresponding percentages shown by the returns of the inquiry of 1896 was 92.5. Of the whole amount of our present total $33,984,822 was in currency and $6,863,043 in specie, pretty evenly divided between gold and silver. Of the total deposits nearly half, or $330,907,747, are credited to New York State, and her percentage of checks is 97.7. If we omit New York State altogether, in order to eliminate with absolute certainty the vast mass of speculative transactions occurring on the New York City Stock Exchange which lead some students of this question to doubt whether the figures represent the method of payment in legitimate trade, we have a grand total for the rest of the country of $357,179,935, of which $323,924,144 were in checks. This is approximately 91 per cent.

The highest percentage shown by any State is 97.7, for New York. The lowest is that of the District of Columbia, 76. Massachusetts comes next to New York with 95.6. These are the only two States whose percentages are above 95. California, Illinois, Iowa, Kansas, Louisiana, Minnesota, Missouri, Montana, Nebraska, Oregon, and Wisconsin are all 90 or more.

Following is the table of returns by States:

TABLE XXI.—*Aggregate of all classes of deposits in national, state, and other banks, by States.*

State.	Gold.	Silver.	Total specie.	Currency.	Checks.	Total.	Gold.	Silver	Specie.	Currency.	Checks.
							P. ct.	*P. ct.*	*P. ct.*	*P. ct.*	*P. ct.*
Alabama	$11,573	$49 426	$60,999	$241,846	$1,537,599	$1,840,444	0.6	2.7	3.3	13.1	83.6
Arizona	25,266	7,153	32,419	39,642	311,637	383,698	.8	1.8	8.4	10.3	81.3
Arkansas	7,985	24,799	32,784	159,243	728,148	920,175	.8	2.7	3.5	17.3	79.2
California	1,121,964	164,569	1,286,533	269,840	15,270,261	16,826,634	6.6	.9	7.5	1.6	90.9
Colorado	122,503	38,152	160,655	215,684	2,484,912	2,861,251	4.2	1.3	5.5	7.6	86.9
Connecticut	4,850	34,709	39,159	662,045	4,648,464	5,350,068	.1	.6	.7	12.4	86.9
Delaware	308	5,541	5,849	79,292	661,329	746,470	------	.7	.7	10.6	88.7
District of Columbia	771	14,748	15,589	446,530	1,459,369	1,921,418	------	.7	.7	23.3	76.0
Florida	2,137	52,845	54,982	165,904	1,391,520	1,612,406	.1	3.2	3.3	10.3	86.4
Georgia	14,267	83,268	97,535	361,784	2,654,679	3,114,016	.5	2.6	3.1	11.6	85.3
Idaho	26,260	30,349	56,609	57,186	634,520	748,315	3.5	4.0	7.5	7.6	84.9
Illinois	171,622	220,206	391,828	3,141,816	49,810,741	53,344,385	.3	.4	.7	5.9	93.4
Indiana	127,384	136,425	263,809	893,118	5,196,209	6,353,136	2.0	2.1	4.1	14.1	81.8
Iowa	55,164	78,102	133,266	478,448	6,358,266	6,969,980	.8	1.1	1.9	6.8	91.3
Kansas	37,216	68,524	105,740	335,919	4,466,085	4,907,744	.7	1.4	2.1	6.8	91.1
Kentucky	37,288	79,113	116,401	338,428	3,651,306	4,106,135	.9	1.9	2.8	8.2	89.0
Louisiana	1,691	63,676	65,367	303,014	3,489,696	3,858,077	------	1.6	1.6	7.9	90.5
Maine	939	11,248	12,187	278,642	1,404,088	1,694,917	------	.6	.6	16.5	82.9
Maryland	5,974	28,742	34,716	627,997	4,356,602	5,019,315	.1	.5	.6	12.6	86.8
Massachusetts	12,352	103,180	115,532	2,467,830	55,345,314	57,928,676	------	.2	.2	4.2	95.6
Michigan	40,080	82,291	122,371	758,738	4,530,455	5,411,564	.7	1.5	2.2	14.0	83.8
Minnesota	136,745	80,292	217,037	620,194	9,835,891	10,673,122	1.2	.8	2.0	5.8	92.2
Mississippi	3,116	31,381	34,497	93,032	597,628	725,157	.4	4.3	4.7	12.8	82.5
Missouri	75,164	170,074	245,238	1,222,244	25,113,312	26,580,794	.3	.6	.9	4.6	94.5
Montana	33,141	14,693	47,834	90,952	1,245,970	1,384,756	2.3	1.1	3.4	6.6	90.0
Nebraska	31,445	56,947	88,392	432,721	8,598,529	9,119,642	.3	.7	1.0	4.7	94.3

TABLE XXI.—*Aggregate of all classes of deposits in national, state, and other banks, by States*—Continued.

State.	Gold.	Silver.	Total specie.	Currency.	Checks.	Total.	Gold.	Silver.	Specie.	Currency.	Checks.
							P. ct.	*P. ct.*	*P. ct.*	*P. ct.*	*P. ct.*
Nevada	$33,163	$4,526	$37,689	$7,209	$297,745	$342,643	9.6	1.3	10.9	2.1	87.0
New Hampshire	1,222	9,425	10,647	139,303	895,311	1,045,261	.1	.9	1.0	13.3	85.7
New Jersey	28,448	50,439	78,887	1,503,386	8,449,498	10,031,771	.2	.5	.7	15.0	84.3
New Mexico	7,798	5,427	13,225	36,743	226,352	276,320	2.8	1.9	4.7	13.3	82.0
New York	193,835	217,926	411,761	7,180,316	323,315,669	330,907,747	------	------	.1	2.2	97.7
North Carolina	3,502	34,058	37,560	156,473	1,109,417	1,303,450	.2	2.6	2.8	12.0	85.2
North Dakota	2,355	13,945	16,300	120,269	873,864	1,010,433	.2	1.3	1.5	11.9	86.6
Ohio	261,116	187,180	448,296	1,831,117	14,620,340	16,899,753	1.5	1.1	2.6	10.9	86.5
Oklahoma	7,802	47,127	54,929	261,623	1,439,920	1,756,472	.4	2.7	3.1	14.9	82.0
Oregon	179,516	26,380	205,896	41,965	3,236,493	3,484,354	5.1	.7	5.8	1.3	92.9
Pennsylvania	501,474	316,949	818,423	4,869,003	48,332,387	54,019,813	.9	.5	1.4	9.1	89.5
Rhode Island	4,879	12,928	17,807	308,319	1,679,525	2,005,651	.2	.6	.8	15.4	83.8
South Carolina	1,367	33,771	35,138	116,135	553,345	704,618	.2	4.8	5.0	16.4	78.6
South Dakota	9,275	16,257	25,532	142,396	968,378	1,136,306	.8	1.4	2.2	12.5	85.3
Tennessee	11,586	54,612	66,198	333,156	2,738,851	3,138,205	.3	1.7	2.0	10.7	87.3
Texas	29,287	128,955	158,242	626,432	5,899,587	6,684,261	.4	1.9	2.3	9.4	88.3
Utah	44,590	15,222	59,812	44,277	915,669	1,019,758	4.4	1.5	5.9	4.4	89.7
Vermont	1,773	8,821	10,594	119,743	630,401	760,738	.2	1.2	1.4	15.8	82.8
Virginia	14,948	39,393	54,341	404,298	3,435,721	3,894,360	.4	1.0	1.4	10.4	88.3
Washington	212,453	52,931	265,384	143,660	3,067,449	3,476,493	6.1	1.5	7.6	4.1	88.3
West Virginia	12,277	21,343	33,620	189,205	996,666	1,219,491	1.0	1.8	2.8	15.5	81.7
Wisconsin	85,844	62,658	148,502	602,319	7,535,398	8,286,219	1.0	.8	1.8	7.3	90.9
Wyoming	12,480	4,122	16,602	25,386	239,278	281,266	4.4	1.5	5.9	9.0	85.1
Total	3,768,195	3,094,848	6,863,043	33,984,822	647,239,813	688,087,678	.6	.4	1.0	5.0	94.0

Distribution of aggregate deposits by banks.—Of the whole amount of over $688,000,000 shown in our tables, the national banks reported more than $548,000,000. The state banks returned about $90,000,000 and the loan and trust companies about $40,000,000. The percentages run from 31.8 in the mutual savings banks to 95.3 in the national banks. The returns, put in this form, bring out strikingly again the overwhelming importance of the national banks in our commercial activity, although their number is so much smaller than that of the others. They bring out, too, the fact already commented on, that even the mutual savings banks receive part of their deposits in the form of checks. The table follows:

TABLE XXII.—*Aggregate of all classes of deposits, by banks.*

	Gold.	Silver.	Total specie.	Currency.	Checks.	Total.	Gold.	Silver.	Specie	Currency.	Checks.
							P. ct.	*P. ct.*	*P. ct.*	*P. ct.*	*P. ct.*
National banks	$2,366,411	$1,996,482	$4,362,893	$21,450,908	$522,475,534	$548,289,335	0.4	0.4	0.8	3.9	95.3
State banks	1,123,850	828,643	1,952,493	7,487,078	83,438,180	92,877,751	1.2	.9	2.1	8.1	89.8
Private banks	34,993	61,511	96,504	532,741	2,666,807	3,296,052	1.0	1.9	2.9	16.2	80.9
Loan and trust companies	85,759	160,046	245,805	3,200,476	36,029,583	39,475,864	.2	.4	.6	8.1	91.2
Stock savings banks	106,672	41,461	148,133	328,895	2,145,736	2,622,764	4.0	1.6	5.6	12.5	81.9
Mutual savings banks	50,510	6,705	57,215	984,724	483,973	1,525,912	3.3	.4	3.7	64.5	31.8
Grand total	3,768,195	3,094,848	6,863,043	33,984,822	647,239,813	688,087,678	.6	.4	1.0	4.9	94.1

The aggregate deposits of all classes in reserve cities.—If we look at the returns from the selected reserve cities only, New York leads again with 98.5, Boston is second with 97.5, St. Louis is third with 95, Chicago is fourth with 94.9, Philadelphia is fifth with 93.2. The other reserve cities have a percentage of checks in total deposits amounting to 88.9, and the average for the country is 96.4. Of the whole amount of deposits in reserve cities, New York City alone has more than half, while the five leading cities have all but $45,000,000. The following table gives the details:

TABLE XXIII.—*Aggregate of all classes of deposits in representative reserve cities.*

	Gold.	Silver.	Total specie.	Currency.	Checks.	Total.	Gold.	Silver.	Specie.	Currency.	Checks.
							P. ct.	*P. ct.*	*P. ct.*	*P. ct.*	*P. ct.*
New York	$109,189	$98,668	$207,857	$3,711,650	$238,895,129	$242,814,636				1.5	98.5
Chicago	98,624	88,602	187,226	2,136,828	42,638,200	44,962,254	0.2	0.2	0.4	4.7	94.9
St. Louis	28,706	56,746	85,452	668,774	14,035,732	14,789,958	.1	.4	.5	4.5	95.0
Boston	3,749	27,375	31,124	1,296,880	48,869,885	50,197,889				2.5	97.5
Philadelphia	103,715	83,152	186,867	1,989,502	28,601,109	30,777,478	.3	.2	.5	6.3	93.2
Total	343,983	354,543	698,526	9,803,634	373,040,055	383,542,215			.1	2.5	97.4
Other reserve cities	451,959	306,008	757,967	4,353,844	40,210,603	45,314,414	.9	.6	1.5	9.6	88.9
Total	795,942	660,551	1,456,493	14,157,478	413,250,658	428,856,629	.2	.1	.3	3.3	96.4

The aggregate percentage shown in country deposits.—For purposes of comparison the following table has been prepared to show the aggregate deposits and the percentage of checks in the returns from the banks of certain States, omitting the returns from banks in cities of 25,000 or more. The table shows that in Iowa 90 per cent of the returns of the deposits were in credit documents; in Kansas, 89.7; Nebraska, 86.9. The tables which have already been given showing the aggregate returns by States will show that other agricultural States range within about the same limits.

TABLE XXIV.—*Aggregate deposits, all banks of certain States, less those from cities of more than 25,000, in 1902–3, according to Census Bulletin No. 20.*

State.	Gold.	Silver.	Total specie.	Currency.	Checks.	Total.	Gold.	Silver.	Specie.	Currency.	Checks.
							P. ct.	*P. ct.*	*P. ct.*	*P. ct.*	*P. ct.*
Illinois	$46,649	$101,269	$147,918	$780,743	$5,226,713	$6,155,374	0.8	1.6	2.4	12.7	84.8
Iowa	22,574	57,090	79,664	348,294	3,934,272	4,362,230	.5	1.3	1.8	8.0	90.2
Kansas	29,616	58,131	87,747	277,552	3,147,340	3,512,639	.9	1.6	2.5	7.8	89.7
Nebraska	8,624	36,006	44,630	315,298	2,381,918	2,741,846	.3	1.3	1.6	12.5	86.9
Texas	22,487	92,792	115,279	410,023	2,765,781	3,291,083	.7	2.8	3.5	12.5	84.0
Grand total	129,950	345,288	475,238	2,131,910	17,456,024	20,063,172	.7	1.7	2.4	10.6	86.9

COLLATERAL EVIDENCE AS TO THE USE OF CHECKS.

Change in small bills.—If that part of the population of the country which makes payments wholly or partly with cash is increasing more rapidly than the rest of the country, the kind of currency which this part of the population uses might be expected to increase more rapidly than the total volume of currency. Table XXVI shows the total volume of currency outstanding, by five-year periods, by denominations, calculated from figures given in the reports of the Treasurer of the United States. Of course the amount outstanding is not the amount in circulation, yet the errors probably average up about the same from year to year, so that changes in the amount outstanding may be taken as a fair illustration of changes in the amount in active use.

We give, first, the sum of the amounts of currency of all denominations annually outstanding, for five-year periods. The second column gives corresponding data for currency of denominations up to and including $20. The next column gives the ratio of these small denominations to the total per million. The other columns give similar data for other denominations. There is no marked increase corresponding to the increase of the population, but it is with the increase of the population rather than the volume of business to which this part of our currency should show a particular sensitiveness. The ratios for the five-year periods show a periodicity, with, on the whole, an upward tendency, but the increase is by no means great enough to take care of the increased volume of business in the period in question.

TABLE XXV.—*Proportion of bills of different denominations in total currency for five-year periods.*

Period.	Total currency all denominations.	Denominations ones to twenties, inclusive.	Ratio of small denominations to all currency per 1,000.	Fifties, hundreds, and five hundreds.	Ratio fifties, etc., to total per 1,000.	Thousands, five thousands, and ten thousands.	Ratio thousands, etc., to total per 1,000.
1884–1888	$4,702,224,357	$3,228,457,377	$686	$812,366,980	$172	$648,400,000	$138
1889–1893	5,103,897,225	3,845,319,870	753	702,794,855	137	755,782,500	148
1894–1898	5,738,679,974	4,249,387,274	740	683,603,200	119	805,683,500	140
1899–1903	7,187,514,768	5,557,586,793	773	799,175,475	111	830,752,500	115
1904–1908	10,020,161,546	7,556,993,446	754	1,041,590,600	104	1,421,577,500	141

If now the total volume of business has been expanding, as we know it has, and that part of the currency which is used by the wage-earners has not been expanding regularly, it must be that the increased volume of payments have been made either with bills of large denominations or settled by means of credit. If we study the increase in the volume of bills of large denominations we find that they have been increasing irregularly in about the same way that the denominations of $20 and less have been doing.

These remarks apply to our paper money only. No account has been taken of the outstanding volume of silver dollars because that has been approximately constant for the period under discussion, nor has the gold been taken into account because very likely it is mostly in the banks.

Evidence from the number of bank accounts.—The banks were asked to classify their accounts according to the balances on hand on the day of the report. They returned the number of accounts whose balance was under $500, the number whose balance was between $500 and $2,500, and the number with a balance over $2,500. The aggregate of the first class is 11,975,000, that of the second class is 2,548,995, and that of the third class is 567,104. Undoubtedly a good many savings accounts are included by other than the savings banks. It would have been possible to determine the number of savings accounts returned by the stock savings banks and the mutual savings banks, and this would have been done if there had been less uncertainty as to the number of savings accounts returned by the other classes of banks. However, 590 savings banks in California, Connecticut, Iowa, Maine, Massachusetts, Michigan, New Hampshire, New Jersey, New York, Ohio, Philadelphia, and Rhode Island had 2,699,620 accounts, each under $500. This would give us, as a rough estimate, 3,700,000 accounts of less than $500 in the stock and mutual savings banks, leaving 8,200,000 such accounts in the other classes of banks. Allowing a due proportion of these as savings accounts, we have probably 8,000,000 of accounts under $500 in the commercial banks which reported. Of course these are by no means all individual accounts nor can the smallness of the balance be taken as a sure index of the amount of business done by the owner of the account nor his economic status in the community. Nevertheless, on the whole, we may conclude that so large a number of accounts with this small balance is another indication of the widespread use of the banking facilities accessible throughout our country.

TABLE XXVI.—*Aggregate individual and other deposits and number of accounts on the books of all banks reporting, by States.*

State.	Individual deposits.	Other deposits	Number of accounts—		
			Under $500	$500 to $2,500.	Over $2,500.
Alabama	$24,898,026	$4,036,485	86,858	11,499	3,026
Arizona	9,322,650	1,978,610	20,078	3,283	813
Arkansas	31,230,493	4,578,112	53,635	5,900	1,185
California	341,589,527	80,679,248	430,483	87,646	22,283
Colorado	66,442,700	36,056,363	92,257	14,464	3,900
Connecticut	257,560,173	12,593,075	292,496	85,805	20,034
Delaware	22,288,415	1,135,993	37,955	5,337	893
District of Columbia	49,343,953	6,504,163	80,897	10,542	2,732
Florida	20,535,874	6,757,196	56,459	6,987	8,517
Georgia	58,124,754	8,292,185	107,694	12,219	2,605
Idaho	16,817,636	6,202,739	28,191	3,956	737
Illinois	548,278,194	406,499,161	734,020	132,988	35,382
Indiana	164,211,949	57,823,714	443,751	58,203	19,831
Iowa	163,796,484	105,452,062	307,554	54,691	11,988
Kansas	123,250,330	38,902,800	249,204	31,731	7,030
Kentucky	69,076,361	24,465,031	195,772	24,764	4,232
Louisiana	46,689,719	25,366,307	61,600	9,975	4,466
Maine	103,768,656	8,636,980	191,506	52,535	4,418
Maryland	109,379,645	38,420,665	142,982	22,875	6,998
Massachusetts	808,474,694	175,165,927	643,790	241,725	22,403
Michigan	161,958,211	84,528,544	360,609	75,290	10,045
Minnesota	596,654,632	94,354,687	189,820	30,830	11,868

TABLE XXVI.—*Aggregate individual and other deposits and number of accounts on the books of all banks reporting, by States*—Continued.

State.	Individual deposits.	Other deposits.	Number of accounts—		
			Under $500.	$500 to $2,500.	Over $2,500.
Mississippi	$17,899,066	$3,405,478	54,025	5,934	1,509
Missouri	247,969,392	191,596,364	313,689	44,720	11,160
Montana	27,590,700	19,774,553	29,733	5,706	1,675
Nebraska	81,046,766	51,262,704	154,973	26,165	5,117
Nevada	5,661,635	1,357,204	7,604	1,601	393
New Hampshire	59,009,848	5,346,784	94,163	21,261	3,449
New Jersey	281,493,047	36,903,499	429,970	81,883	76,454
New Mexico	6,043,657	3,349,163	16,448	1,673	352
New York	2,507,391,259	946,165,776	1,957,790	601,474	137,815
North Carolina	24,201,986	6,994,006	83,993	10,881	2,740
North Dakota	22,378,580	17,437,549	46,402	5,752	1,519
Ohio	371,223,757	145,612,899	688,493	199,902	20,896
Oklahoma	30,574,574	11,083,734	120,025	12,283	1,996
Oregon	49,416,145	17,514,617	65,073	14,354	3,071
Pennsylvania	989,771,318	318,046,548	1,764,827	309,177	49,806
Rhode Island	103,251,597	27,051,301	96,868	36,709	7,283
South Carolina	16,151,922	3,868,275	52,768	5,949	1,561
South Dakota	27,745,955	14,634,966	59,945	8,943	1,983
Tennessee	54,962,798	28,302,427	140,649	17,706	4,369
Texas	133,400,967	43,570,006	285,498	38,458	8,737
Utah	24,139,757	10,382,593	56,749	8,934	1,446

Vermont	53,940,808	2,987,359	86,479	22,565	976
Virginia	68,538,478	19,243,739	171,433	21,365	4,580
Washington	52,294,380	19,729,439	84,840	16,194	3,285
West Virginia	39,195,722	12,885,005	119,241	16,158	3,657
Wisconsin	105,898,165	74,337,788	170,532	27,179	5,086
Wyoming	7,698,347	4,242,619	15,179	2,824	803
Total	9,202,583,702	3,265,516,442	11,975,000	2,548,995	567,104

FINAL CONCLUSIONS AS TO THE AVERAGE PROPORTION OF PAYMENTS MADE WITH CHECKS AND OTHER CREDIT INSTRUMENTS.

The conclusion reached in the inquiry of 1896 was that at least 80 per cent of the total business of the country at that time was settled by means of credit paper. The average per cent of the retail deposits made in the form of credit instruments, on the basis of the returns of that year, was 67. In the present returns it is 73 per cent. The discussion in the report of 1896, which has been repeated in part in the present discussion, with some additional points, led to the conclusion that "40 per cent is as low as could in reason be claimed to be correct and that 55 per cent is, all things considered, probably about correct." This is for retail trade.

From the present discussion, the writer is of the opinion that this is probably too low. Undoubtedly the use of checks has grown considerably in the past fifteen years. The number of national banks increased from 3,689 in July, 1896, to 6,893 last April, while the number of state and private banks and loan and trust companies is now about 14,550 as against about 5,700 thirteen years ago. The percentage of increase in the number of banks in the past thirteen years is about 128. The "banking power" of the United States as measured by the Comptroller of the Currency[a] has increased 242 per cent since 1890. In the meantime the population of the country is estimated to have increased from about 70,000,000 in

[a] Reports of Comptroller, 1896, p. 691, and 1908, p. 458.

1896 to about 90,000,000 now. In other words, the banking power of the country has been increasing more rapidly than the population. Meantime the business of the country, as measured by the total bank clearings in 1896 and 1908 has increased from $51,977,799,114 to $126,238,694,398.

The total estimated circulating medium of the country has increased from $1,506,434,966 to $3,038,000,000. As the population of the country increases, very likely an increasing proportion of the people belong to the wage-earning class, or to the class just above, with relatively small incomes. If so, the smaller number of the population with the larger income would do a larger proportion of the business, and it is this class who most commonly make their payments with checks. These reflections are especially applicable in a period of prosperity such as this country has on the whole experienced in the past fifteen years. Consequently, it is altogether likely that the percentage of the volume of ordinary payments made by check has been increasing somewhat, as the figures of the bank returns would seem to show. In the opinion of the writer it would not be far out of the way to assume that 60 per cent of the retail trade of the country, under existing conditions, is paid for with checks.

We have found no reason to think that the figures obtained for the wholesale trade are not representative. So far as the writer is aware, no one has ever produced any evidence that invalidates the truth of the common belief that 90 per cent or more of the wholesale business of the country is done by means of credit paper. In getting at our final average we may therefore take the figures on the face of our returns as substantially correct. If now we take the percentage of checks in the retail payments at 60 and the percentage in the wholesale payments at 95 and weight these in the proportion of the deposits returned for the two classes of dealers, we get 86 as the average percentage of retail and wholesale business done with checks and other credit paper.

It is not a matter of great importance whether we take the figures of "all others" at their face value or lessen them by a considerable amount to meet the objections that have been discussed as to the duplication of checks, the deposits by speculators, etc. The writer is of the opinion that this form of demand for payment should not be omitted. If, nevertheless, we omit from the third class of deposits those of the New York City banks, where the greatest speculative transactions take place, allow $6,000,000 for retail business not "banked," and then weight the percentages of the respective classes according to the volumes of deposits with the $6,000,000 added to the retail total and retail cash, and New York City out of the "all others" total, we reach a final average percentage of 88 as that which represents that part of the trade of the country which from day to day is settled by means of checks and other credit paper.

The conclusion reached in 1896 was that 80 per cent was a fair probable average. Considering the facts that the volume of business has increased more rapidly than population, that we have probably one bank to every 4,000 people, that the country has seen a long period of prosperity, there doubtless has been some increase in the use of checks. Surely we may conclude that the 1896 percentage was not too high. Very likely a figure between 80 and 88 would be about right.

Is the use of checks and credit instruments increasing? It has been said that the use of checks is not increasing, because the percentage shown in the bank inquiries of various dates, as described in this paper, has not shown a steady increase. On June 30, 1881, the percentage was given as 95.1; on September 17, 1881, it was 94.1; on July 1, 1890, it was 92.5; on September 17, 1890, it was 91; on September 15, 1892, it was 90.6; on July 1, 1896, it was given as 92.5; and on March 16, 1909, it is 94. These figures can not be used as the basis of an argument that the proportion of checks used in payment has increased. That the absolute volume of business settled in this way is increasing, no one denies. The variation in these percentages seems to indicate a larger proportion of this kind of settlement in June and July than in the fall. Still it would not be safe to accept this inference as true without further evidence. The opposite, however, certainly is not true. The movement is probably periodic.

SUMMARY.

We may summarize the results of our inquiry and inferences therefrom briefly as follows:

1. In the first place, it is very clear that a large proportion of the business of the country, even the retail trade, is done by means of credit instruments. While it is probably true that wage-earners, as a class, do not

commonly use checks, it is also true that a great many of them do. Moreover, the use of checks is common among people who derive their income from other sources, even though it be not larger than the well-paid day laborer. We are justified, therefore, in concluding that 50 or 60 per cent of the retail trade of the country is settled in this way.

2. There is no reason to modify the percentage of checks in the wholesale business of the country. The figures of the table are probably as nearly correct as any that could be gotten. Over 90 per cent of the wholesale trade of the country is done with checks and other credit documents.

3. The very general use of checks is shown in the deposits of "all other" depositors. The average is close up to that of the wholesale trade, and while many corporations, public and private, are doubtless represented here, and many speculative transactions are included, there is no reason for excluding any one of those in determining the proportion of business done, whatever we may think of its legitimacy from the point of view of public morals or public utility.

4. The use of checks is promoted in a measure by the payment of wages by check. It appears from our investigation that of weekly pay rolls reported by the banks, aggregating $134,800,000 for the week ending March 13 last, 70 per cent was in checks. These pay checks are probably cashed largely by the merchants and would appear in their accounts mainly on the following Saturday or Monday. Some doubtless got into our deposits

on the Tuesday for which we have returns. However, they may be counted, in part at least, as checks used in the settlement of transactions, because in most cases they would be given in settlement of an account, the owner getting back the difference between his account and the check.

5. The great use of checks is shown also by the large number of accounts under $500. This evidence is not conclusive, but shows a tendency. Of course, the accounts include not only those of individuals, but of firms, corporations, and others.

6. We may therefore safely accept an average of 80 to 85 per cent as the probable percentage of business of this country done by check.

7. The fact that so large a proportion of business is done with credit paper may or may not be a good thing. Whether it is or not depends on circumstances. If any part of the country is compelled to use checks because of the lack of currency, when it would prefer the latter, the situation is an evil.

8. The transaction of so large a volume of our business by checks is an element of danger in times of stringency and crisis. In such times the uncanceled balance of credit transactions creates a larger demand for money, but the habit of settling by check has meantime kept the available amount of money at a minimum.

9. Consequently there ought to be some means of supplying additional currency when credit as a means of payment diminishes. This currency ought to be as safe and as uniform as the ordinary currency, and it should

be capable of being quickly emitted and recalled. That is, it should possess elasticity.

10. The large money circulation of the country is explained by the facts that our prices and wages range high, that our people probably carry a larger average amount of money on their persons than do foreigners, that some portion of our currency has been destroyed or lost or hoarded, and that some of our money is abroad in the hands of money brokers and others. Finally, as our business grows, the amount of money needed as reserve to perform this vast volume of business transactions increases, too.

11. The amount of money released by our credit transactions is not equal in amount to the volume of credit instruments, for there must always be enough to settle the uncanceled balances called for in money from day to day.

12. This demand for reserve has an influence in determining the value of money on general prices just as has the demand for money for direct payment.

13. The volume of credit transactions very likely tends to increase as population and business grow. It does not increase uniformly, however, but by periodic movements. That is to say, the rate of increase of credit transactions, as compared with the whole volume of business, grows, as it were, by jerks and at a decreasing rate.

THE BEARING OF THESE INVESTIGATIONS ON THE MONETARY SITUATION.

Several important questions are closely related to the inquiry which has been reported and discussed. Among them are these:

1. What is the amount of money rendered unnecessary by the use of credit paper?

2. What is the influence of the vast volume of credit transactions on the value of money or the level of prices?

3. Why is it that our per capita circulation is so large and where is the money in active circulation?

4. Does this discussion show the need of more money for circulation, or may we safely rely upon our method of credit payments to meet the business needs of the country?

5. If more money is needed, under what conditions can it be best supplied?

1. We will take these questions up in order. It is not a correct view of the case to suppose that the credit paper used in settling debts displaces a volume of money equal to itself. The amount of money displaced is the difference between the amount that would be needed in a purely money régime and the amount needed to pay the uncanceled balances of the credit transactions. Now, the same unsettled balance may result from very different volumes of business. This is not the place to discuss what factors make the uncanceled balance large or small, nor do we know any way of telling beforehand what volume of business may be settled by credit cancellation in a community with a given money circulation. In a city where there is no clearing house and the banks exchange checks from day to day the volume of business settled by cancellation of checks, on the basis of a given amount of money as a reserve, will be smaller than can be so handled when the credit machinery is made more perfect by the establishment of a clearing house. The process is well illustrated

in times of stringency when the clearing-house banks pool their reserves. This is only another way of saying that a larger volume of transactions is canceled and a smaller balance left to drain the reserve. Therefore, the amount of money displaced by the use of credit paper in a community with the simplest form of credit machinery would be the whole volume of the transactions, minus the reserve necessary to settle balances. If we could separate all the transactions of the day or week into aggregate credits and debits to be settled at the same moment, the amount of money necessary to settle them would be the part of the balance settled immediately with cash, plus the amount necessary as a reserve for the part carried over on the books of the banks. Obviously, now, the amount necessary for reserves is a very variable one, depending not only on the total amount of business, but also upon that part of the unsettled balances which is called for in money form immediately. It is for this reason that the volume of credit business that can be done on a particular reserve is a very variable one. It is also very unstable. Credit built upon credit, as so many of our transactions are, trembles and falls at very slight shakings of confidence in the future. A comparatively slight depression of the market, a comparatively small change in the amount of credit transactions, may produce a large uncanceled balance and make necessary a much greater amount of money. The more our credit machinery expands the more delicate it becomes.

No one can say, therefore, with definiteness what is the amount of money released if 75 or 80 per cent of our business transactions are settled by means of credit paper. This is a matter in which the long experience of practical bankers is the only safe guide, because the amount in question is changing from day to day as the conditions change. No simple rule about it can be laid down. Certainly, however, it is not 75 per cent of the money which would be necessary if all transactions were settled with money. It is an amount varying from one-third to one-fifth of uncanceled credit balances, according to the perfection of the banking machinery, the state of credit, prosperity, and public confidence.

One point needs to be carefully borne in mind. However great the volume of credit exchanges, however extensive the use of credit may become in a community, they can never fully displace sales for direct money payment. The extensive use of credit is not of itself a sign that a community is well off. Credit is used in poor as well as in rich communities. Its extensive use in a poor and undeveloped country is likely to indicate a lack of capital rather than an abundance of wealth. Every community tends to use the cheapest medium of exchange accessible to it. If its capital is of very high value for producing goods for direct consumption, a community will be averse to investing much of it in a medium of exchange.

This is the reason why undeveloped countries, as our own was a century ago, try to effect their exchanges by means of credit paper to a larger extent than wealthier communities. Under such conditions paper money is commonly thought to be the cheapest medium of exchange. If, now, part of the money exchanges are replaced with credit exchanges, the amount of money released, or the amount without which the community could now get on, would be the whole amount formerly used in money payments, provided these payments now done on credit exactly canceled one another, and we could be sure that they would continue to balance one another forever. We know, however, that we can not be sure of that; we know that transactions are not likely to cancel one another completely from time to time; hence the amount of money released by the substitution of credit payments for direct money payments is the amount formerly used minus the reserve necessary to do this credit business. The important point, however, is that less money is necessary. How much less we can not be sure. We can get some light on the subject, however, by noting the volume of business done by credit paper and the balances which from time to time are carried as a basis of settlement.

It is important to note also that an increase in the volume of credit transactions does not necessarily mean that we must get a proportionate increase in our reserve of money. Every refinement of the credit mechanism makes it possible to do a larger volume of business on the same reserve.

Of course, it will not do to over-emphasize the importance of credit exchanges, vast as they are. Credit and credit documents can not replace money altogether. They reduce the amount necessary, but against them some reserve must always be kept, accessible for emergencies in the settlement of balances. The volume of business that can be done by credit paper depends on several circumstances. Obviously, in the first place, it depends upon the banking facilities of the country. If the banks are widely distributed, if they are willing to deal in transactions small enough to be within the reach of large numbers of people, many more transactions will be settled through them than would otherwise be the case. This fact undoubtedly explains in large measure the development of what may be called the "banking habit" among the people of the United States. Undoubtedly our people pay by check much more commonly and much more largely than people of any other country. We settle smaller transactions by check; our banks are willing to carry smaller accounts. Indeed, the rapid industrial development of our country is probably due in no small degree to our system of independent banks and the facility with which we have permitted banks to be established. The small independent bank in the country community has felt that its interests and success were bound up with the interests and success of the community, and, therefore, has undoubtedly been willing to do more for the general interests than a branch of a large bank in some remote commercial center would have felt like doing, even if it had been justified in doing so. The small capital with which we have permitted banks to be established also has undoubtedly been a contributing factor to our rapid economic development, as well as to the promotion of the banking habit among our people.

In the next place, the density of population is, of course, an important factor for the growth of credit exchanges. A larger volume of business is settled by bank paper in a commercial center than in an agricultural community, even though the proportion of total business thus settled may not be larger. However, it is necessary that there should be a certain number of people within reach of a common center in order to have a bank established there. Of course the smaller the bank the fewer the people thus required. Thus again our inclination in the past to favor the establishment of the small independent banks has facilitated the spread of banking and promoted the volume of business settled in the country districts by credit payment and stimulated the banking habit among our people.

Finally, the general education and intelligence of the mass of the people is an important factor. Men do not use banks unless they have confidence in them, and they have come to be regarded as a settled part of the ordinary commercial mechanism of the community. Our people are people of a wide general education and high order of intelligence. They understand the place and work of the bank in a community much better than the same number of people, for example, in a European country. This fact is strikingly brought out by a study of the proportion of retail business settled by means of checks in what are called the "foreign" districts of our large cities, on the one hand, and in an agricultural community on the other. The European immigrant is not a man who has had banking connections in his home country, and he does not use them here, even though the facilities are more numerous.

Such evidence as there is seems to indicate that payment by check has shown an increase during the past few years:

(*a*) In the first place, the returns of our reports show a larger percentage in retail trade. This evidence, of course, is by no means conclusive, but the checks could not be deposited if they were not drawn; therefore, whether they are largely "cashed" checks or checks received in payment of purchases, the fact that they are deposited in a larger degree indicates a wider use.

(*b*) The prosperity of the farmers in the Central West has enabled many to have bank accounts who fifteen years ago could not carry balances. The writer's information from central Illinois is strongly in this direction.

(*c*) The third evidence is found in the growth of the number of small banks, especially in the country districts. Since national banks have been permitted to establish themselves with a capital of $25,000 their number has increased from 3,617 to 6,926.

(*d*) The appearance of a considerable proportion of checks in the deposits of mutual savings banks is also, to some degree, significant. Of course the credit documents received in the deposits of these banks may be to a considerable extent money orders. Nevertheless their deposits show a certain use of credit paper by the patrons of these banks.

On the other hand, the increase of that part of the population which consists of the wage-earning class, by whom the use of checks is small, is undoubtedly greater than that of our other classes of population. However, the wealthy classes, though fewer in number, have more to spend and their use of checks raises the proportion of credit paper in payments.

We can not expect any social movement to continue steadily in one direction for an indefinite time. Such evidence as inquiries of this character furnish seems to show that there is a certain ebb and flow in the proportion of checks used in business payments. With a given amount of money a certain proportion of it can be used for bank reserves on which to build credit transactions. For a time the volume of business will increase more rapidly than the money supplies, so that the proportion of credit business to the whole will increase, the improvement of the credit machinery in the meantime facilitating the movement. But the perfection of the facilities for utilizing to the utmost a given reserve, or a slowly increasing one, will come to a stop after a time, and it will be necessary to increase the money supply for any further expansion of credit. In the language of business, another unit of capital must be added to plant. The unit added to the social capital devoted to exchange—that is, the additional amount of money—will be larger than is necessary for most profitable immediate use, consequently the proportion of money exchanges will for a time show an increase. We may conclude, therefore, that the volume of business done on credit gradually increases as the population and total amount of business are enlarged, but at a decreasing rate and with occasional or periodic retardations.

2. *Relation of credit exchanges to the volume of money and prices.*—It is pertinent to inquire, now, what effect, if any, this great settlement of indebtedness by means of credit paper has upon the value of money. Evidently, it can influence this value, or the general price level, only as it changes the amount of demand for money. We have seen reason, now, to think that 80 per cent of our business transactions are settled by means of credit paper. Credit paper cancellation enables a larger amount of business to be done with the same amount of money and has an effect in determining the value of money by increasing the demand for reserves. Francis A. Walker, who may be taken as a representative of the extreme opponents of the doctrine that the extensive use of credit documents has a large influence on prices, insists that the growth of settlement by credit paper and the general transfer of credit paper by indorsement, the extension of bank deposits and the cancellation of indebtedness based thereon, have practically no effect on prices. "These transactions are, so far as concerns the use and by consequence the value of money, the same essentially as if they had been acts of barter. Exchanges in this category do not involve the employment of money, and they are therefore to be counted out when we are considering the causes and conditions which determine the value of money. They constitute no part of the demand for money." [a]

[a] Francis A. Walker: Discussions in Economics and Statistics, I: 199.

Admitting the partial truth of all this, it still holds that the use of credit paper in effecting credit exchanges makes possible a far larger volume of business than could otherwise be done, and that this increased volume of business must in some way influence prices seem undeniable. Mr. Walker and those who agree with him insist that its effect is nil. He urges that all transactions by direct barter, and by indirect barter or credit, are made upon the basis of prices determined by the direct money exchanges and that they thus have no influence whatever on the price level. "Were barter goods to be multiplied fourfold (but not at the expense of the goods exchanged for money) this would have no effect upon prices, since it would alter neither the demand for nor the supply of money."[a]

Again, it is urged that the volume of business shown by bank deposits or credit transactions does not represent truly the trade of the country. We are told by many that there is a vast amount of credit transactions embodied in banking and clearing-house statistics which may be termed "fictitious." That is to say, they are not a part of the necessary work of exchange in a community. For example, the cotton and wheat crops are sold several times over on the exchanges of the country, but not all these purchases and sales are a necessary part of the process of getting the cotton from the planter to the manufacturer. These sales, we are told, are purely speculative and born out of the credit organization, which, it is urged, merely makes the transactions pos-

[a] Francis A. Walker: Ibid., 198.

sible. If this credit organization did not exist, these multifarious and unnecessary speculative purchases and sales would not be carried on. In a sense, of course, this statement is true. In a sense, these speculative purchases and sales are not necessary to get the raw material to the manufacturer. In a sense, also, it is true that the jobbers, commission merchants, and other middlemen are not "necessary" to get the goods from the manufacturer to the consumer. All the existing agencies are necessary, however, to get the cotton or the wool to the manufacturer and the goods to the consumer at the price at which they buy them, under the existing machinery of transportation and exchange.

These exchanges actually exist. All the purchases involved constitute a part of the demand for means of settlement. Therefore they are to be regarded as a proper part of the exchange business of the country, and in some degree they must influence the need for money.

The influence of the volume of business settled by means of credit paper on the value of money, or the general level of prices, is far greater than Mr. Walker admits. The demand for money to effect exchanges includes, first, demand for money for direct exchanges; second, demand for reserves for credit exchanges. Some goods exchange by direct barter and still more probably by indirect barter. If these last exchanges just canceled one another, the credit paper that grows out of them would also cancel, and no balances would remain to be settled with money. Usually, however, they do not cancel and the balance must be settled with cash; hence a reserve is necessary. We never can tell whether credit exchanges will cancel; experience shows, indeed, that they never do cancel, and in the absence of certainty it is necessary for every community through its banks to keep a reserve of money for the purpose of settlement. Even if at some time they do cancel, we could never be sure that the next day or the next month or the next "season" would not give the community or the country or the world a disproportionate production of some goods as compared with others, which would impair the equality of cancellation in exchange and create a new balance of indebtedness, for the settlement of which money would be necessary. Or a new supply of money may become available and so disturb the equality of cancellation, create a new level of prices, and therefore require a balance for settlement in the shape of a larger reserve. This demand for reserve is certainly one of the influences that go to determine the value of money. In short, the demand for money includes a demand for direct payment and a demand for reserve. Disregarding for our present purpose all other factors, the value of money or the general level of prices will settle at a point where a unit of money may be used either for direct payment or for reserves. Thus we see that the volume of credit exchanges is of great importance, not only in enabling us to determine the volume of business done, but because of the influence on prices when acting through bank reserves.

3. *Our monetary circulation.*—Our per capita circulation, as estimated by the Comptroller of the Currency, has increased from $21.10 in 1906 to $34.72 in 1908. This is larger than the per capita circulation of other great

industrial and commercial countries with the exception of France. Why is it necessary and where is it? It is necessary, perhaps, for the following reasons:

(*a*) A larger amount of money is needed in this country because, in the first place, our prices range higher. If the prices of articles commonly consumed range 20 per cent higher than they do abroad, the people who buy them and pay for them with money need a larger amount to make their purchases. The same cause makes a larger reserve necessary to exchange a given volume of goods by credit. The demand for money, therefore, both for reserve and direct money transactions, is greater on account of the higher scale of prices.

(*b*) The same kind of reasoning applies to our wage scale. Whether the wage scale be the cause of the higher cost of living or the higher cost of living be the cause of the higher wage scale, more money is needed to pay wages. If wages are paid directly in cash, more money will be needed in proportion to the trade If wages are paid with checks, more money will be needed by the amount that the reserve must be increased to furnish a basis for the checks.

(*c*) Our country is more sparsely settled than England, France, or Germany. In spite of the large increase in the banking facilities of the country, it still remains true that very many places are remote from banks, so that business, so far as it is not barter, will probably be carried on with money. It is necessary, therefore, to have a larger amount of money than if population were denser. We have seen that the proportion of credit paper in the deposits of the agricultural parts of the country is higher. This condition is probably due as much to the difficulty of getting a sufficient amount of money as to the desire to use the bank-deposit system of payment.

(*d*) It may be that our spirit of individualism plays some part. So large a proportion of our wage-earning population have come from conditions where they had opportunity to handle very little money, that they like to carry money on their persons. It makes them feel, as one man said to the writer, "more independent." To quote the same informant, they would "rather pay higher prices and have more money to pay with."

(*e*) Doubtless there is a good deal of hoarding by people who distrust banks or are not near enough to use them. It might be urged that no larger proportion of people here hoard than is the case in Europe. Without disputing this, it is true, however, that if only the same proportion hoard and in the same relative amounts as is done by corresponding classes of the population, the absolute amount thus withdrawn would be larger because of our higher scale of wages and prices.

It is a dangerous thing to attempt, but we may make a rough estimate of the amount of money necessary for business in this country, somewhat as follows:

If we add returns for the nonreporting banks according to their ratio to the whole number and the various classes of deposits, we get in round numbers $990,000,000 as the bank deposits of the day. Of this amount 5 per cent, let us say, was in money, amounting to about $50,000,000. If we add $20,000,000 for business not "banked" we get $70,000,000 as the amount of money passing in the business of one day. How often does this turn over? Probably once in about twenty-one days. For the week is a common wage period; three to ten days are the payment period of many business houses which take advantage of discounts; and, of course, thirty days are also common. Let us take twenty days as the average.[a] Then $1,400,000,000 is the amount of money used in the turnover. The banks have $1,500,000,000. Take $100,000,000 to $200,000,000 as the amount abroad hoarded, lost, and destroyed. This gives us a grand total of $3,000,000,000 to $3,100,000,000, or approximately our reported circulation.

4. *Do we need more money?*—It is sometimes urged that an increasing use of credit renders a larger volume of money unnecessary; or at any rate that the increase in the need for a medium of exchange may be met by our very admirable elastic system of bank deposits. There are two or three considerations that must be urged in reply to this last opinion. As we have already noted, the use of credit paper is not of itself proof that a community is wealthy. Indeed this circumstance may show the very opposite condition. Some of our agricultural communities which are using checks so largely may be doing so because of the difficulty of getting money, or they may be doing so by choice. In other words, the large use of credit paper may under some circumstances mean that it is difficult to get currency. We can not be sure without knowing the

[a] I am indebted to Professor Irving Fisher for this estimate for 1896. It is based on the report of that year.

circumstances of the particular case. It is the opinion of the writer that this is in part an explanation of the large use of deposit banking in this country.

In the next place, the settlement of a very large proportion of exchanges by means of credit paper introduces a delicacy of character into the trading mechanism of a community which may cause it to be more easily upset. The larger the volume of credit settlements in proportion to the volume of money settlements, the greater the panic when confidence breaks down and the balance of canceled credit transactions thereby is made larger. A breakdown of confidence means an increase in the amount of transactions that must be settled by ready money. Therefore it is not a safe condition for the country to have the amount of actual money so small for its retail transactions that when confidence fails, the strain on it will be severely felt. It would be better for the country to have a smaller volume of credit transactions and a larger volume of direct money payments. If the habits of the people preclude this, then some means should be provided of supplying readily and efficiently the increased demand for ready money which occurs on account of a breakdown of confidence and the increase of the uncanceled balances of credit transactions. In other words, sources of additional currency supply which will flow out rapidly when it is needed to the places where it is needed, and will retreat with equal efficiency when the emergency passes, is an especial desideratum in a country where the proportion of transactions settled by credit paper is very large.

5. The additional supply of circulating medium necessary in times of stringency can be supplied in any one of three ways. In the first place, it may be issued under some arrangement by the existing independent banks of the country in their various communities. This is virtually an increase of credit currency. In the second place, it might possibly be supplied from some central bank to the existing banks in the various communities. In the third place, the existing credit currency, United States notes, might be retired and their place taken with specie which, in time of stress, could be gathered in to a greater or less extent in return for an increased volume of bank notes to be issued in either one of the first two ways.

It is not the province of this paper, however, to discuss this matter. Therefore the writer contents himself with simply mentioning these three ways.

DIAGRAM OF THE PERCENTAGE OF CHECKS IN AGGREGATE DEPOSITS BY STATES.

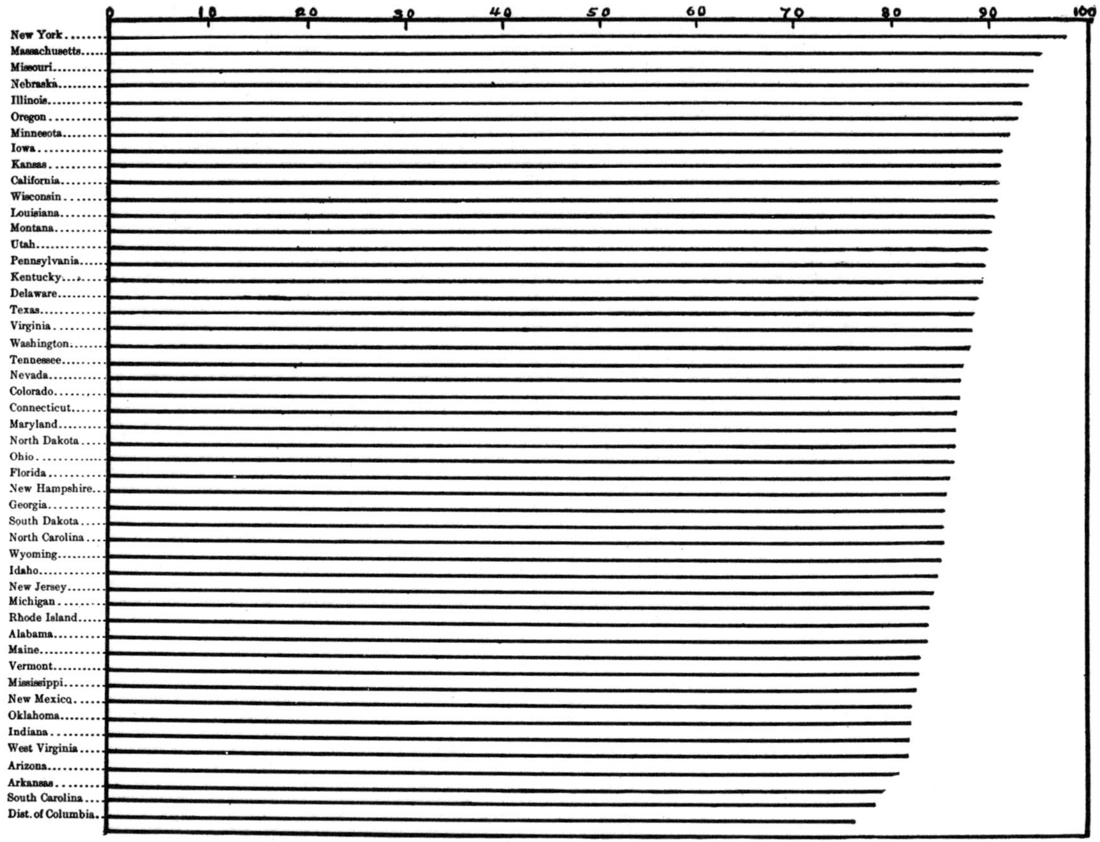

DIAGRAM OF THE PERCENTAGE OF CHECKS IN RETAIL DEPOSITS BY STATES.

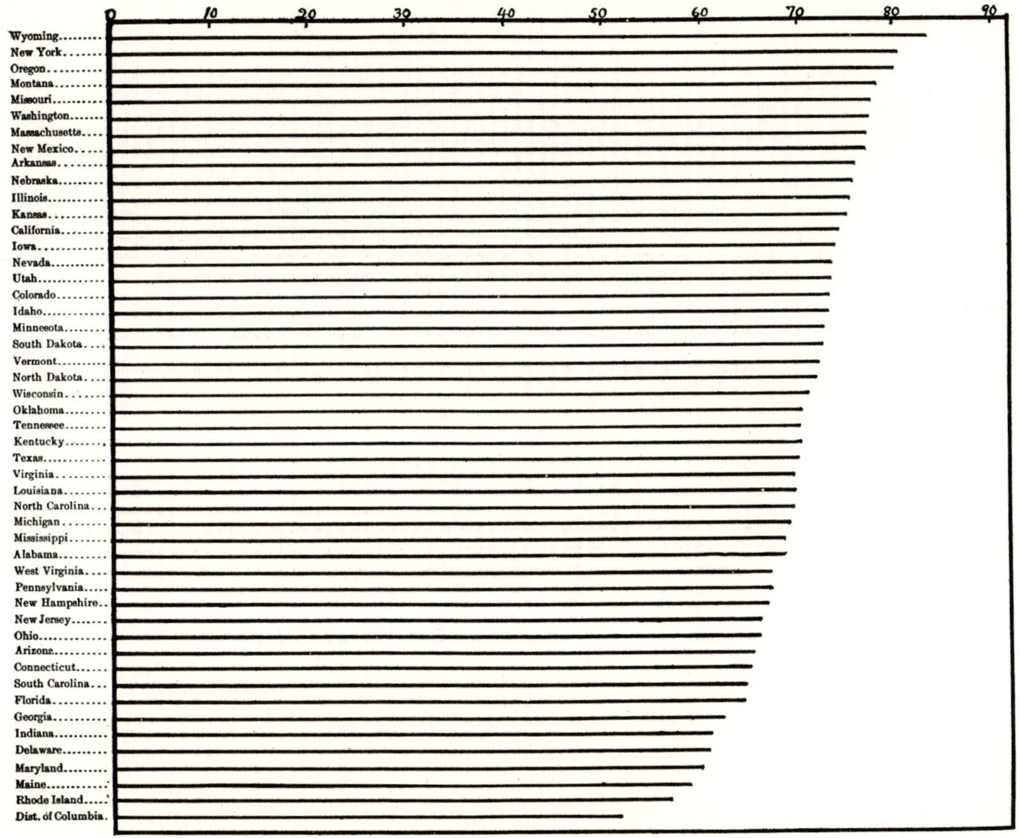

DIAGRAM OF THE PERCENTAGE OF CHECKS IN RETAIL DEPOSITS BY CLASSES OF BANKS.

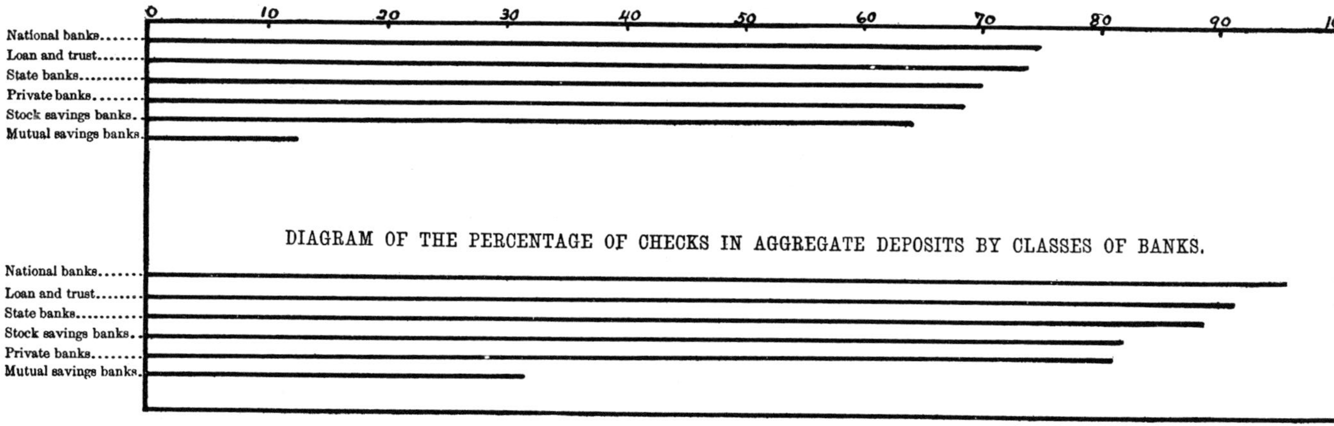

SELECT BIBLIOGRAPHY.

ANDREW, A. P.: Credit and the Value of Money. Publ. Amer. Econ. Assoc., 3d ser., VI: 103–107.

BABBAGE, CHAS.: Analysis of the Statistics of the Clearing House During the Year 1839. Journ. Stat. Soc., Lond., XIX: 28.

BARNETT, R. W.: The Effect of the Development of Banking Facilities, etc. Journ. Inst. Bankers, II: 73, esp. 78.

CONANT, C. A.: Extension of the Clearing System. Bank. Mag., N. Y., LXX: 433.

DUN, JOHN: The Banking Institutions, Bullion Reserves, etc., of the United Kingdom. Journ. Stat. Soc., Lond., XXXIX: 1.

ESSARS, PIERRE DES: La Vitesse de la Circulation de la Monnaie. Journ. de la Soc. de Statist. de Paris, Apr., 1895, 143 ff.

FARRER, Sir T. H.: What do we Pay With? or, Gold, Credit, and Prices. London, 1889.

FISHER, IRVING: A Practical Method of Estimating the Volocity of Circulation of Money. Journ. Stat. Soc., Lond., LXXII, Pt. III.

FISHER, WILLARD: Money and Credit Paper in the Modern Market. Journ. Pol. Econ., Chicago, III: 391–413.

GARFIELD, JAMES A.: Speech in Cong. Rec., Nov. 16, 1877, p. 462.

GILBART, J. W.: The Laws of the Currency in Scotland. Journ. Statist. Soc., XIX: 144–169. Especially pp. 157, 167, 168. London.

KEMMERER, EDWIN WALTER: Money and Credit Instruments in their Relation to General Prices. New York, 1907. 2d ed., 1909.

KINLEY, DAVID: Credit Instruments in Retail Trade. Journ. Pol. Econ., III: 203–217. Chicago, 1895.

Credit Instruments in Business Transactions. Journ. Pol. Econ., V: 157–174. Chicago, 1897.

Credit Currency and Population. Journ. Pol. Econ., X: 72–93. Chicago, 1901.

Money. A Study of the Theory of the Medium of Exchange. Pp. 43, 44, 199–223. New York, 1904.

Report to Comptroller of the Currency, 1894. (See Report of the Comptroller.)

Report to the Comptroller of the Currency, 1896. (See Report of the Comptroller.)

The Relation of the Credit System to the Value of Money. Publ. Amer. Econ. Assoc., 3d ser., VI: 84–94. New York, 1905.

KNOX, JOHN JAY: Address to the American Bankers' Association. Proceedings of the Convention of the American Bankers' Association, 1881, pp. 33–49. New York, 1881.

LANDRY, A.: La Rapidité de la circulation monétaire. Rev. d'Econ. Pol., 1905.

LUBBOCK, Sir JOHN: The Country Clearing. Journ. Statist. Soc., XXVIII: 361–371. London, 1865.

MACLEOD, HENRY DUNNING: The Theory and Practice of Banking. 5th ed., 2 vols. London, 1892.

MARTIN, JOHN B.: An Inquiry into the History, Functions, and Fluctuations of the Bank Note Circulation in the United Kingdom, Continental Europe, and the United States. Journ. Inst. Bankers, I: 273–341, especially 282–292. London, 1880.

MUHLEMAN, MAURICE L.: Monetary and Banking Systems. New York, 1908.

PALGRAVE, R. H. I.: Notes on Banking in Great Britain and Ireland, Sweden, Denmark, and Hamburg, etc. Journ. Statist. Soc., XXXVI: 27–157, especially 80–86. London, 1874.

POWNALL, GEORGE H.: The Proportional Use of Credit Documents and Metallic Money in English Banks. Journ. Inst. Bankers, II: 629–675. London, 1881.

Report of the Comptroller of the Currency, 1881, pp. 11–23. Washington, 1882.

Report of the Comptroller of the Currency, 1890, pp. 19 ff. Washington, 1890.

Report of the Comptroller of the Currency, 1892, pp. 31–39. Washington, 1892.

Report of the Comptroller of the Currency, 1894, pp. 17–24. Washington, 1895.

Report of the Comptroller of the Currency, 1896, pp. 57–98. Washington, 1896.

Review of the Annual Report of the Comptroller of the Currency of the United States, 1894. Journ. Inst. Bankers, XVI: 83–85. London, 1895.

SPRAGUE, O. M. W.: Distribution of Money between the Banks and the People since 1893. Quar. Journ. Econ., XVIII: 513–523. Boston, 1904.

VEBLEN, T. B.: The Use of Loan Credit in Modern Business. Chicago, 1903.

WILLIS, H. PARKER: Credit Devices and the Quantity Theory. Journ. Pol. Econ., IV: 281–308. Chicago, 1896.

INDEX.